Substance Misuse

RESEARCH HIGHLIGHTS 5 3

Research Highlights in Social Work

This topical series examines areas of particular interest to those in social and community work and related fields. Each book draws together different aspects of the subject, highlighting relevant research and drawing out implications for policy and practice. The project is under the editorial direction of Professor Andrew Kendrick, Head of the School of Applied Social Sciences at the University of Strathclyde, Scotland.

Substance Misuse

The Implications of Research, Policy and Practice

Edited by
Joy Barlow MBE

RESEARCH HIGHLIGHTS 53

Jessica Kingsley *Publishers*
London and Philadelphia

Acknowledgements

I would like to thank all of the contributors to this volume who have given wholeheartedly of their expertise, knowledge and time to make this volume a success. As usual, my heartfelt thanks are also due to my Personal Assistant Vincenta Hamilton who has worked timeously on this endeavour, with her usual good humour and fortitude.

Finally many thanks to Gerald Barlow without whose support nothing would be possible.

Joy Barlow, July 2009

Research Highlights in Social Work 53

Editor: Joy Barlow

Secretary: Elaine Webster

Editorial Advisory Committee:

Professor Joyce Lishman	Editorial Director – Head of School, School of Applied Social Studies, The Robert Gordon University, Aberdeen
Ms J. Barlow MBE	University of Glasgow
Mr S. Black	Edinburgh
Prof. I. Broom	Robert Gordon University, Aberdeen
Ms S. Hunter	University of Edinburgh
Mr S. Jones	Jessica Kingsley Publishers
Prof. A. Kendrick	University of Strathclyde
Prof. B. McGettrick	Liverpool Hope University
Prof. G. McIvor	Lancaster University
Ms K. Skinner	The Scottish Institute for Excellence in Social Work Education
Dr J. Taylor	University of Dundee
Dr H. Wilkinson	University of Edinburgh

Robert Gordon University
School of Applied Social Studies
Faculty of Health and Social Care
Garthdee Road Aberdeen AB10 7QG

First published in 2010 by
Jessica Kingsley Publishers
73 Collier Street
London N1 9BE, UK
and
400 Market Street, Suite 400
Philadelphia, PA 19106, USA

www.jkp.com

Library of Congress Cataloging in Publication Data

Substance misuse : the implications of research, policy, and practice / edited by Joy Barlow.

　　p. cm.

　　Includes bibliographical references and index.

　　ISBN 978-1-84310-696-8 (pb : alk. paper) 1. Drug abuse. 2. Drug abuse--Treatment. 3. Drug abuse--Prevention. I. Barlow, Joy.

　　HV5801.S8343 2010

　　362.29--dc22

　　　　　　　　　　2009024852

British Library Cataloguing in Publication Data

A CIP catalogue record for this book is available from the British Library

ISBN 978 1 84310 696 8

eISBN 978 0 85700 219 8

Contents

Part III Treatment and Recovery, and the Wider Impacts of Substance Misuse

Part IV Prevention

Part V Integrated Services and Workforce Development

Tables and Figures

Introduction

Joy Barlow

The problems associated with substance use are never far from media headlines. There is a growing body of knowledge from the perspectives of medicine, sociology, psychology, justice and ethics which continues to frame the context of substance misuse. 'The war on drugs' is hotly debated, and everyone seems to have an answer.

'Only the wisest and stupidest of men never change' said Confucius 2000 years ago. Although there have always been changes in policy affecting substance use, we are in perhaps one of the most turbulent periods at the present time. We might well echo the words of the Price Waterhouse Change Interventions Team in 1995, which defined events as 'more like a white-water kayak race'. Practitioners need to know what to hold on to at this turbulent time, and this is the aim of the book – to give examples from current research and practitioners' experience, and links between policy and practice, which will assist those who work with people affected by substance misuse, their families and carers.

It is hoped that the audience for this book, primarily social workers or students of social work, will be augmented by practitioners from other disciplines who have a role to play in the field of substance misuse. Substance misuse permeates the day-to-day work of many professionals, and (as readers will see) current policy, particularly as it pertains to drugs, gives all professionals a role to play in recovery.

Contributions to this volume are mainly from the United Kingdom, but some international authors are included. Some chapters have two contributions, where the links between policy and practice can be highlighted by examples from different authors. In other chapters authors have commented upon both research and practice within the one contribution. The book is arranged in five parts:

1. The historical context of drug and alcohol policy.

2. Alcohol and tobacco.

3. The treatment context in which recovery from substance misuse might take place, and the wider impact of substance misuse.

4. Prevention, including the impact of social exclusion and the needs of the black and minority communities.

5. Conclusions about integrated working and messages for the workforce.

Terminology in the substance misuse field is fraught with difficulty, and it must be accepted that a number of different terms are used in this volume. Some of the substances discussed are rightly defined as being 'misused'; other authors use the terms 'problem drug and alcohol use'. I have allowed authors to use terminology relating to the context of their experience.

1. The history of drug and alcohol policy
How we got to where we are now

In the first chapter Charlie Lloyd considers the pathways of policy that have brought us to where we are now. He describes the seminal points in both drug and alcohol policy, and discusses the current position of policies, which are at a crossroads. He notes the importance of changes in policy as experienced in the devolved jurisdictions of the United Kingdom. He concludes that whilst there are many new policies, they are still at an early stage of development. We await to see national policy translated into local policy and action, at a time of economic recession.

2. Alcohol and tobacco
Alcohol

In his article on alcohol in Chapter 2, Jack Law examines attitudes, beliefs and practice. He discusses the lack (until very recently) of emphasis on alcohol as a substance capable of causing significant harm to individuals and society. He considers the basic issues of legality, price and availability, and calls for a greater understanding of their impact on shaping practice.

In their contribution to the subject of alcohol, Gerard Vaughan and Megan Larken illustrate the concepts of collaboration and partnership in the context of alcohol policy and regulations from a New Zealand perspective. They give examples of active and creative relationships which are required in the field of alcohol policy in New Zealand, particularly in working with Mäori, the indigenous people of New Zealand, on alcohol policy and intervention.

Tobacco

In her article on second-hand smoke in Chapter 3, Sally Haw relates the history of the Scottish smoke-free legislation. She describes in detail the impact of the Scottish smoking ban from the point of view of seminal evaluation studies. These include compliance with legislation; the improvement in air quality and reduction in second-hand smoke exposure; health impacts and socio-culture and behaviour change. She concludes that implementation of the legislation has been accompanied by high levels of compliance, and the impact on health and socio-culture has been much greater than expected.

In their contribution to the subject of tobacco and the impact of behaviour change, Linda McKie, Margaret Black and Anne Bryce describe a community-development approach to smoking cessation. They discuss the implications for work through this approach, and for organisations that provide support for tobacco control. They illustrate the importance of the community development approach for evaluation practice. Linda and her colleagues have very useful advice to practitioners on how to organise and deliver smoking cessation services which promote behaviour change.

3. Treatment and recovery, and the wider impacts of substance misuse

Treatment and recovery

At the beginning of Chapter 4, Brian Kidd invites the reader to consider the clinical approach to the treatment of problem substance use. He discusses factors which are currently influencing the debate. He discusses in depth the clinician's role in treatment, and the required support from essential services if problem substance users are to be given the optimum treatment for recovery. He considers in detail the role of harm reduction from a clinical perspective; he concludes that the recovery focus may bring resolution to the debate between harm reduction and abstinence.

In an accompanying article Neil McKeganey questions the effectiveness of current services for facilitating recovery for those experiencing problem drug use. He focuses specifically on the Drug Outcome Research in Scotland study (DORIS), and gives detailed analysis of the several studies comprising the DORIS cohorts. Neil asks some big questions that will challenge practitioners to consider their current practice. He particularly raises the issue of assessing those service users for whom abstinence is an achievable goal. He faces us all with questions about what sort of services we shall need to deliver in the future.

The role of employment

In Chapter 5 Joanne Neale and Peter Kemp begin by examining the role that employment can play in the recovery from problem drug use. They give the reader insight into the use that must be made in this area of research findings and policy. They discuss the vital question of why policy makers are so interested in the economic viability of recovering drug users, and set forward arguments about the reduction or withdrawal of social security benefits. They conclude with important messages for practitioners about what will make it possible for those individuals experiencing drug problems to enter and remain in paid work.

In the accompanying article Bernadette Monaghan, former Chief Executive of Apex Scotland, illustrates with examples from practice the significant points raised by Joanne and Peter in the previous contribution. The work of Apex in various parts of Scotland is described, examining various service designs and how they facilitate the progression to paid employment. Case studies are quoted to give the reader a flavour of the outcomes of services. The conclusions indicate that a number of routes may be required to build up self-confidence and self-belief, which are necessary staging posts in the journey to recovery.

Parental substance misuse

The two contributions to Chapter 6 deal with the aspect of drug and alcohol misuse that is probably the most highlighted and discussed in recent years – the impact of parental substance misuse on parenting and its effects on children. The Advisory Council on the Misuse of Drugs report of 2003 – *Hidden Harm – Responding to the Needs of the Children of Problem Drug Users* – sets the scene for significant cultural and practice change for both substance misuse and child welfare and safeguarding services.

In his contribution Donald Forrester takes a 'root and branch' approach to the problem. He faces the reader with very hard observations, based on research, about the work of social workers in child protection. He pulls no punches about the considerable and intractable problems that practitioners and indeed society face, and what needs to change. This chapter argues that work with families affected by parental drug misuse is synonymous with effective childcare work in general. Once again in this book, practitioners are challenged to consider their own practice, and to look for better alternatives.

In the accompanying contribution, Joyce Nicholson describes how a specific training programme has sought to bring alternative new practice to provide better outcomes for children affected by parental substance misuse. Drawing on her own experience as a specialist STRADA (Scottish Training on Drugs and Alcohol) trainer, Joyce describes in detail the training programme developed for a particular local authority area in Scotland. She discusses the practitioner's response to training, and provides evidence from different perspectives of ways in which both cultural and practice change may take place. Both she and Donald lay great stress on the need to develop reflection in practice. She concludes with important statements about ownership of new ways of working for all practitioners, and the pivotal role played by management.

The role and importance of the family

Again in recent years the substance misuse field has begun to recognise that those with problems do not exist in isolation. Most of them will have families. In her article about the family in Chapter 7, Vivienne Evans describes the role and work of Adfam, a leading national charity working with families of substance misusers in England and Wales. Her contribution describes the impact of substance misuse on the family from research and practice perspectives. She indicates the benefit of work involving families, and describes the essential requirements of such services. She notes some of the deficits in this field of work and makes recommendations for the future.

Maurizio Coletti's accompanying contribution is from an Italian perspective and considers how to make families a part of treatment. Using research evidence he discusses the relationship between problematic drug use and family. He describes the various treatment interventions and the role that the family can play in these interventions. He points the practitioner to specific ways of working with the family, and considers examples of good practice in family therapy.

Drugs and crime

Finally in this section about treatment and the wider implications of substance misuse, Toby Seddon's chapter considers the issues of drugs and crime, and looks at the less than straightforward links between them. Drawing on significant research data, he sets out key findings and considers concepts and thematic issues that may be missed in the 'dense thicket' of research evidence. This is a robust research chapter, which easily signposts the practitioner to further reading, and importantly asks the reader to consider questions hitherto unexplored in practice.

4. Prevention

Redefining drug prevention

In their introductory chapter to the topic of prevention, Harry Sumnall and Lisa Jones set the scene for discussion on prevention from a wide perspective and then home in on specific approaches. They discuss mass media interventions and targeted prevention strategies. They conclude with messages for practitioners about the planning of prevention initiatives within the wider context of the lives of young people, and suggest some of the limitations of traditional prevention strategies.

Drug prevention and children

In his chapter, Richard Ives adds information about prevention with children and young people to Harry Sumnall and Lisa Jones's overall review of prevention. It looks first at the level of knowledge of, and involvement with, drugs among children and young teenagers – any attempts at prevention have to take this as a starting point. The chapter also looks more closely at some of the drug education and prevention programmes aimed at children and younger teenagers; discusses campaigns aimed at parents; and considers some aspects of the UK government's FRANK brand. To conclude, some of the challenges of drug prevention are discussed, and some ways forward suggested.

Social exclusion

The following two contributions in Chapter 11 consider the wider impact of social exclusion, and consider education and prevention. Jane Fountain reports on a project, funded by the Department of Health, carrying out needs assessment among Black and minority ethnic drug misusers. It is a project rooted in the various communities surveyed, using community organisations to carry out the needs assessment. The article provides the reader with evidence of the barriers to accessing drug services, issues of language and culture, and the use of the media. Explicit recommendations are made to improve practice and service delivery. Of all the contributions to this book, it is the one in which the voice of people affected by drug misuse is most clearly heard.

In his article, James Egan considers the relationship of poverty and social exclusion with harmful paths of substance use. The discussion ranges over the bigger picture of socio-economic deprivation, and critiques the welfare-to-work model as a route out of poverty and social exclusion. As with the article on employment by Joanne and Peter (Chapter 5), James calls into question the current moves towards benefit changes for drug and alcohol misusers. He concludes with significant implications for practice, including the use of Motivational Interviewing (a strategy also discussed by Donald Forrester in Chapter 6), the use of the cycle of change, and the importance of acting upon coexisting levels of poverty and widening inequalities. He suggests a move away from focusing on individual motivation to a more assertive role in addressing socio-economic disadvantage in all its forms.

5. Integrated services and workforce development
Integrated services
In this penultimate chapter Neil Hunter describes the integrated service approach adopted by Glasgow City Council. He rehearses the research evidence for the importance of integrated team working, and discusses in detail the experience of setting up such teams across a wide metropolitan area with seemingly intractable drug and alcohol problems. Neil describes in detail the service development and design of the community addiction teams, and gives a clear indication of the benefits of integrated teams, including transaction between a range of professionals. Throughout the chapter the reader is given very clear information about how to bring about better integrated working, and the contribution of such services to the success of the 'Road to Recovery' strategy.

Workforce development

In the final chapter I have considered what the foregoing chapters have told the reader about the significant changes required in service design, and therefore those needed in workforce development. Taking examples from the experience of STRADA (Scottish Training on Drugs and Alcohol) and wider research, I have addressed what we mean by workforce development and who we are addressing as the workforce; what skills are needed to equip the workforce to do the job competently and confidently; what we know about developing the workforce and what works. I encourage the reader to consider the impact of learning and development on practice, the importance of attitudes and values, and links between theory and practice in all forms of workforce development. Finally, I make a number of suggestions for the future that should equip the workforce to assist in better outcomes for those affected by drug and alcohol problems, and for their families, carers and communities.

PART I

The History of Drug and Alcohol Policy

CHAPTER 1

How We Got to Where We Are Now

Charlie Lloyd

In considering where we are now in terms of current drug and alcohol policy, it is useful to look back at the pathways that have taken us here. Laws, policies and strategies are, and always have been, primarily driven by actual or perceived trends in drinking and drug use (and associated problems). So in considering how and why particular laws have been passed or particular policies forged, it is also necessary to look at the problems that have led to them.

This chapter therefore provides a brief history of how we got to where we are now – in terms of the history of drug and alcohol consumption and legislative and policy responses to this consumption – before turning to a consideration of where we are now – in terms of current drug and alcohol strategies in the UK.

Viewed historically, the drug that has had the most impact on the way we live, over the longest period, and which has caused the most damage, public concern and legislative responses to it, is alcohol. Public fears concerning other drugs have a much more recent history, with legislative control not occurring before the late 19th century. Given the very different and largely separate histories of drinking and drug use, and policy responses to them, alcohol and drugs are here dealt with separately.

Alcohol

A short history of drinking and legislative responses to drinking

It is impossible to find out when alcohol was first intentionally consumed but as Edwards (2000) points out, alcohol must have been around 'as soon as it was possible to gather fruit, add water and wait a few days for enzymatic action to do its work' (pp.3–4). Throughout recorded history, alcohol has played an important role in the large majority of civilisations. Wine was consumed in Ancient Egypt, Greece and Rome.

A key event in the history of alcohol was the development of distillation, which became widespread over the 16th and 17th centuries. While, initially, distilled alcohol was primarily used for medical purposes, gin came to be consumed in large amounts in 18th-century London (the 'Gin Craze'). Between 1700 and 1735 gin consumption rose from 500,000 gallons to five million gallons (Thom 2001). The causes of this drink epidemic were political and economic: the government had acted to help farmers find a market for excess grain by encouraging the fermentation and distillation of the grain to produce gin, and thereby also to prevent the reliance on foreign spirits. The tax on distilling was abolished and gin was allowed to be sold without a licence. This led to the rapid escalation in gin drinking and the attendant social consequences famously portrayed in Hogarth's etching *Gin Lane*.

Up until the 20th century, legislative controls were primarily 'linked to economics, politics and social order rather than to individual and public health concerns' (Thom 2001, p.18). For example, in the Middle Ages, local licensing control grew out of concerns that public houses had become 'unruly hotbeds of political dissent' (Thom 2001, p.19). This led to an Act in 1495 which allowed alehouses to be closed on the agreement of two justices of the peace. Then the disease model of alcohol addiction, which saw addiction to alcohol as a disease of the brain, became increasingly influential. Seeing problem drinkers as suffering from an illness rather than a moral weakness led to more sympathetic responses: treatment and rehabilitation rather than disapproval and punishment. The Temperance Movement also drew on this new understanding of alcoholism. Temperance had its roots in the US but soon spread to Europe, where large numbers of people 'took the pledge' and refrained from drinking. Despite being a widespread social movement, the Temperance Movement had very limited success in bringing about any legislative control in the UK – this in contrast with the US, where the Temperance Movement was influential in bringing about prohibition, which lasted from 1920 to 1933. It was rather the need to keep the population fit and able to work during World War I that brought about increased legislative control on drinking. The Defence of the Realm Act 1914 brought in controls over pub opening hours and the strength of beer; and it increased taxation. Similar motivations lay behind the State Management Scheme (1916) which led to the nationalisation of breweries and pubs in three areas where large armaments factories existed.

Alcohol use declined after the turn of the century and remained at a low level between the wars. However, from 1960 onwards there has been a quite dramatic increase in alcohol use up until the present day (British Medical Association 2008). While the disease concept had been influential over the course of the 19th century, its influence waned over the first half of the 20th but was rediscovered under the new term 'alcoholism' in the 1940s. This was particularly influential in the expansion of specialist provision for alcoholics in the 1950s and 60s (Edwards 2000). The 1970s witnessed a move towards focusing on alcohol misuse and problem drinking (rather than alcoholism) at a population level (Kneale and French 2008; Thom 2001). This new public health paradigm led to an increasing focus on 'universal' approaches, such as substance-use education, public awareness campaigns, and lower-level interventions, such as community-based detoxification and brief interventions. The adoption of 'units' as the standard measure of alcohol in the 1980s rendered problem drinking more quantifiable and, therefore, more visible. This public health approach has continued to gain in influence over the intervening years and is now increasingly reflected in recent policy documents emanating from the Department of Health.

In the 21st century, public concern about drinking has grown exponentially. Disorderly drinking in town and city centres has caused a growing level of public disquiet, as has drinking among young women. The public health lobby has proved increasingly effective in getting its voice heard, with frequent opportunities provided by growing figures on alcohol consumption and on alcohol-related illness and death. Alcohol has therefore become a major policy issue – increasingly eclipsing illicit drugs as the substance abuse issue of the day.

Current alcohol policy

The first overarching UK drug strategy was introduced in 1995, and this led to increasing pressure from the voluntary sector for a similar overarching strategy for alcohol. In 2004 this finally arrived in the shape of the Alcohol Harm Reduction Strategy for England (Cabinet Office 2004). Since then, there has been a flurry of policies reflecting the political salience of the alcohol issue. The Licensing Act 2003 came into effect in 2005, and a new English policy document, *Safe. Sensible. Social.* (Department of Health *et al.* 2007) came out in 2007. In Scotland, a quite radical consultation document came out in 2008: *Changing Scotland's Relationship with Alcohol: A Discussion Paper on Our Strategic Approach* (Scottish Government 2008a: henceforth the Discussion Paper); and the Welsh drug and alcohol strategy *Working Together to Reduce Harm* (Welsh Assembly Government 2008) included a range of measures focusing on alcohol.

The main elements of these policies were:

1. Public health and the need for culture change

2. Education and information

3. Treatment

4. Crime, disorder and licensing

5. Taxation.

1. PUBLIC HEALTH AND THE NEED FOR CULTURE CHANGE

The increasing dominance of the public health paradigm in alcohol policy has been accompanied by a growing realisation that, if any difference was to be made to alcohol-related health problems, policy had to make an impact on the large numbers of people who drink over the recommended levels, not just the problem drinkers or alcoholics. This has led to strong calls for culture change in *Safe. Sensible. Social.* (SSS), the Discussion Paper and in the Welsh strategy. It has also led to an emphasis on all groups who drink too much, rather than just the familiar target of young people.

Two means of realising such culture change are proposed: public campaigns and influencing the price and availability of alcohol. The UK strategy in particular promises sustained national campaigns that will 'challenge public tolerance of drunkenness' and raise public knowledge of alcohol units, so that people can more readily estimate the amount they are drinking. However, the main means proposed of reducing drinking levels at the population level, particularly in the Scottish document, is through attempting to influence how alcohol is priced, made available and sold. There is a tacit recognition that, in order to encourage people to drink less, governments will have to address the considerable force of the alcohol industry pushing people in the opposite direction. SSS promised a review of the effectiveness of the industry's Social Responsibility Standards for the Production and Sale of Alcoholic drinks in the UK. This was subsequently undertaken and showed that these voluntary standards 'are currently having negligible impact in either reducing bad practice or promoting good practice on the ground' (KPMG 2008). In 2009, the UK government (Home Office 2009) published a consultation document on a new, mandatory code of practice for alcohol retailers in England and Wales, which includes a ban on 'irresponsible promotions' (such as 'Women drink free' and 'All you can drink for £x').

The Scottish *Discussion Paper* also included a ban on reduced-price and loss-leading promotions. However, it went much further by proposing a minimum retail price, preventing promotion of alcohol in stores, and introducing separate check-outs for people buying alcohol. By such measures, the Scottish Government aimed to 'denormalise' alcohol and reduce consumption. Since the publication of the discussion document, the Scottish Government has decided to go ahead with these measures. However, initial attempts to introduce a minimum price through licensing powers were foiled by opposition parties and the change will therefore have to be made through legislation.

2. EDUCATION AND INFORMATION

One potentially important source of information on drinking is the bottle or can in which it is bought. The UK government has been putting increasing pressure on the producers to include unit information and health messages on alcohol containers. While initially it was hoped that this would be done voluntarily, there have been increasing threats of coercion.

It is noticeable that there is very little focus in any of the alcohol strategy documents on school-based alcohol education, presumably reflecting scepticism about the potential for such approaches to have an impact on drinking.

3. TREATMENT

There is good evidence that brief alcohol interventions delivered by GPs in a primary healthcare setting can have an impact on drink problems (e.g. Kaner *et al.* 2007). The main focus in all three strategy documents is on early identification of alcohol problems and early, brief interventions.

4. CRIME, DISORDER AND LICENSING

Over the past decade, there has been growing public and media disquiet about alcohol-related disorder in town and city centres. In England

and Wales the Licensing Act 2003 came into effect in November 2005 and was introduced amid a furore in the media about the potential for extended licensing to aggravate the problems already being experienced. The introduction of flexible opening hours was well-publicised. The Act also expanded court and police powers to close licensed premises temporarily due to disorder problems, and included provision for licences to be reviewed prior to their expiry. Evaluation of the Act has shown little impact on public order and crime (Department of Culture, Media and Sport 2008).

Relevant sections of the Violent Crime Reduction Act 2006 came into effect in England and Wales in June 2008. They introduced Drinking Banning Orders, whereby individuals could be banned from drinking in particular premises; and Alcohol Disorder Zones, which allow local authorities to impose charges on licence holders in designated ADZs, to recoup the costs of alcohol-related disorder (including policing costs).

5. TAXATION

There is good evidence to show that increasing the price of alcohol through taxation significantly reduces drinking (Babor *et al.* 2003; Booth *et al.* 2008). While alcohol duty and taxation are the preserve of the UK parliament, the need to impact consumption through taxation is referred to by both the Scottish Government and the Welsh Assembly. By comparison, taxation is 'the elephant in the room' when it comes to the UK government's strategy, with no discussion of the issue. This may represent inter-departmental tensions. In 2006, Patricia Hewitt, then Secretary of State for Health, took the highly unusual step of calling on another government department – the Treasury – to 'really increase' taxes on alcohol. This pressure from the Department of Health appears to have been successful: the March 2008 budget included an increase in alcohol duties of 6 per cent above the rate of inflation, with increases of 2 per cent above inflation promised in each of the following four years.

Conclusions on alcohol policy

Historically, there have been waves of public concern about alcohol that have taken different forms. We currently appear to be on the crest of one such wave. Alcohol consumption and alcohol-related health problems have both risen over the past 20 years (NHS/Information Centre 2009; Smith and Foxcroft 2009). Public concern has likewise risen, with increasing anxiety about town- and city-centre disorder, young women and alcohol-related ill-health. Alcohol has therefore become a major focus for policy makers across the UK. In England, the government has gone from a resounding silence prior to 2004 to producing three substantial policy documents in a four-year period.

A central feature of this new policy focus on alcohol is the recognition that changing a socially embedded behaviour like alcohol requires a radical cultural shift. The Scottish strategy is clearest in seeing this, requiring a 'denormalisation' of alcohol and its consumption and seeing the alcohol industry as a potential impediment to such a shift. Indeed, the recent rush of policy documents has witnessed a growing impatience with the alcohol industry and a growing determination to introduce mandatory controls on how alcohol is sold in the UK.

Drugs
A short history of drug use and policy responses

A hundred and fifty years ago, opium, cannabis and coca (the plant from which cocaine is derived) were all perfectly legal. Opium in particular was widely used, widely advertised and could be purchased from a corner shop as easily as we buy aspirin today. Laudanum – an alcoholic extract of raw opium – was one of the most widely used medicines, taken by many for a wide range of medical complaints. However, this widespread use was not without social concern. In particular, early disquiet focused on the large number of overdose deaths (both accidental and intentional) occurring among babies, children and adults. The first legislation to introduce limited controls on these drugs (The Pharmacy and Poisons Act 1868) was primarily a response to this problem. Public concern about the use of opium – and increasingly cocaine – continued to grow after the turn of the century, with a number of highly publicised deaths of young women associated with cocaine use, and a scandal surrounding the use of cocaine by the armed forces en route to the trenches in World War I. Nevertheless, reflecting the increasing importance of the international dimension in dictating drug policy, the real impetus for further legislative control came from the need to institute an international agreement, the Hague Convention, in UK Law.

Britain was not the only country to have suffered from opium addiction: indeed Britain played a major role in ensuring that such problems were rife elsewhere and profiting from them. Over the 18th and 19th centuries, a trade deficit with China led to British merchants selling opium grown in India to China. Despite many attempts to control and prevent this trade by the Qing Dynasty, it continued to flourish and caused a serious problem of opium addiction in China. The two Opium Wars therefore resulted from China's attempts to stamp out this trade – attempts that were effectively resisted by Britain, which won both of these wars.

The British therefore had a strong investment in the international trade in opium. However, by the late 19th century, opinion around the world, and particularly opinion in America, was turning against the trade. Such pressures eventually led to the international Hague Convention, which introduced international controls over the production, distribution and use of opium (and its derivatives) and cocaine. The Convention was enacted in the UK through the Dangerous Drugs Act 1920.

So drugs like morphine, heroin and cocaine were supposedly restricted to medical use from the 1920s onwards. However, these drugs were still widely prescribed – usually, initially for pain relief but, as patients became addicted to the drugs, prescription continued. Moreover, some doctors were clearly prescribing irresponsibly – either to others or to support their own habits. Concerns about such prescribing led to the setting up of the Rolleston Committee in 1924. The committee's report concluded that morphine and heroin prescription for addiction should be limited to two key groups: those undergoing gradual withdrawal from the drug; and those for whom the drug cannot be withdrawn because of the severity of their addiction. This formed what has since been described as 'the British System' of treatment, lasting up until the 1960s, whereby heroin addicts were prescribed pharmaceutical heroin.

Over subsequent decades there continued to be problems with rogue prescribers of heroin and cocaine, and it proved difficult to take action either under the Dangerous Drugs Act or the guidance set by the Rolleston Committee. The most notorious of these rogue prescribers was the psychiatrist, Lady Frankau, who prescribed 600,000 heroin tablets in the single year of 1962. Such problems, coupled with an increasing number of new, younger heroin users, led to the Dangerous Drugs Act 1967, which introduced specialist centres for treating addicts (Drug Dependency Units) and restrictions on the rights of doctors working outside these units to prescribe heroin and cocaine to addicts.

By this stage in history, the number of known heroin users was escalating, and in the late 1960s the illegal importation of heroin became established, possibly partly as a result of the restrictions on prescription brought in by the Dangerous Drugs Act 1967. 'Recreational' drug use was also taking off, with cannabis, amphetamines ('speed') and LSD increasingly being used.

The next major piece of drug legislation was primarily a response to another international agreement (the United Nations Single Convention on Narcotic Drugs, 1961). The Misuse of Drugs Act 1971 still constitutes the main legislative basis for current drug policy and practice, and classified controlled drugs into Classes A, B, and C with the severity of punishment set by the class. The maximum penalty for possession of a Class A drug was set at seven years; Class B, five years and Class C, two years. Higher sentences were specified for production, supply and intent to supply. Some drugs – most notably cannabis – have been moved across these classes since the 1971 Act and new drugs have been added to the list. Commonly used drugs are now classed as shown in Table 1.1.

TABLE 1.1 CURRENT CLASSIFICATION OF THE COMMONLY USED CONTROLLED DRUGS (CORRECT AS OF JULY 2009)

Class A	Class B	Class C
Heroin	Cannabis	Benzodiazepines
Methadone	Amphetamines	Buprenorphine
Cocaine	Barbiturates	GHB
Ecstasy		Ketamine
LSD		
Psilocybin		
Mushrooms		
Meth(yl)amphetamine		

The 1980s witnessed the birth of what we currently understand as 'the drug problem'; that is, extensive recreational drug use among young people, and a sizeable population of addicted problem drug users who cause considerable harm to themselves, their families and communities. A new wave of heroin use emerged in urban areas around the UK. This took a very different pattern from the heroin use of the 1960s, consisting mainly of adolescents and young people, and involving inhalation ('smoking' or 'chasing the dragon') rather than injection. Large numbers of young people were introduced to heroin at this point in history – many believing that they would not become addicted because they were 'smoking' the drug. This proved to be a catastrophic mistake: they did become addicted and many ended up injecting as a more efficient way to take the drug. While the number of known heroin addicts stood at just over 2000 in 1980, this figure had increased to more than 10,000 by 1987 (Mold and Berridge 2007).

Another public health catastrophe soon added further misery to the developing heroin epidemic. In 1986, research published by a GP in Edinburgh and his colleagues found that 51 per cent of a sample of 164 Scottish intravenous drug users were HIV positive (Robertson *et al*. 1986). Other research in Edinburgh and Dundee also found high rates of HIV infection among intravenous drug users.

These findings caused considerable alarm among policy makers and changed UK drug policy in a radical way. Fifteen pilot syringe and needle exchange projects were launched in 1987. The Advisory Council on the Misuse of Drugs[1] was asked to consider the issue and in 1988 published a report which concluded that 'HIV is a greater threat to public and individual health than drug misuse'. The conclusions of this report, coupled with a positive evaluation of the pilot projects and support from the government, led to the proliferation of needle exchange programmes around the UK. This action signalled a dramatic shift of policy in the direction of harm reduction – whereby the aim of policy and practice should be to reduce the harms associated with drug use – rather than necessarily a reduction in use or no use at all. The evidence suggests that, as a result of this rapid response, the UK has avoided the HIV epidemics that have occurred among injecting drug users in many other countries around the world.

Yet another significant development in the late 1980s was the appearance of widespread ecstasy use in dance venues and 'raves'. By 1995, an estimated 1.5 million ecstasy tablets were being used every weekend.

In 1995, the first overarching English drug strategy was introduced: *Tackling Drugs Together* (HM Government 1995). The main targets were crime, young people and public health – the latter emphasis reflecting the 'harm reduction' response to the spread of HIV among injecting drug users. The strategy also set up Drug Action Teams – local policy structures including representatives from the key agencies with an interest in drug issues. In 1997, Tony Blair's New Labour government was elected and with it came the new post of Anti-Drugs Coordinator (or 'Drugs Tsar') and, a year later, a new ten-year drug strategy, *Tackling Drugs to Build a Better Britain* (HM Government 1998). This strategy targeted young people, communities, treatment and drug availability. Notably, reducing the health risks associated with drug use was no longer listed as one of the key objectives.

---

1   A standing body of experts that advises the government on a range of drug policy
     issues, including the classification of drugs, set up by the Misuse of Drugs Act 1971.

The defining policy initiative over this ten-year strategy has been the rapid increase in funding for drug treatment. Between 2001/02 and 2008/09, central government funding (known as the 'Pooled Treatment Budget') nearly tripled: from £142 million to £398 million, reflecting the central aim of the Labour government's drug policy of reducing crime through treating problem drug users (Duke 2006; Reuter and Stevens 2007).

Current drugs policy

The year 2008 was a bumper year for drug strategies, with new strategy documents coming out for the UK (HM Government 2008), for Scotland (Scottish Government 2008b) and for Wales (Welsh Assembly Government 2008). Their key elements are summarised below under the four 'pillars' of drug policy: prevention, enforcement, treatment and harm reduction.

PREVENTION

As its name suggests, the UK strategy, *Protecting Families and Communities*, contains a strong focus on the family and, in particular, families where there are drug-using parents. A two-pronged approach is outlined accordingly: on the one hand parents will be provided with better information and support to prevent and reduce the harm associated with their children's drug use; and on the other, more accessible treatment and support for drug-using parents, including greater support for kinship carers, such as grandparents, who frequently care for the children of their drug-using offspring (Barnard 2007). The Scottish and Welsh strategies lay a similar, strong emphasis on children with drug-using parents, particularly in the Scottish strategy where a chapter is devoted to the children affected by parental substance misuse. These children are to be given prominence in the framework for integrating children's services, known in Scotland as *Getting It Right For Every Child*.

ENFORCEMENT

Protecting Families and Communities puts a strong emphasis on working closely with communities to achieve enforcement, involving neighbourhood policing and local intelligence. As described earlier, the mission lying at the heart of the previous ten-year strategy has been to identify problem drug users in the criminal justice system and divert them into treatment. To achieve this, there had been a steady progression in the drug testing of offenders and resources for their treatment. *Protecting Families and*

Communities seems to have marked the end of this progression. It is clear that no further resources are forthcoming, and suggestions for ways to increase further the proportion of offenders diverted into drug treatment are limited. There is, nevertheless, a strong focus on improving treatment in prison, as there is in the Scottish strategy.

The Welsh strategy is candid on the subject of enforcement: 'we have arguably made less impact in this area over the period of the previous strategy than in other areas... Illegal drugs still appear to be easy to access and the prices have continued to drop' (p.48). Akin to the English strategy, reference is made to the importance of community policing.

TREATMENT

It is in the area of treatment that the most radical changes are apparent. The English strategy proposes 'a radical new focus on services to help drug users to re-establish their lives' (p.30). The issue of 'social reintegration' appears frequently throughout the documents and is, perhaps, the most significant feature of the new strategy, reflecting a shift away from concentration on the potential for drug treatment towards reducing drug use and crime. The strategy proposes 'more personalised approaches...which have the flexibility to respond to individualised circumstances' (p.29) and provide access to accommodation, education, training and employment.

One element of this integration strategy has attracted considerable public attention, as the Home Secretary explained:

> We do not think it is right for the taxpayer to help sustain drug habits when individuals could be getting treatment to overcome barriers to employment... In return for benefit payments, claimants will have a responsibility to move successfully through treatment and into employment. (HM Government 2008, p.6)

At time of writing, the Welfare Reform Bill is currently being debated in the House of Lords. The Bill includes new powers to require claimants to answer questions about their drug (and possibly alcohol) use, attend a 'substance-related assessment', undergo a drug test and attend drug treatment as part of a 'rehabilitation plan'. Benefits may be withdrawn from claimants if they fail in any of these requirements.

The Scottish strategy, *The Road to Recovery*, is driven by a single strong imperative – to make 'recovery' the main goal of drug treatment. As the Scottish Minister for Community Safety says in the foreword, 'this commitment to recovery, to responding to the desire of people who use drugs to become drug-free, lies at the heart of this strategy' (p.*iv*). It is very rare to read a policy document that is so clearly focused on a single idea: the word 'recovery' appears 143 times. There has been a quite lengthy and heated debate in Scotland about the aims of drug treatment (as there has been throughout the UK: Roberts 2009), and this debate has clearly had its impact on the Scottish strategy. On the one side has been those who pin their colours to the 'harm reduction' cause (reducing the harm associated with drugs, rather than necessarily the drug use itself); and, on the other, those who support the cause of abstinence (ceasing to use drugs). The Scottish document is clearly aligned with the second camp.

As part of this mission, *The Road to Recovery* states that a range of appropriate treatment and rehabilitation services must be available in all areas of Scotland and that treatment services must integrate with a wider range of generic services. This focus on non-medical services to aid social integration is akin to the English strategy's focus on reintegration. Linked to this more holistic approach, is a strong emphasis on person-centred care and individual care plans.

There is a strong focus throughout the Welsh strategy on involving service users: putting them 'at the heart of policy, planning and service design' (p.31). While this is a feature of the other strategies, it finds particular expression in the Welsh document.

On the issue of reintegration/recovery, the Welsh strategy points out that:

> for many substance misusers, it is the provision of wrap around services, alongside the appropriate treatment and aftercare services, that will be pivotal to reducing the harm caused by their substance misuse and to the ability to maintain or re-establish themselves in the community. (p.36)

The strategy advises that Community Safety Partnerships (the local inter-agency structures responsible for commissioning treatment services) 'should consider wrap around services as a core component of treatment for all substance misusers' (p.36).

HARM REDUCTION

While one of the three key objectives of *Tackling Drugs Together* (HM Government 1995) was 'reducing the health risks and other damage caused by drug use', by the time of New Labour's strategy in 1997, harm reduction had been significantly played down. *Protecting Families and Communities* included only a limited reference to 'continuing to promote harm minimisation measures including needle exchange and drug-assisted treatments that encourage drug users to enter treatment, in order to reduce the risk of overdose for drug users and the risk of infection for the wider community' (pp.29–30).

The Scottish strategy clearly sets up harm reduction as being in opposition to the central mission of recovery: 'the provision of interventions for those suffering from problem drug use has, in recent years focused on harm reduction…this [strategy] proposes a new approach to tackling problem drug use, based firmly on the concept of recovery' (p.21).

In stark contrast to these words, the Welsh strategy points out that if the levels of blood-borne viruses among injecting drug users are to be reduced,

> there will need to be an expansion in harm reduction services for drug misusers. The services provided must include needle exchange, harm minimisation advice, blood-borne virus testing and vaccination for hepatitis B. Access to these must be easy and convenient and include better provision via outreach services. (p.32)

Concluding comments on drug policy

The history of drug policy shows how successive waves of concern about drug use and associated problems, including overdose and HIV, have shaped legislative and policy responses. The international dimension has been influential, with a number of international agreements finding expression in British legislation, including the current Misuse of Drugs Act 1971. The main aim of these laws has been the control of drugs. However, following the discovery of the HIV epidemic, harm reduction became a key element of policy and practice and was amalgamated with other aims within the first overarching drug strategy of 1995. With New Labour, two years later, came a new central goal for drug policy – crime reduction; and this chimed well with a harm-reduction philosophy, in that the main vehicle for stabilising heroin users came from the harm-reduction stable: methadone maintenance. There has therefore been a period of some consensus between the harm-reduction 'reformers' and policy makers in Westminster, although their ultimate goals have been somewhat different. However, this comparatively quiet period may be at an end, with a radical new policy agenda that has been embraced (to different degrees) by the 2008 British drug strategies – recovery. What this new agenda will actually mean in terms of change on the ground is a crucial question, as it requires the involvement of – and dedication of resources from – agencies for which drug users may be very low on their list of priorities, such as housing, employment, training and education. The real test for drug policy in the coming years will be the extent to which these mostly laudable and radical aims concerning the reintegration of drug users are translated into radical change on the ground in a time of budget-squeezing national recession.

Overall conclusions

Alcohol is a legal drug that is consumed by a large majority of people in the UK. Its legality brings considerable scope for control: the market is visible and can be manipulated though policy and the law, as it has been over hundreds of years (with variable effects). By contrast, the drug market is largely uncontrollable – it is hidden and rarely disturbed by government or criminal justice agency intervention. The levers available to government to influence these markets, and thereby the consumption of these markets' products, are therefore very different. Another important difference stemming from the legal status of these drugs is the existence of a powerful and legitimate alcohol industry, which is perfectly within its rights to lobby government and seek to influence public opinion. Its black market reflection, the market in drugs controlled by the Misuse of Drugs Act 1971, appears to have very limited influence – at least in the UK.

These fundamental differences tend to send policy makers down very different paths. Nevertheless, the Welsh Assembly has opted to include drugs and alcohol within one strategic document. This is a significant political move – in that it inevitably draws attention to the continuity of psychoactive substances, something that has been fiercely resisted in the past. It also has practical ramifications in that it naturally leads to policies primarily designed for one side of the equation being applied to the other. Thus, the Welsh strategy's focus on wrap-around treatment seems to be applied to alcohol, as well as illicit drugs. For dependent users of alcohol, this may have important implications in terms of more holistic interventions.

However, the policy responses to alcohol and illicit drugs are largely different. The new focus in the drugs field is now on the rehabilitation of problem drug users: 'reintegration' to the UK government; 'recovery' to the Scottish Government; 'wrap-around services' for the Welsh. There is no new significant pot of funding for this work akin to that released for the New Labour policy of treatment in the criminal justice system. The

UK government is setting up pilot projects in England that will focus on the potential to redistribute resources and work in partnership in order to realise these new goals. Whether learning from these – and the Scottish Government's call for a change in culture – will be enough to realise real changes in how dependent drug users experience treatment on the ground remains to be seen.

The new wave of alcohol policies are no less radical in their intent. The growing awareness of the damages caused to society by harmful drinking and the ubiquitous, embedded, 'normalised' nature of drinking in our society has led governments in the UK to consider how the current drinking culture might be changed. One logical answer is communication and information campaigns that aim to make people reflect on their own alcohol consumption and give them the tools to calculate their consumption – and this approach is given strong emphasis. However, there is also a growing frustration with the alcohol industry and its perceived influence on drinking culture. The language of policy documents appears to have moved on from earlier talk of 'partnership' to actions that would restrict the way in which alcohol is promoted and sold.

These are therefore very interesting times in the UK drug and alcohol policy fields. However, many of these new policies are still at an early stage of development and a key issue for the future is whether and how these national strategies are translated into local policy and action – and, critically, whether the current economic recession will stymie the brave new world of the reintegration of drug users, on the one hand, and more coercive approaches to the alcohol industry on the other.

References

Babor, T.F., Caetano, R., Casswell, S., Edwards, G., Giesbrecht, N., Graham, K., Grube, J., Gruenewald, P., Hill, L., Holder, H., Homel, R., Österberg, E., Rehm, J., Room, R. and Rossow, I. (2003) *Alcohol: No Ordinary Commodity – Research and Public Policy.* Oxford and London: Oxford University Press.

Barnard, M. (2007) *Drug Addiction and Families.* London: Jessica Kingsley Publishers.

Booth, A., Brennan, A., Meier, P.S., O'Reilly, D.T., Purshouse, R., Stockwell, T., Sutton, A., Taylor, K.B., Wilkinson, A. and Wong, R. (2008) *The Independent Review of the Effects of Alcohol Pricing and Promotion.* Sheffield: University of Sheffield.

British Medical Association (2008) *Alcohol Misuse: Tackling the UK Epidemic.* London: British Medical Association.

Cabinet Office (2004) *Alcohol Harm Reduction Strategy for England.* London: Prime Minister's Strategy Unit.

Department of Culture, Media and Sport (2008) *Evaluation of the Impact of the Licensing Act 2003.* London: Department of Culture, Media and Sport.

Department of Health, Home Office, Department for Education and Skills, and Department for Culture, Media and Sport (2007) *Safe. Sensible. Social. The Next Steps in the National Alcohol Strategy.* London: Department of Health.

Duke, K. (2006) 'Out of crime and into treatment? The criminalisation of contemporary drug policy since Tackling Drugs Together.' *Drugs: Education, Prevention and Policy 13,* 5, 409–415.

Edwards, G. (2000) *Alcohol. The Ambiguous Molecule.* London: Penguin.

HM Government (1995) *Tackling Drugs Together: A Strategy for England 1995–1998.* London: HMSO.

HM Government (1998) *Tackling Drugs to Build a Better Britain: The Government's Ten-Year Strategy for Tackling Drugs Misuse.* London: The Stationery Office.

HM Government (2008) *Drugs: Protecting Families and Communities. The 2008 Drug Strategy.* London: Home Office.

Home Office (2009) *Safe. Sensible. Social. Selling Alcohol Responsibly: A Consultation on the New Code of Practice for Alcohol Retailers.* London: Home Office.

Kaner, E.F.S., Dickinson, H.O., Beyer, F.R., Campbell, F., Schlesinger, C., Heather, N., Saunders, J.B., Burnand, B. and Pienaar, E.D. (2007) 'Effectiveness of brief alcohol interventions in primary care populations.' *Cochrane Database of Systematic Reviews,* Issue 2. Art. no. CD004148.

Kneale, J. and French, S. (2008) 'Mapping alcohol: Health, policy and the geographies of problem drinking in Britain.' *Drugs: Education, Prevention and Policy 15,* 3, 233–249.

KPMG (2008) *Review of the Social Responsibility Standards for the Production and Sale of Alcoholic Drinks.* London: Home Office.

Mold, A. and Berridge, V. (2007) 'Crisis and opportunity in drug policy: Changing the direction of British drug services in the 1980s.' *Journal of Policy History 19,* 1, 29–48.

NHS/The Information Centre (2009) *Statistics on Alcohol: England, 2008.* London: NHS.

Reuter, P. and Stevens, A. (2007) *An Analysis of UK Drug Policy.* A monograph prepared for the UK Drug Policy Commission. London: UKDPC. Available at www.ukdpc.org.uk/docs/UKDPC%20 drug%20policy%20review.pdf, accessed on 26 June 2009.

Roberts, M. (2009) *Drug Treatment at the Crossroads. What It's for, Where it's at and How to Make It Even Better.* London: Drugscope.

Robertson, J.R., Bucknall, A.B.V., Welsby, P.D., Roberts, J.J.K., Inglis, J.M., Peutherer, J.F. and Brettle, R.P. (1986) 'Epidemic of AIDS related virus (HTLV-III/LAV) infection among intravenous drug abusers.' *British Medical Journal 292,* 527–529.

Scottish Government (2008a) *Changing Scotland's Relationship with Alcohol: A Discussion Paper on Our Strategic Approach.* Edinburgh: Scottish Government.

Scottish Government (2008b) *The Road to Recovery: A New Approach to Tackling Scotland's Drug Problem.* Edinburgh: Scottish Government.

Smith, L. and Foxcroft, D. (2009) *Drinking in the UK. An Exploration of Trends.* York: Joseph Rowntree Foundation.

Thom, B. (2001) 'A Social and Political History of Alcohol.' In N. Heather, T.J. Peters and T. Stockwell (eds) (2001) *International Handbook of Alcohol Dependence and Problems.* Chichester: Wiley.

Welsh Assembly Government (2008) *Working Together to Reduce Harm: The Substance Misuse Strategy for Wales 2008–2018.* Cardiff: Welsh Assembly Government.

PART II

Alcohol and Tobacco

CHAPTER 2

Is Alcohol Different?

Alcohol: Attitudes, beliefs and practice

Jack Law

At long last we are addressing the impact of our drinking behaviour on our health and well-being and the quality of life in our communities. But, focusing on alcohol is a much greater challenge than we perhaps first assume. Its legality, its easy availability, its allure as a lifestyle product, and its symbolic status all influence our attitudes, beliefs and practice. By more fully understanding these issues, it is argued, we can raise our awareness of the problems, and develop the policies and practices we need to address alcohol-related harm.

It is a truism that alcohol is 'no ordinary commodity', but our awareness of its extraordinariness is diminished by its ubiquity and visibility.

Alcohol, tobacco and illegal drug use

The debate about alcohol in Scotland and the rest of the UK has been overshadowed by that about the illegal use of drugs, despite most policy makers and practitioners knowing that in many respects alcohol misuse was a far greater problem. So, the social and health impact of illegal drug use took priority over alcohol misuse. It is only in the last few years that we have begun to rethink our beliefs about alcohol, and to develop some quite radical and innovative policy proposals to reduce the impact of alcohol-related harm in Scotland through changing our culture.

The fact is that every now and again we like to change our state of mind. We enjoy the stimulus, the relaxation, and the 'altered state' which some substances can give us. We enjoy the disinhibition and apparent relaxation which, albeit temporarily, comes from taking drugs. Alcohol, at least in Western societies, is the most easily available and the drug of choice.

While alcohol and tobacco have been relatively freely available to the global market for centuries, the availability of other mind-altering drugs has increasingly been the subject of state regulation. The difference between alcohol, tobacco and other drugs is that the former continue to be legally obtained and openly taken, whereas most other legal drug use is confined to substances which are, by and large, provided after assessment by a recognised professional for reasons of treatment.

Furthermore, whereas tobacco use is recognised as being without question harmful, and illicit drug use as socially, economically and personally extremely harmful, the personal, social and health risks of alcohol consumption have been underplayed to the extent that in our society they are habitually ignored, or indeed in some circumstances considered to be an attractive dimension of alcohol use.

Alcohol as a symbol

Alcohol use also carries symbolic meaning. It is associated with spiritual beliefs, with personal and social bonding and with other social rituals. Its symbolic resonance makes it in many respects quite unique. When we consider our attitudes and beliefs, the symbolic power of alcohol should not be underestimated, for this has a subconscious influence on our awareness about its misuse. In other words, it sets up contradictory and often confusing beliefs about a drug which on the one hand is associated with well-being and harmony, whereas on the other quite clearly contributes to significant health problems and social harm.

It is important to understand some fundamental issues about alcohol if we are to consider seriously how to address alcohol problems in our society. By doing so we will begin to understand how they impact on our ability to intervene and change the relationship we have with alcohol, and to change our culture. Our attitudes, beliefs and values about alcohol shape our consciousness, awareness, understanding and ultimately our ability to engage in the problems that arise from its misuse. We are influenced by three basic issues – legality, price and availability; and by understanding their impact we should be able to understand more clearly how to shape practice.

Legality and alcohol-related harm

It is legal to sell and buy alcohol to people above a certain age. It is legal to drink alcohol in most public places, in some designated public spaces and in the home. But it is not legal to sell to someone who is under age or intoxicated, or to drink in some public places. Yet despite these rules, we know and indeed tolerate them being flouted by appearing to celebrate the behaviours which arise from intoxication. It is only in the last few years in Scotland that we have begun to experience a change in public attitudes towards the lax application of licensing laws and tolerance of public drunkenness.

Traditionally the public debate about alcohol in Scotland has been about health risks, treatment services and the anti-social behaviour associated with excessive drinking. Only occasionally have the regulations governing the sale of alcohol been considered as a useful means of tackling alcohol-related harm. Despite the best intentions, the changes in legislation in Scotland in 1976 did not deliver the intended outcomes of reducing behaviours associated with excessive consumption. The fully coming into force in 2009 of the Licensing (Scotland) Act 2005 marked a change of approach. Scotland's new licensing law is based on five key principles, one of which is 'the protection and improvement of public health'. In other words, the law is based on harm-reduction principles, which resonate with other social and health policies related to reducing alcohol-related harm.

The implications for policy and practice are profound, for what this means is that licensing policy and decision making at local level must take account of public health and safety considerations. In other words, licensing decisions must address not only business concerns but also issues about the quality of life of communities and the well-being of their citizens. This strikes at the very heart of issues about alcohol-related harm and draws the retailer into making a contribution to the reduction of harm.

Furthermore, it acts as a counterbalance to an approach which focuses solely on the consequences of consumption, for example drink-driving laws, by considering the other side of the relationship between the drinker and the retailer, matters such as marketing and retailing practices, availability and price.

The Act also established Local Licensing Forums whose membership is drawn from local communities and representatives from health and social services. Their role is to work with Licensing Boards on the impact of their decisions on communities. There are now 40 Local Licensing Forums in Scotland, most in their infancy, but each beginning to engage with

Local Licensing Boards on local issues. Their value lies in community engagement, for this is an important way of changing our alcohol culture by working in communities not just on issues arising from the sale of alcohol, but challenging behaviours which contribute to social and health harms. By turning these issues into matters of public concern, local people are empowered and able to influence changes in behaviour that will have a positive benefit to their communities. By working with communities on the impact of licensing decisions on communities, the long-term impact should reduce social disturbance and free up resources to enable those with more deeply seated alcohol-related problems get the support they need.

So, in terms of public policy, the means by which the sale of alcohol is regulated is a powerful tool in tackling alcohol-related harm and a useful vehicle in creating meaningful partnerships between communities, the retail sector and public bodies. But this requires better-informed decision making and practice by all those involved in the regulation and sale of alcohol products. From April 2008 all local government elected members, licensees and bar staff have to be trained in licensing law, and with the introduction of Licensing Standards Officers we have a dedicated workforce whose role it is to improve compliance with and implementation of the law. It is expected that this will lead to improved decision making and retail practices and reduce the sale of alcohol to young people who are under the legal age and provide local businesses with the opportunity to engage in positive relationships with communities.

Globalisation and alcohol-related harm

The alcohol industry is essentially global; its reach is enormous for it penetrates every continent of the world. Marketing, advertising and price have to be considered in the context of a global alcohol industry which continually searches for new markets to develop, new partnerships to create through mergers and acquisitions, and new ways to sell its products. Like any global industry alcohol manufacturers seek to protect and develop their interests through influencing trade agreements and government policy. While no ordinary commodity, alcohol is an important economic commodity. It provides countries with export incomes, governments with revenues and people with jobs. A priority for alcohol producers and retailers is to create the optimum conditions for trade, which tends to mean as few restrictions on commercial enterprise as possible. International trade agreements such as the WTO General Agreement on Trade and the EU single market policy treat alcohol like any other commodity and take no account of the impact of marketing and price on alcohol-related harm. This has resulted in tax reductions in Denmark, Finland and Poland, with increases in consumption and in the incidence of alcohol-related harm. These agreements reduce the government's room for manoeuvre in developing effective policy measures on price – which are proven to be effective in reducing alcohol-related harm.

Price and alcohol-related harm

Unlike most other drugs, alcohol is freely available on the market, albeit usually subject to some restrictions. For most commodities price is a determinant of its value. In other words there tends to be a corresponding relationship between price and perceived value: the lower the price the lower the perceived value of a commodity. So it could be argued about alcohol.

Unlike many other commodities, there is a clear and unambiguous inverse relationship between the price of alcohol and alcohol-related harm. In other words, the lower the price the greater the harm. Not only is this a distinguishing feature of alcohol but it demands different policy responses from those relating to other products. Unsurprisingly, the alcohol industry rejects this position in the face of overwhelming evidence, and indeed continues to lobby and challenge policy initiatives based on price.

Alcohol products are also marketing tools. Cut-price alcohol is used as a marketing technique to entice customers into stores and encourage them to buy other products while there. In this sense alcohol is an 'extraordinary commodity' in that it appears to be used quite unashamedly as a cheap way of attracting customers.

Given the evidence that harm diminishes as price increases, the challenge for policy makers is clear. The 'protection and improvement of the public health' principle embodied in Scottish licensing law creates an opportunity for public health and related practitioners to influence the practice of cheap alcohol sales. This can be done if Licensing Boards' policies make the connection between the impact of the sale of cheap alcohol on the quality of life and well-being of our communities.

We know that some sections of our populations are more price-sensitive than others. Paradoxically those who are alcohol-dependent respond quickly to price increases by buying less. We also know that young people, especially those under the legal age to purchase alcohol, are also price-sensitive. So, if the practice of selling cut-price alcohol were to stop, we would see a positive change in some drinking behaviour. The implications for social work and health practice are self-evident: less time and resources spent on dealing with the consequences of alcohol-related incidents, leaving more available to treat the causes of dependence or problem behaviour.

Marketing, advertising and alcohol-related harm

Commercial interests in alcohol can be broken down into two distinct sectors – production and retail, each of which can be subdivided into segments with their own identifiable interests. All have one thing in common: to maximise consumer interest in their products. The methods by which alcohol products are brought to consumers' attention are central to achieving this aim. The practices adopted by many retailers in the UK make it increasingly apparent that alcohol products are used to attract consumers into stores from which they will purchase other non-alcohol-related products.

The importance of advertising and marketing processes cannot be overstated; for not only do they increase consumers' awareness of alcohol products, they also influence their consciousness and understanding of alcohol and diminish awareness of alcohol-related harm. The power of alcohol-related imagery is so important that even the industry itself agrees that its form and content should be regulated. But what difference does this make to policy makers and practitioners?

Well, we are all consumers, and just as likely to be influenced by sophisticated marketing techniques as anyone. The more we see alcohol promotions and advertising the less we are likely to think about the harm associated with its misuse and to spot the harm its misuse has on our lives and the lives of others. So perhaps it is no surprise that it has taken us quite some time to develop robust policy approaches to alcohol-related harm!

By promoting cut-price alcohol and stacking alcohol products high at key points in a store, consumers are encouraged to buy more of the product than they need. We all find it hard to resist a bargain, we all insist we will store those extra purchases for another day, but most of us consume the alcohol we have purchased more quickly than we intended. This is because our sense of the special value of that product is diminished because it is so cheap. Alcohol isn't bread, biscuits or beans! It is a drug, the sale of which is restricted by law, which may be consumed by adults and only in moderate quantities. But current marketing techniques serve to diminish our awareness and consequently our understanding of the risks we run, because we drink routinely and often consume more than we plan. This may explain why the UK's consumption of alcohol products has doubled in the last 40 years, rising from 5.7 litres of pure alcohol per person per year in 1960 to 11.3 litres in 2005. This is a huge challenge for it forces us to think critically about some of the very deeply held beliefs about alcohol which shape our social and drinking culture.

Our understanding of alcohol

Price, marketing and availability all have an impact on our consciousness and on our understanding of alcohol. Most people in Scotland drink alcohol, many of us to the point of intoxication and with little apparent personal harm or harm to others. We all believe we understand and know alcohol, and yet as has been demonstrated during an Alcohol Awareness week, when we are at home we tend to quaff larger measures and more frequently than is safe for our health and well-being. Unit-awareness is poor. Often we don't know the alcohol content of most of the drinks we consume, and many of us believe it is safer or preferable to be intoxicated by alcohol rather than by illicit drugs. Scotland's alcohol culture is typified as one which celebrates drunkenness. Our attitudes and cultural beliefs about alcohol have existed for generations, and this has served to diminish our understanding and appreciation of the harm alcohol misuse has on our society. Cheap and easily available alcohol reinforces that culture. Very few of us are immune to our culture, and this is the challenge for practitioners.

Alcohol Focus Scotland provides training to licensees and bar staff, part of which is about raising alcohol awareness. Around 20 per cent of those who undertake training claim to have changed their drinking behaviour for the better as a result of the course. Were we to do the same with social and health service practitioners the impact could be considerable. Not only would we have a healthier workforce, but we would also improve the likelihood of earlier intervention, more targeted interventions with individuals, and safer communities.

Arguably, improving our understanding and awareness of alcohol-related harm is the single most important starting point if we are serious about changing our culture and reducing harm. By raising our own awareness we challenge our own beliefs about alcohol, open ourselves to the earlier identification of harm, influence behaviour before it becomes harmful and contribute to making the change in our alcohol culture we so badly need.

The importance of partnerships in alcohol policy and regulation

Gerard Vaughan and Megan Larken

'The work of many'

Concepts of collaboration and partnerships are heard in a variety of public health contexts; and little wonder, as achieving complex public health goals requires collective action. Collaboration and partnerships are also important in the context of alcohol policy and regulation. For the Alcohol Advisory Council of New Zealand (ALAC), a Crown entity mandated to reduce alcohol-related harm, partnerships and relationships are integral to all that we do. Our strategic direction has adopted the Māori proverb *Ehara taku toa i te toa takitahi, engari, he toa takitini* – Success is not the work of one, but the work of many. Why are partnerships so important for reducing alcohol-related harm? This article will explore partnership initiatives in New Zealand, with some examples.

Different types of relationships

First, what do we mean by partnerships in the context of alcohol policy? Is it different from collaboration? One useful explanation is that a partnership is the most intensive form of collaboration at the end of a continuum of relationship types, starting with co-existence as the least intensive, and moving through to networking, co-operation, collaboration, and finally partnership (Craig and Courtenay 2004). (We would also add 'consultation' to this continuum.) The term 'collaboration' denotes working together on a project in a way that involves sharing power, perhaps even trading off or modifying one of your own objectives in order to achieve the most important shared objectives of the group. 'Partnership' denotes an even closer, ongoing relationship of working jointly and sharing resources. Having a definitional framework helps us to think about what type of relationship is needed for any given set of circumstances, depending on the nature of the job at hand and the organisations involved. This is important in alcohol policy because one may be dealing with stakeholders ranging from liquor industry groups to advocates of abstinence, as well as agencies that do not have alcohol and drugs as a core focus. This article will touch on activities in New Zealand that involve relationship types along the entire spectrum described above, not just partnerships in the strict sense of the word.

A basis for collaboration

Work in the alcohol field is particularly amenable to a collaborative approach. First, alcohol affects such a wide range of social and health outcomes that anyone working in alcohol policy or implementation will accumulate wide-ranging networks; these set the foundation for collaboration. Second, because alcohol is a legal, regulated drug, a wider range of tools and strategies must be used to regulate alcohol compared with the tools available to regulate illegal drugs (the classic example being licensing systems). Historically, strategies have aimed to control access, availability and affordability, but increasingly we are also seeking ways to modify social and physical drinking environments.

A modern regulatory system

In New Zealand, collaborative relationships have to be especially active and creative. This is partly because the regulatory framework (primarily the Sale of Liquor Act 1989) is so liberal that people working to reduce alcohol-related harm end up using non-regulatory options to the fullest. The object of the Act is to 'establish a reasonable system of control over the sale and supply of liquor to the public with the aim of contributing to a reduction of liquor abuse, so far as that can be achieved by legislative means'. Sometimes, debates about alcohol policy seem to present a black and white choice between legislative means and 'individual responsibility'. In reality, there is a varied landscape in between these two choices. An effective, modern regulatory system runs on a combination of regulatory authority, persuasion, social pressure, monitoring and enforcement measures. The most perfectly evidence-based and logical law will fail in practice without an underpinning of some measure of social consensus for the need for such a law and the fairness of the penalties therein. The New Zealand scene is heavily reliant on the persuasion and social pressure end of the regulatory pyramid, and to really maximise these effects, it is essential to communicate, co-operate, collaborate and innovate.

A national protocol

One good example of collaboration is the National Protocol on Alcohol Promotions. This is a voluntary code jointly developed by ALAC, the

Hospitality Association of New Zealand (HANZ), the New Zealand Police and Local Government New Zealand. The purpose of the code is to provide guidelines on the application of section 154a of the Sale of Liquor Act 1989. This Act prohibits 'the promotion of any event or activity held or conducted on the premises, that is intended or likely to encourage persons on the licensed premises to consume alcohol to an excessive extent'. The law doesn't provide details of what is and is not an acceptable promotion, so the National Protocol provides some examples of what may or may not comply with the spirit of the law. For instance, a complimentary standard drink upon arrival is deemed acceptable, but not a promotion involving multiple free drinks over a short time period. Premises that breach the code risk being prosecuted and fined under section 154a of the Act.

A community-based example

An example of collaboration, unique to New Zealand, is Te Ara Poka Tika, or Project Walkthrough. Under the Māori Community Development Act 1962, Māori wardens have powers and responsibilities to monitor licensed premises, and prevent drunkenness and disorderly behaviour.[1] There had been limited use of their powers in recent years, so the project took the traditional role and gave it a more contemporary focus. Te Ara Poka Tika is an inter-agency community-based programme involving local city councils, police, Te Puni Kokiri (the government's Māori development department), ALAC, the Māori Wardens Association and the wardens themselves.

Issuing licences

The role of New Zealand local government in regulating alcohol is different from larger countries. While councils have a wide brief in terms of promoting community well-being, they do not hold budgets for police services, which are centrally driven. Health services are allocated by district health boards, but public health services are still funded by the Ministry of Health (a central government agency). The Sale of Liquor Act gives each of New Zealand's 73 territorial authorities or councils the responsibilities and powers of a District Licensing Agency (DLA). A DLA issues licences for the sale of liquor to the public and certifies managers who are in control of those premises. They are also empowered to carry out other activities consistent with the purpose of the Act. These activities include working with other regulatory bodies, such as police and public health services,

---

1   There were precursors to the Māori warden service as early as the 1870s, as Māori organised themselves in response to changes brought by Europeans to New Zealand.

and monitoring licensees' compliance with the conditions of their liquor licence and the requirements of the Act. The workloads associated with this latter activity can put pressure on DLA priorities, especially in small territorial authorities with multiple demands on limited resources and staff time. A recent report on liquor licensing by the Auditor General included a finding that:

> DLAs must work closely with the Police and public health services. These working relationships were generally close, with evidence of effective collaboration. However, information was not always well coordinated between the three. Moreover, each approaches the liquor licensing function with different expectations and priorities, and has different resources available for this work. In our view, a formal agreement between the local DLAs, the Police, and the public health services – such as a protocol – to record the common goals, differing roles, and agreed approach to processing applications, sharing information, and pooling resources would help...such arrangements can serve as an enduring record and practical operating framework for working together. (Office of the Auditor General 2007, p.6)

Alcohol Accords

Alcohol Accords are collaborative frameworks achieved through a consultative and co-operative relationship between licensees, District Licensing Agencies, local councils and other interested stakeholders. Their purpose is to reduce local alcohol-related harm and ensure a safe and prosperous night-time economy. Depending on the nature of the locality and the type of Accord, groups may include security companies, taxi companies, bus companies, sports clubs, interest groups or community groups.

The book *Raising the Bar*, from Australia, found that 'the lack of evidence of the effectiveness of accords suggests that partnerships that emphasise purely voluntary compliance with good practices do not generally produce strategies that are sufficiently powerful or focused to reduce violence' (Graham and Homel 2008). Experience in New Zealand confirms this; but we have also found that licencees will co-operate with voluntary initiatives when the alternative is enhanced, targeted monitoring by enforcement agencies. For example, in Christchurch, a voluntary one-way door policy[2] set at 4am was implemented in 2006 (in October 2008 it changed to 3am).

ALAC commissioned an evaluation of the policy in 2007. Although there was a small increase in overall crime and violence in the inner city, serious violent offences decreased on Saturday-Sunday nights by 22 per cent. The evaluation also found a consistent shift toward improved perceptions of safety in the central business district at night. There was a unanimous view that relationships between stakeholders had been significantly improved and this was widely noted as an important achievement of the Accord. Critical success factors include the significant hands-on involvement of frontline police, and early formation of the Accord Management Team with strong licensee representation. According to the evaluation, the literature supports the importance of active leadership provided by licensees (Kirkwood and Parsonage 2007).

A further strength of collaborative arrangements such as Alcohol Accords is that they have the effect of building moral mandate, transparency and community spirit. It is not the local police officer approaching the local publican with his or her own judgment on a matter of concern, it is the police acting on behalf of the Accord. Accords also improve the efficiency of police resources because maximum use is made of self-regulation. Social responsibility amongst licensees is enhanced, with the group providing a pathway to help with dealing with disorderly behaviour on the premises and social problems they may come into contact with. For example, in the far north of New Zealand, one licensee who ran an off-licence bottle store was concerned about a customer who would buy alcohol for her partner, and the licensee knew the woman was a victim of partner abuse. Through the network the licensee had established via the Accord, the licensee was able to get advice and help for the family from a local social service provider.

Gaps in legislation

With regard to off-licences, progress in using self-regulatory and relationship-based strategies has been hampered by a lack of legislation to back it up. There is no off-licence equivalent to section 154a's ban on promotions likely to encourage excessive consumption, even though the operating environment for off-licence liquor sales is geared for bulk-buying and high-volume sales strategies. To address pricing issues would require

---

2   A 'one-way door' or 'lockout' policy means that patrons may exit the premises at the appointed time but no new ones may enter.

legislation. Pricing is an issue that cannot be solved via collaborative efforts alone because the requisite discussions between industry people would contravene the Commerce Act's provisions barring restrictive trade practices. In fact, one obstacle for Alcohol Accords has been when the Commerce Commission has intervened in response to complaints from some licensees opposed to the direction of Accord discussions. It is a challenge for police and DLAs to navigate the complexities of competition law while conducting Accords.

The lack of tools and strategies for off-licence practices is just one gap in the legislation. Another pressing problem is the lack of efficient avenues for local government regulation. Few councils have used to the fullest the regulatory tools available to them because these can be difficult and expensive, open to legal challenge and requiring a watertight evidence-base at micro-level. Consequently, some localities have simply too many licensed premises and communities are protesting. ALAC believes there is a need for a licensing system with a re-balanced basis for decision making about alcohol outlets, one which clearly takes into account the evidence-base for social impacts at a macro and district-wide level, as well as taking a precautionary approach and giving some weight to community feeling.

Ongoing consultation and collaboration have led to an increased understanding of deficiencies in the Sale of Liquor Act, and a wide consensus of belief has emerged that the legislation is out of step with alcohol market conditions and community views. The Liquor Licensing Authority is the central body charged with hearing disputed applications for liquor licences and disputed sanctions. In a recent decision refusing an off-licence application in Porirua East (an area with high levels of deprivation), the judge cited the object of the Act, and he stated: 'We used to refute the argument that the establishment of an off-licence would lead to an increase in liquor abuse and/or disorderly behaviour in the local community. Experience has persuaded us that such consequences are realistic.'

There is currently an amendment bill (the Sale and Supply of Liquor and Liquor Enforcement Bill) before Parliament in New Zealand with the primary aim of giving more power to communities and local authorities to deal with issues surrounding alcohol outlets by giving legal status to local licensing policies. In addition, a root and branch review of liquor legislation is being conducted by the New Zealand Law Commission, an independent Crown entity that includes a high level of stakeholder consultation.

Looking ahead

So what is the future of partnerships and collaboration to reduce alcohol-related harm in New Zealand? We are starting to see co-location of services, such as in the far north, and this is a welcome development. We would also like to see funding of full-time dedicated positions for local or regional alcohol coordinators in such places as the police, public health service or local authority.

Here we have discussed the importance of partnerships in alcohol policy and regulation. However, to get the legislation right also takes leadership on the part of governments. We have drawn on examples within New Zealand showing how collaboration at different levels is occurring between sector groups. With the development of the Global Alcohol Strategy, collaboration and partnerships between countries, particularly to deal with cross-border issues, will be important. International progress will benefit from sharing learning about what is already working within different countries.

References

Craig, D. and Courtenay, M. (2004) *The Potential of Partnership: Key Learnings and Ways Forward Based on Waitakere City Experiences*. Auckland: Local Partnerships and Governance Research Project.

Graham, K. and Homel, R. (2008) *Raising the Bar: Preventing Aggression in and Around Bars, Pubs and Clubs*. Portland, OR: Willan Publishing.

Kirkwood, L. and Parsonage, P. (2007) *Evaluation of the Christchurch City One-Way Door Intervention: Final Report*. Wellington: Alcohol Advisory Council of New Zealand.

Office of the Auditor General (2007) *Liquor Licensing by Territorial Authorities*. Wellington: OAG. Available at http://www.oag.govt.nz/2007/liquor-licensing/docs/oag-liquor-licensing.pdf, accessed on 24 June 2009.

CHAPTER 3

Fresh Air?

Second-hand smoke

Sally Haw

Second-hand smoke (SHS) is made up of exhaled mainstream smoke and side-stream smoke from the lit end of the cigarette. It contains a noxious mix of toxins and human carcinogens and there is overwhelming evidence that it is an important cause of lung cancer, coronary heart disease, respiratory disease and stroke in non-smokers. SHS exposure has also been found to exacerbate unstable angina and increase the risk of chronic obstructive pulmonary disease (COPD), upper and lower respiratory tract infections, and sudden infant death syndrome (SIDS) (US Department of Health and Human Services 2006).

SHS exposure in the home is associated with the greatest burden of disease, causing an estimated 10,700 deaths in the UK per annum (Jamrozik 2006). However, before the introduction of legislation that banned smoking in enclosed public places, SHS exposure at work was estimated to kill more than two employed people per working day (617 deaths per year), including 54 deaths in the hospitality industry each year in the UK (Jamrozik 2006).

Scottish smoke-free legislation

With the growing concern about the adverse health effects of SHS exposure and recognition of the failure of UK-level action to reduce SHS exposure through a voluntary charter for the hospitality sector (Plunkett *et al.* 2003), the Scottish Executive launched the first Scottish tobacco control action plan *A Breath of Fresh Air for Scotland* in 2004. This included proposals for a Scottish debate on second-hand smoke.

A national consultation was launched in June 2004, to which there were over 53,000 responses from organisations and individuals, representing the largest response ever to a Scottish consultation. The great majority of respondents, 82 per cent, endorsed the idea that further action was required to reduce exposure to second-hand smoke, and 80 per cent indicated that they would support a law creating smoke-free enclosed public places, with few exemptions (Scottish Executive 2004).

In December 2004 proposals for comprehensive smoke-free legislation were formally presented to the Scottish Parliament in the form of the Smoking, Health and Social Care (Scotland) Bill. It was eventually approved by Members of the Scottish Parliament (MSPs) on 30 June 2005, by a majority of 97 to 17 with one abstention and received Royal Assent on 5 August 2005.

The Smoking, Health and Social Care (Scotland) Act 2005 came into force at 6am on 26 March 2006. The legislation makes it an offence to smoke or to allow smoking in virtually all enclosed public and workplaces, including pubs and restaurants. There are only a few exemptions, including residential accommodation; designated rooms in adult care homes and hospices, psychiatric units and off-shore installations; designated hotel rooms, prison cells and police interview rooms; and private cars.

Smoke-free legislation came into force in Wales on 2 April 2008; in Northern Ireland on 30 April 2008; and in England on 1 July 2008.

Impact of the Scottish smoking ban

The decision to implement comprehensive smoke-free legislation was widely regarded as one of the most significant developments in public health policy for a generation, and so to assess its impact a comprehensive evaluation strategy was developed (Haw *et al.* 2006). The evaluation focused on eight key outcome areas – compliance with the legislation; second-hand smoke exposure; smoking prevalence and tobacco consumption; tobacco-related morbidity and mortality; knowledge and attitudes; socio-cultural adaptation; economic impacts on the hospitality sector; and health inequalities. Assessment of each of the outcome areas was based on a combination of secondary analyses of routine health, behavioural and economic data as well as a portfolio of eight research projects especially commissioned to address specific questions. The research studies focused on intermediate impacts up to one year after the implementation of the legislation, while the routine data will permit changes to be monitored over a much longer period – three years in the first instance. In the rest of this chapter, we report on findings on levels of compliance; changes in second-hand smoke exposure; health impacts; and socio-cultural and behavioural change.

Compliance with smoke free legislation

Environmental health officers (EHOs) are responsible for enforcement of the legislation and data on inspections of bars and other workplaces indicated that right from the very start compliance with the legislation was high. In the first three months following implementation, there were 32,000 inspections of which 97 per cent were compliant with the smoking regulations. In spite of fewer inspections, which by autumn 2008 had fallen to about 8000 per quarter, compliance with smoking regulations has been maintained. At the same time compliance with the requirement to display no smoking signage increased from 80 per cent to 97 per cent by autumn 2008 (Scottish Government 2009).

A detailed ethnographic study of eight bars in three contrasting communities conducted by Eadie and colleagues (2008) sheds further light on compliance. They found that staff in all study bars attempted to enforce the ban. Three factors – high public awareness of the law, concerns about licensee liability and perceptions that the legislation had been 'imposed' upon the licensed trade – were all thought to have helped staff to challenge customer violations. Having outdoor drinking areas to which smokers could be directed also facilitated enforcement. In general, instances of non-compliance were thought to be unintentional, the majority being attributed to attention lapses or absent-mindedness, usually by older customers and customers under the influence of alcohol or lack of awareness among customers from outside Scotland.

However, in bars located in deprived communities compliance was lower and there was less support for the legislation than in more affluent communities (Eadie et al. 2008; Richmond, Haw and Pell 2007). Nevertheless, all bar staff attempted to enforce legislation, with fear of prosecution cited as the main motive for enforcing the ban. Interestingly, knowledge of enforcement process, fines and personal liability was often poor, with most study participants overestimating the financial value of fines (Eadie et al. 2008).

Combined with findings from Hyland et al. (2009), who also reported dramatic reductions in observed smoking in restaurants, cafes and other workplaces as well as in pubs, it appears that within a year of implementation, the Scottish ban had become largely self-enforcing. However, given that fear of prosecution was given as the primary motivation for enforcing the ban – continued visible monitoring by EHOs and swift action when violations occur are likely to be important in maintaining compliance in coming years.

Improvement in air quality and reduction in SHS exposure

Studies of the impact of smoke-free legislation on SHS exposure have been conducted in other jurisdictions where complete bans have been introduced, for example in the US (Eisner, Smith and Blanc 1998), Norway (Ellingsen *et al.* 2006), the Republic of Ireland (Allwright *et al.* 2005) and Italy (Gasparrini *et al.* 2006). These studies have typically found falls of 80–90 per cent in air- and bio-markers of SHS exposure within a few days, weeks or months of introduction of smoke-free legislation.

Semple, Creely and colleagues (2007) set out to measure changes in air quality in a sample of 41 pubs in two Scottish cities by monitoring $PM_{2.5}$. These are very small respiratory particles most of which in indoor air come from SHS. Baseline measurements were made during an eight-week period leading up to implementation of the legislation and then again two months after implementation. They found that two months after the legislation had been introduced, $PM_{2.5}$ concentrations had fallen by 86 per cent and that air quality in the majority of Scottish pubs was now equivalent to that of outdoor air (Semple, personal communication).

The improvement in air quality in bars was also reflected in self-reported SHS exposure and salivary cotinine measures obtained from a cohort of bar workers recruited from 72 bars. Cotinine is a metabolite of nicotine present in body fluids, and in non-smokers is a bio-marker of SHS exposure in the previous three to four days. Among non-smoking bar workers, salivary cotinine concentrations fell by 89 per cent one year after legislation (Semple, MacCalman *et al.* 2007), indicating that the reductions in SHS exposure observed at two months were sustained for a full year after the legislation had been introduced.

While the evidence of the impact of smoke-free legislation on occupational, particularly bar workers', exposure is now extensive, relatively little has been done to assess the impact of legislation on levels of SHS exposure in the general population. However, two repeat cross-sectional studies in the Scottish evaluation – a household survey of adults (Haw and Gruer 2007) and a school-based survey of Primary 7 (10- to 12-year-old) school children (Akhtar *et al.* 2007) – set out to do this. Measures of SHS exposure were based on both self-reported exposure and salivary cotinine concentrations.

In both non-smoking adults and children salivary cotinine concentrations fell by 39 per cent post-legislation. However, the reductions in SHS exposure were not similar across all groups. In adult non-smokers from non-smoking households, average cotinine concentrations fell by 49 per cent compared with a 16 per cent reduction among non-smokers from smoking households, which was not statistically significant. Similarly in Primary 7 pupils, the reduction in cotinine concentrations was greatest among children from homes where neither parent smoked (51% fall) and among children from homes where the father figure smoked (44% fall). In children from homes where either only the mother or both parents smoked only an 11 per cent and non-significant reduction was observed.

In both adults and children, the reduction in salivary cotinine was associated primarily with reductions in reported SHS exposure in public places. However, despite the continuing very high levels of home exposure in some groups, particularly children, neither study found evidence of displacement of smoking from public places into the home.

Respiratory health of bar workers

A number of studies have reported improvements in the respiratory health of bar workers linked to new smoke-free law. Both US (Eisner *et al.* 1998) and Irish studies (Allwright *et al.* 2005; Goodman *et al.* 2007) found improvements in lung function as well as reductions in reported respiratory (wheezing, coughing, phlegm) and sensory (irritated eyes, sore throat) symptoms.

Menzies *et al.* (2006) replicated the Eisner study findings reporting improvements in respiratory and sensory symptoms in Dundee bar workers together with a 5.1 per cent mean improvement in lung function two months post-legislation. However, seasonal factors including differences in temperature and rates of respiratory infections between collection of baseline measures in February and at follow-up in May cannot be ruled out as alternative explanation of these findings.

As part of the national evaluation, Ayres and colleagues (2009) followed over 190 bar workers from over 70 bars over a longer 12-month period, thus eliminating possible seasonal confounders. They found that reported improvements in respiratory and sensory symptoms were maintained one year after their workplaces had become smoke-free. In non-smokers, the

largest reductions in individual symptoms were in the proportion of bar
workers reporting phlegm production (which fell from 33% to 14%) in the
proportion reporting irritated eyes (which fell from 39% to 11%) and in
the proportion reporting sore throat (which fell from 44% to 25%) about
one year after the ban. Interestingly, improvements were also obtained in
the respiratory health of smokers with the proportion reporting wheezing
fell from 48 per cent immediately before the ban to 31 per cent one year
later, while reports of irritated eyes fell from 35 per cent to 25 per cent
in the same time period. Measures of lung function were also obtained
from bar workers participating in the study, but no improvement was
observed. The research team suggest that this may have been due in part to
methodological problems associated with measuring lung function in the
field rather than in a clinical setting (Ayres, personal communication).

Reductions in heart attack in the general population

Second-hand smoke exposure is associated with a number of cardiovascular
changes, including epithelial dysfunction, platelet aggregation, oxidative
stress, inflammation, decreased energy production in the heart muscle,
and a decrease in the parasympathetic output to the heart. The multi-
dimensional impacts of SHS exposure on the cardiovascular system provides
some explanation of a much greater than expected risk associated with
passive smoking and cardiovascular disease compared with active smoking
(Barnoya and Glantz 2005). There are now eight published studies that
have analysed routine hospital admission data for heart attack (Barone-
Adesi *et al.* 2006; Bartecchi *et al.* 2006; Cesaroni *et al.* 2008; Juster *et al.*
2007; Khuder *et al.* 2007; Lemstra, Neudorf and Opondo 2008; Sargent,
Shepard and Glantz 2004; Seo and Torabi 2007). All report reductions
in the number of hospital admissions for heart attack following smoking
bans. However, there are a number of methodological issues; in particular,
problems associated with small numbers of cases and/or consistency of
diagnosis over time, as well as lack of information on smoking status.
To overcome these problems, a prospective study of admissions for acute
coronary syndrome (ACS) to nine general hospitals was conducted as part
of the Scottish evaluation (Pell *et al.* 2008). Using a standard case definition
of chest pain plus raised troponins (a marker of damage to the heart muscle)
in admission blood sample, data were collected from consenting patients on
smoking status and exposure to SHS. In addition, admission blood samples
were tested for cotinine. Pell and colleagues found that the number of
ACS admissions fell from 3235 in the ten-month period leading up to the

ban (June 2005 to March 2006) to 2684 in the same ten-month period post-ban – a 17 per cent reduction overall. In smokers the reduction was 14 per cent compared with 19 per cent in ex-smokers and 21 per cent in never smokers. The overall reduction of 17 per cent compares with a 4 per cent reduction in ACS admissions over a similar period in England and a mean annual reduction of 3 per cent in ACS admissions in Scotland in the ten-year period preceding the study. This study provides a robust assessment of the impact that smoking bans can have on population health and confirms the findings from the other studies.

Socio-cultural and behavioural change

A number of the studies in the national evaluation have collected data on behavioural and socio-cultural change and, although presenting a much more complex and not entirely consistent picture, there is evidence the Scottish smoke-free legislation has been accompanied by a number of marked behavioural and socio-cultural adaptations.

Martin, Ritchie and Amos (2008) conducted a complex longitudinal qualitative study of four communities. They report that despite pre-legislation hostility and bravado that there would be mass flouting of the law particularly in deprived communities, there was a high degree of compliance, albeit sometimes accompanied by continuing resentment. There was some enthusiasm in study participants about the aesthetic changes to public places and the impact of the legislation on their own and others' smoking, but it was also clear that some groups – especially older men whose social lives centred around bars – experienced a sense of loss as their smoking and drinking companions stayed at home.

Hyland et al. (2009) found that once implemented there was growing support for the legislation among both Scottish non-smokers and smokers. In the rest of the UK, where at the time of the study legislation had not yet been implemented, support also increased over the same period, but the increase in support was much greater in Scotland. Support for the legislation among bar workers also increased, while at the same time concerns about the economic impact of the legislation among bar workers fell quite considerably (Hilton et al. 2007). This is consistent with Hyland and colleagues' (2009) conclusion that the Scottish legislation had not had a major impact on reported frequency of visiting bars and restaurants overall. However, notably in Scotland, non-smokers reported visiting bars more often post-legislation.

Martin *et al.* (2008) also reported that implementation of the legislation was associated with changes in smoking behaviour. Changes occurred in all four localities but were greatest in disadvantaged communities where there was a greater overall reduction in reported consumption of tobacco, including quitting. Two mechanisms were postulated. First, previously context-specific routine and habitual smoking behaviour was disrupted by the smoking legislation. Second, stigma associated with being a more visible smoker reduced consumption. This was acutely experienced, (particularly by women who smoked) even in communities where smoking had previously been prevalent and been both accepted and acceptable.

However, while some smokers may have quit smoking as a result of the smoking ban there is little evidence that this occurred consistently across Scotland. Data from the Scottish Household Survey (Scottish Government 2008a) indicates that smoking prevalence declined from 26.2 per cent in 2005 to 25.0 per cent in 2006 and to 24.7 per cent in 2007, which is in line with the underlying trend pre-legislation. Over-the-counter sales of nicotine replacement therapy (NRT) did increase in the three months leading up to the Scottish legislation (Lewis, Haw and McNeill 2008), but this did not continue post-legislation. One year post-legislation, Hyland and colleagues (2009) also failed to find differences in smoking cessation indicators in Scotland compared to the rest of the UK, and reported NRT use actually decreased in Scotland relative to the rest of the UK post-legislation. In combination these data suggest that there was an acceleration of quitting in the build-up to the legislation but that this was not sustained once the legislation came into force.

While the results on smoking prevalence are disappointing there is some evidence of changing norms about exposing others to SHS in private places. Martin and colleagues report that post-legislation, there was better understanding and an increased awareness of the effects of second-hand smoke, which is consistent with more stringent home smoking restrictions following the Scottish ban reported by both Haw and Gruer (2007) and Hyland *et al.* (2009).

In summary

On 26 March 2006, the Smoking, Health and Social Care (Scotland) Act came into force, prohibiting smoking in virtually all enclosed public places. Implementation of the legislation was accompanied by very high levels of compliance and the impacts on SHS exposure among bar workers and the general population, health and socio-cultural norms have been much greater than expected.

The national evaluation of the Scottish legislation found:

- an 86 per cent improvement in air quality in bars, with air quality in most post-legislation equivalent to outdoor air

- an 89 per cent reduction in SHS exposure in bar workers

- a 39 per cent reduction in SHS exposure in adults and 11-year-old children

- improvements in the respiratory health of bar workers

- a dramatic 17 per cent reduction in hospital admissions for acute coronary syndrome

- an increase in support for the legislation post-implementation among both smokers and non-smokers but with evidence of less support in more deprived communities

- an increase in awareness of the risks associated with SHS and some evidence of changing social norms around exposing others to SHS

- some evidence of more stringent home smoking restrictions post-legislation

- some evidence that smokers, particularly women, experienced feelings of stigma associated with more visible smoking

- some evidence of social isolation among older male smokers who no longer frequented pubs following the smoking ban.

The evaluation did not find:

- any evidence of displacement of smoking from public places into the home

- consistent evidence of increased quitting associated with the legislation.

However, while the Scottish smoke-free legislation has been a great success, it is clear that some adults and children who live in smoking households continue to be exposed to very high levels of SHS while at home. Further action on this is urgently required.

Second Chance Learning: A community-development approach to smoking cessation

Margaret Black, Anne Bryce and Linda McKie

The aim of this brief case study is to describe the evaluation of a community-development smoking cessation project. We also draw out the implications of this work for the community-development approach, for organisations that provide support for tobacco control and for evaluation practice.

A community-development approach is one in which a group of people, who may be defined by geography, workplace, interest, age group or other criteria come together to define their needs, consider how those needs might be met, and to decide collectively on priorities for action (Jones 1991). In the specific case of tobacco control, a community-development approach is one in which a group of people in a given locality (or organised around a specific topic) defines its health needs in relation to tobacco; considers how those needs can be met; and decides collectively on priorities for action.

The Inverclyde Tobacco Strategy was a project implemented in an area in which deprivation levels are high and smoking is the norm, and through which small grant funding of £5000 was made available to each of the three pilot initiatives, from April 2000 to March 2001. The project was supported in several ways. For example, it was decided to consult with people working at community level at all stages of the project. Moreover, the project aimed to support initiatives that acknowledged the (often complex) role that smoking plays in people's lives, and as a concomitant to that, recognised disparate experiences and needs amongst those who wished to address their tobacco use. Thus smoking cessation was not the sole goal of the project: there was a wider aim to promote a culture in which attempting to stop smoking was acceptable. This was done by taking a flexible approach and supporting work which aimed to enhance the self-confidence of participants, thereby increasing their confidence in their ability to address their own smoking as well as tobacco control in their local communities (Health Promotion Department, Argyll and Clyde Health Board 2000).

This case study considers the evaluation of one pilot initiative, hosted by Second Chance Learning.

The evaluation

The evaluation team[1] collected information on the training provided to participants, the work of each of the initiatives, and the work of the Health Board Tobacco Steering Group on a continuing basis. In the light of the Health Promotion Department's wish that the evaluation should 'tell the story of the [strategy] and its achievements at the end point...[and] support an evolving and developing process', particular attention was paid to documenting and understanding approaches and methods that have provided support to participants and raised awareness more generally (Shaw 1999). The evaluation included both formative and process approaches, employing a range of methods including semi-structured interviews with project staff, focus group and telephone interviews with participants and, when appropriate, monitoring of smoking status. Data was collected from April 2000 to May 2001, primarily by one of the authors, Margaret Black. Further information was derived from attendance at Steering Group and other meetings. The range of methods used provided the potential for triangulation. Analysis of the data was undertaken by the members of the evaluation team who individually reviewed the data to draw out themes which were then discussed and agreed with other team members. In keeping with the approach of a formative evaluation, the team provided regular feedback to those involved in the strategy so as to encourage reflection, and change where appropriate. In addition, the process element ensured the team could provide in-depth descriptions of how the various dimensions of the strategy were established and operated, as well as charting progress to outcomes and future work. The team also conducted focus groups with the Argyll and Clyde Tobacco Steering Group (Black *et al.* 2001).

Second Chance Learning

Second Chance Learning (SCL) was a community-based education project established in 1987, and was located in a relatively deprived part of Greenock, in an area with a preponderance of local authority housing. Unemployment is high, and in the wider Inverclyde area economic activity is decreasing. SCL had a strong community-development ethos, and offered its users accredited training courses, as well as discussion and support groups. One of SCL's objectives was to encourage hard-to-reach groups, (people on low incomes, the unemployed) into learning situations

---

1   The evaluation team comprised two of the authors and the third author was, at the time of the evaluation, health board officer responsible for community-development projects on tobacco cessation.

(Second Chance Learning 2001). It had a well-established management committee, which included members of the local community and students at SCL. There was a high degree of trust between the committee and the staff, and it is worth noting that although there was a friendly and informal atmosphere within the project, this existed within a formal and structured approach to its continuing development.

SCL faced particular challenges in that the population of the Inverclyde area is decreasing, and the residual population includes a significant number of people for whom the transition from benefits to work is perceived to have potentially adverse financial implications. Although SCL had been in existence for many years, there remained misconceptions about its remit. Some people believed that it was available only for the unemployed, but conversely, when more affluent students were attracted, the sight of smart cars in the car park could leave the more disadvantaged members of the local community feeling that SCL was not for them. This had implications for SCL's aim of attracting students who might not be reached by more traditional educational establishments.

When there was interest in a topic, SCL staff and users would spend time looking at the issues and agreeing the way in which they wanted to approach it. The numbers of users involved in this preparation might be small, or it could be all the users who potentially would be involved in the particular class or activity, as it was in the case of the tobacco work. Generally, users were realistic about the level of resources available, and staff were experienced in accessing resources from a variety of sources. Activities might be started with a relatively small number of students, knowing that numbers were likely to increase over time.

The nature of SCL's involvement in the Inverclyde Tobacco Strategy derived from an initial investigation of the problem, in which potential group members considered what might be appropriate support interventions for the circumstances of their community (Kirkwood 1991). They met in this capacity for some weeks before becoming committed to act on their smoking, and this methodology sat very comfortably with SCL's preferred way of working, summarised by the project manager as 'SCL doesn't do for, it does with'. The outcome of the discussions by this original group was that the objective of SCL's tobacco initiative should be to provide help with stress management, confidence building, and assertiveness; as well as advising on the avoidance of weight gain; and providing opportunities for development in other aspects of participants' lives. With support from the local pharmacy, SCL was also able to give help with nicotine replacement therapy.

Membership of the groups came not only from existing users, but also by way of referrals from the Greenock Health Centre tobacco initiative. Activities included stress management; confidence building; and advice about diet and exercise, since some group members had concerns about the possibility of weight gain. A health visitor came to measure blood pressure and peak-flow readings; and for those who had given up, improvements in these figures were very encouraging. Reflecting SCL's wish to respond to the needs of the participants, the activities of a second group were different: for example they wanted more of the 'fear factor' – information and images to illustrate the dangers of continuing to smoke. Between the two groups (13 members in all), 12 participants stopped smoking, although nine started again – citing, for example, the stresses of the Christmas period as the trigger. Though there was some drop-off in numbers, members continued to meet, as an amalgamated group, following the formal end of the tobacco initiative. Some of the members whose quit attempts had been unsuccessful were encouraged by their continued membership of the group to plan to try again. Members also performed their own rap and drama sketches for the local community and for schools.

For SCL staff, the success of the tobacco initiative was not only that some group members were able to quit, but also that they understood better why they had wanted to smoke, and so became more able to develop strategies to cope with these issues. It was important that intermediate indicators such as these are given weight not only by individual initiatives, but also by the Health Board and the steering group, since most smokers will try many times to stop before achieving that absolute success (Department of Health 1998). Relying only on quantitative measurements will tend grossly to understate the progress that is made by the participants.

Implications for current and future practice
Using an inequalities-sensitive lens

In 2008, two Scottish Government policy documents, *Equally Well*, the report of the Ministerial Task Force on Health Inequalities, and *Achieving Our Potential: A Framework to Tackle Poverty and Income Inequality in Scotland*, set out the actions required to tackle poverty and address inequalities in health. Public sector bodies are now required to take action within their spheres of responsibility to address inequalities:

- by acting on poverty, social exclusion and worklessness
- by tackling discrimination and promoting equality

- by ensuring that children and young people have the best start in life, so that all can realise their potential and avoid poverty in later life.

These reflections offer a review of the work and evaluation of Inverclyde Tobacco Initiative within this policy context.

STRENGTHS

During the life of the initiative there was an attempt to engage with all service users affected by tobacco use in order to seek their views, their involvement in and their ownership of the initiative. This non-judgmental, inclusive approach was successful on a number of fronts:

- the reduction of stigma associated with smoking
- the reduction of stigma associated with quitting in a community where smoking is the norm
- the identification of perceived support needs e.g. confidence building.

IMPLICATIONS FOR EVALUATION

There is significant value in ensuring that all those involved in this type of project work, whether as staff or participant, are engaged in the process of the development of the evaluation plan. This can reinforce the message that giving up smoking is a process (potentially a long one) that must acknowledge the full implications of smoking in a person's life, and the circumstances of that life.

IMPLICATIONS FOR CURRENT AND FUTURE PRACTICE

Continued smoking in a society where smoking is no longer the norm is associated with inequalities: low-income communities such as in Inverclyde have higher rates of smoking prevalence. And while it was recognised that smoking served a number of social functions within the community (e.g. coping with stress, rewarding self, relaxation), the focus of the group was primarily on smoking as a problematic, individual behaviour. So, for example, the group looked at ways of managing stress rather than finding solutions to the causes of stress such as money worries, isolation, unemployment – issues which are socially and politically mediated.

Use of community-based organisations to provide tobacco control support

STRENGTHS

Apart from the more obvious economic benefits of using resources already established within the community, there were a number of other advantages to basing the initiative in a local project. A key issue was that the centre had an established reputation for user-centred work, with an established ethos of equality and acceptance. A process of levelling was at work in SCL where they prided themselves on 'working with rather than doing for' centre users.

IMPLICATIONS FOR EVALUATION

Project workers and participants were invited to discuss achievements and set-backs at local conferences held to feed back interim findings. All present were able to work together to agree how best to use the information, that had been affirmed through debate, to support further progress. Making participants equal partners in the evaluation process in such ways can help to diminish power differentials.

IMPLICATIONS FOR CURRENT AND FUTURE PRACTICE

Power differentials can act as a barrier to people accessing the help they need. For example, 'minority stress', the feeling of difference and/or inferiority that can arise in relation to real or perceived discrimination, can be most acutely felt in those healthcare settings where people from low-income communities have low status and power (i.e. that they are recipients of care rather than equal partners in care planning). An expert-led approach may have merit in treating disease but may be less good at supporting change in the life-style behaviours and social circumstances that underpin ill-health.

Project user involvement in preparation for the Inverclyde Tobacco Initiative

STRENGTHS

Smokers at all stages of the cycle of change were invited to get involved and consider what a smoking cessation service for people like them, might look like. By de-personalising the issue, defensiveness over the subject matter was dissipated and smokers got engaged in determining the content of the imagined service.

IMPLICATIONS FOR EVALUATION

It is vital to think early and widely about anticipated outcomes, outputs and indicators to ensure that these adequately capture what is likely to be a wide range of effort and achievement. The SCL project described itself as providing smokers with the opportunity to 'practise' stopping smoking as a way of encouraging reflection on what would be helpful to them. However, the evaluation team was not in place until after training had been provided and the first group was already trying to give up. Earlier engagement in the process could have reinforced the message that early results based on quitting were not essential for the success of the project.

IMPLICATIONS FOR CURRENT AND FUTURE PRACTICE

This inclusive approach allowed determined smokers to consider what they might not normally consider – what might support them to stop smoking. This process allowed smokers to consider the possibility of change, to build motivation around stopping smoking and to make tentative steps toward behaviour change.

One size doesn't fit all: Appreciation of diversity
STRENGTHS

A learning model was used to support group enquiry into the constituent elements of effective smoking cessation support and the identification of individual participant needs in relation to stopping smoking. It became apparent that different groups identified different support needs, which demanded a range of interventions. Group enquiry was effective primarily in identifying psychological and behavioural issues, such as low self-esteem and weight gain.

IMPLICATIONS FOR EVALUATION

An inclusive and participatory evaluation process has the potential to offer extra opportunities for exploration of the barriers and inhibitors to progress. The tendency to relapse at Christmas, for example, was initially assumed to be related to the increased number of social occasions at which people could be tempted to smoke, and it was only through open discussion with participants that other underlying reasons were identified and acknowledged.

IMPLICATIONS FOR CURRENT AND FUTURE PRACTICE

The use of a group work model to undertake investigative enquiry into effective smoking-cessation activity can both engage and motivate group members in the personal decision to make an active attempt to stop smoking. This can help to identify personal needs such as confidence-building and diet control, and enable programmes to be developed to address these expressed needs. There is also an opportunity to explore underlying issues arising from social inequalities, such as money worries or domestic abuse, and to offer help and support in dealing with these and other issues which will otherwise lessen people's chances of making a successful quit attempt.

Conclusion

To be inequalities sensitive and perhaps to be more effective, smoking cessation services should be located in venues that are credible, acceptable and accessible to low-income and diverse communities. Services should work in partnership with smokers to identify personal and social barriers to stopping smoking and provide appropriate support. This could include referral on to helping agencies such as financial inclusion services. Similarly, behaviour change support requires to be set in the context and realities of people's daily lives and viewed as a process of change that may require a longer lead up period to build motivation and self-confidence prior to a quit attempt, include multiple attempts to stop smoking and opportunities for long-term support.

References

Akhtar, P.C., Currie, D.B., Currie, C.E. *et al.* (2007) 'Changes in child exposure to environmental tobacco smoke (CHETS) study after implementation of smoke-free legislation in Scotland: national cross sectional survey.' *British Medical Journal 335*, 545–549.

Allwright, S., Paul, G., Greiner, B. *et al.* (2005) 'Legislation for smoke-free workplaces and health of bar workers in Ireland: before and after study.' *British Medical Journal 331*, 1117.

Ayres, J.G., Semple, S., MacCalman, L. *et al.* (2009) 'Bar workers' health and environmental tobacco smoke exposure (BHETSE): Symptomatic improvement in bar staff following smoke-free legislation in Scotland.' *Occupational and Environmental Medicine 66*, 339–346.

Barnoya, J. and Glantz, S. (2005) 'Cardiovascular effects of secondhand smoke: Nearly as large as smoking.' *Circulation 111*, 2684–2698.

Barone-Adesi, F., Vizzini, L., Merletti, F. and Richiardi, L. (2006) 'Short-term effects of Italian smoking regulation on rates of hospital admission for acute myocardial infarction.' *European Heart Journal 27*, 2468–2472.

Bartecchi, C., Alsever, R.N., Nevin-Woods, C. *et al.* (2006) 'Reduction in the incidence of acute myocardial infarction associated with a citywide smoking ordinance.' *Circulation 114*, 1490–1496.

Black, M., McKie, L., Allen, E. and Barlow, J. (2001) *Community Based Approaches to Tobacco Control in the Inverclyde Area: The Evaluation of the Inverclyde Tobacco Strategy and Initiatives.* Glasgow: Glasgow Caledonian University.

Cesaroni, G., Forastiere, F., Agabiti, N., Valente, P., Zuccaro, P. and Perucci, C.A. (2008) 'Effect of Italian smoking ban on population rates of acute coronary events.' *Circulation 117*, 1183–1188.

Department of Health (1998) *Smoking Kills: Tobacco White Paper.* London: The Stationery Office.

Eadie, D., Heim, D., MacAskill, S. *et al.* (2008) 'A qualitative analysis of compliance with smoke-free legislation in community bars in Scotland: implications for public health.' *Addiction 103*, 1019–1026.

Eisner, M.D., Smith, A.K. and Blanc, P.D. (1998) 'Bartenders' respiratory health after establishment of smoke-free bars and taverns.' *Journal of the American Medical Association 280*, 22, 1909–1914.

Ellingsen, D.G., Fladseth, G., Daae, H.L. *et al.* (2006) 'Airborne exposure and biological monitoring of bar and restaurant workers before and after the introduction of a smoking ban.' *Journal of Environmental Monitoring 8*, 3, 362–368.

Gasparrini, A., Gorini, G., Marcolina, D. *et al.* (2006) 'Second-hand smoke exposure in Florence and Belluno before and after the Italian smoke-free legislation.' *Epidemiologia e Prevenzione 30*, 6, 348–351.

Goodman, P., Agnew, M., McCaffrey, M. *et al.* (2007) 'Effects of the Irish smoking ban on respiratory health of bar workers and air quality in Dublin pubs.' *American Journal of Respiratory and Critical Care Medicine 175*, 840–845.

Haw, S.J. and Gruer, L. (2007) 'Changes in adult exposure to second hand smoke following implementation of smoke-free legislation in Scotland.' *British Medical Journal 335*, 549–552.

Haw, S., Gruer, L., Amos, A. *et al.* (2006) 'Legislation on smoking in enclosed public places: How will we evaluate the impact?' *Journal of Public Health 38*, 24–30.

Health Promotion Department, Argyll and Clyde Health Board. (2000) *Evaluation of the Inverclyde Tobacco Initiative.* Paisley: Argyll and Clyde Health Board.

Hilton, S., Semple, S., Miller, B.G. *et al.* (2007) 'Expectations and changing attitudes of bar workers before and after the implementation of smoke-free legislation in Scotland.' *BMC Public Health 7*, 206.

Hyland, A., Hassan, L.M., Higbee, C. *et al.* (2009) 'The impact of smoke free legislation in Scotland: Results from the Scottish International Tobacco Policy Evaluation Project.' *European Journal of Public Health.* Doi: 10.1093/eurpub/ckn141.

Jamrozik, K. (2006) 'An Estimate of Deaths Attributable to Passive Smoking in Europe.' In *Lifting the Smokescreen: 10 Reasons for a Smoke Free Europe.* Brussels: European Respiratory Society.

Jones, J. (1991) *Community Development and Health Education: Concepts and Philosophy.* Health Education Unit Occasional Papers, Vol 1. Milton Keynes: Open University.

Juster, H.R., Loomis, B.R., Hinman, T.M. *et al.* (2007) 'Declines in hospital admissions for acute myocardial infarction in New York State after implementation of a comprehensive smoking ban.' *American Journal of Public Health 97*, 2035–2039.

Khuder, S.A., Milz, S., Jordan, T., Price, J., Silvestri, K. and Butler, P. (2007) 'The impact of a smoking ban on hospital admissions for coronary heart disease.' *Preventative Medicine 45*, 3–8.

Kirkwood, G. (1991) 'Education in the community. Fallacy: The Community Educator Should Be a Non-directive Facilitator.' In B. O'Hagan (ed.) *Charnwood Papers: Fallacies in Community Education.* Nottingham: Education Now.

Lemstra, M., Neudorf, C. and Opondo, J. (2008) 'Implications of a public smoking ban.' *Canadian Journal of Public Health 99*, 62–65.

Lewis, S.A., Haw, S.J. and McNeill, A.D. (2008) 'The impact of the 2006 Scottish Smoke-Free Legislation on sales of nicotine replacement therapy.' *Nicotine and Tobacco Research 10*, 1789–1792.

Menzies, D., Nair, A., Williamson, P.A. *et al.* (2006) 'Respiratory symptoms, pulmonary function, and markers of inflammation among bar workers before and after a legislative ban on smoking in public places.' *JAMA 296*, 1742–1748.

Martin, C., Ritchie, D. and Amos, A. (2008) *Evaluation of the Smoke-free Legislation in Scotland: Qualitative Community Study. Final Report.* Edinburgh: Health Scotland.

Pell, J.P., Haw, S., Cobbe, S. *et al.* (2008) 'Smoke-free legislation and hospitalizations for acute coronary.' *New England Journal of Medicine 359*, 482–491.

Plunkett, M., Haw, S., Cassels, J., Moore, M. and O'Connor, M. (2003) *Smoking in Public Places: A Survey of Public House and Restaurant Customers.* Edinburgh: ASH Scotland & HEBS.

Richmond, L., Haw, S. and Pell, J. (2007) 'Impact of socioeconomic deprivation and type of facility on perceptions of the Scottish smoke-free legislation.' *Journal of Public Health 29*, 376–378.

Sargent, R.P., Shepard, R.M. and Glantz, S.A. (2004) 'Reduced incidence of admissions for myocardial infarction associated with public smoking ban: Before and after study.' *British Medical Journal 328*, 977–980.

Scottish Executive (2004) *A Breath of Fresh Air for Scotland – Improving Scotland's Health: The Challenge – Tobacco Control Action Plan.* Available at www.scotland.gov.uk/ Publications/2004/01/18736/31540, accessed on 24 June 2009.

Scottish Executive (2004) *Smoking in Public Places: A Consultation on Reducing Exposure to Second Hand Smoke.* Available at www.scotland.gov.uk/Publications/2004/12/20381/48299, accessed on 24 June 2009.

Scottish Government (2008a) *Scottish Household Survey: Results from 2007.* Available at www.scotland. gov.uk/Publications/2008/08/07100738/0, accessed on 24 June 2009.

Scottish Government (2008b) *Achieving Our Potential: A Framework to Tackle Poverty and Income Inequality in Scotland.* Edinburgh: Scottish Government Publications.

Scottish Government (2008c) *Equally Well: Report of the Ministerial Task Force on Health Inequalities.* Edinburgh: Scottish Government Publications.

Scottish Government (2009) *Smoke-free Legislation: National Compliance Data.* Available at www. clearingtheairscotland.com/latest/index.html, accessed on 24 June 2009.

Second Chance Learning (2001) *Annual Report.* Greenock: Second Chance.

Semple, S., Creely, K.S., Naji, A. *et al.* (2007) 'Second hand smoke levels in Scottish pubs: The effect of smoke-free legislation.' *Tobacco Control 16*, 127–132.

Semple, S., MacCalman, L., Atherton, Naji, A. *et al.* (2007) 'Bar workers' exposure to second-hand smoke: The effect of Scottish smoke-free legislation on occupational exposure.' *Annals of Occupational Hygiene 51*, 571–580.

Seo, D.C. and Torabi, M.R. (2007) 'Reduced admissions for acute myocardial infarction associated with a public smoking ban: Matched controlled study.' *Journal of Drug Education 37*, 217–226.

Shaw, I. (1999) *Qualitative Evaluation.* London: Sage.

US Department of Health and Human Services (2006) *The Health Consequences of Involuntary Exposure to Tobacco Smoke: A Report of the Surgeon General.* US Department of Health and Human Services.

PART III

Treatment and Recovery, and the Wider Impacts of Substance Misuse

CHAPTER 4

Treatment and Recovery

Anything new under the sun?
Brian A. Kidd

Introduction

The approach to the treatment of problem substance use in the UK is at a crossroads. Professionals and lay people are actively debating the purpose of treatment. Politicians are searching for effective solutions to this complex problem. Funding decisions are under media scrutiny and professional opinions about 'harm reduction' or 'abstinence' are being challenged. The outcome of this debate will determine the way substance misuse is tackled in the UK.

From a clinician's perspective, this article summarises the historical events that have led to this crossroads, discusses factors currently influencing the treatment debate and considers keys to success.

Background and context
The British system

Replacement prescribing has been central to treatment for substance misuse in the UK for over a century. Political opinion in the UK has supported this approach despite concern from international partners (Royal College of Psychiatrists 1987). The effectiveness of the British system can be debated. Prescribing opiates to small numbers of high-functioning middle-class addicts has been described as 'a system of masterly inactivity in face of a non-existent problem' (Downes 1988). With approximately 250,000 individuals currently on methadone in the UK, the size of the problem now is very different. In 1964 there were 342 identified addicts in the UK, a massive increase from the 62 known in 1958. By 1968, 2782 were known, with 764 under 20 years old (Royal College of Psychiatrists 1987). In light of public concerns about increasing problems and a perception of over-prescribing by doctors, the 1970s saw increasing controls over addictive drugs and restrictions of medical practice, making treatment of addiction a specialist activity (Stark, Kidd and Sykes 1999). By the 1980s, however, this policy was reversed, recognising that illicit substance use was becoming more widespread and problematic. General practitioners were again encouraged to provide medical care (ACMD 1982, 1984).

Blood-borne viruses (BBV)

HIV/AIDS changed everything. In Scotland the McLelland Committee published a report acknowledging the risk of HIV infection in intravenous drug users, and this heralded a policy change promoting the concept of 'harm minimisation' (SHHD 1986). This espoused the view that, even if drug users continued to use substances, services could reduce the dangers through a range of clinical interventions. In 1988 ACMD acknowledged HIV/AIDS as a public health problem, encouraging the development of community drug teams to engage users (ACMD 1988). The follow-up report recommended increasing treatment capacity by remunerating general practitioners (ACMD 1989). By 1991 national treatment guidelines recommended replacement prescribing with methadone as a key harm-reduction intervention (Department of Health 1991).

Building capacity

Harm reduction was now the focus for clinical services treating substance misuse. Government policy followed clinical opinion. For 15 years national strategies focused on delivering services to increase the capacity of harm-reduction services – particularly methadone prescribing – to prevent an HIV epidemic. By 1999 the evidence base supporting the harm-reduction impact of methadone was developing. New clinical guidance focused on quality standards and medical training to further improve access to appropriate treatment (Department of Health 1999). Descriptive research in the UK supported the view that long-term methadone maintenance was the treatment of choice for injecting opiate-dependent individuals. As well as reducing risk-taking and exposure to BBV, this could reduce risk of death from overdose and improve social functioning (Gossop, Marsden and Stewart 1998, 2001).

Concerns

By the early 2000s harm reduction was well established and was even encroaching on social care. Evidence suggested that prescribing reduced crime, and services were commissioned to give offenders access to methadone. Children's services promoted methadone as a means of reducing risk for drug users' families. However, concerns were raised that harm reduction with methadone had become the treatment of choice for all drug users at the expense of treatments focusing more on progress and normalisation in the context of abstinence. There were issues regarding the lack of a range of available services. The availability and viability of residential (abstinence-based) facilities was reduced. Experts interpreted research as showing a clear cause-and-effect relationship between attempts to come off methadone and relapse or even death (Farrell and Marsden 2003; Gossop *et al.* 2001). Higher doses of methadone were promoted, with dose becoming a measure of 'quality' suggesting that a higher dose reflected better treatment (NTA 2007). In this context the 2007 UK treatment guidelines clarified the evidence base to date (Department of Health 2007).

Evidence-based medicine

Evidence-based medicine is the use of the best available evidence to support practice, the highest level of evidence being consistent findings in a number of high-quality randomised controlled trials. When a strong evidence base is lacking, expert committees review existing literature giving an authoritative view on best practice. Evidence-based medicine allows better understanding of treatment effectiveness – improving outcomes. However, demonstrating the impact of treatment in substance misuse is a challenge. Substance misuse is a severe and enduring condition that is hazardous to individuals as well as having a social impact. It is closely associated with mental health and physical conditions with high levels of morbidity and mortality. It is also a highly politicised area, and its development and the degree of risk it brings are closely associated with deprivation.

The 2007 guideline acknowledges that the evidence base is patchy. For some treatments the evidence base is strong – for example the harm-reduction impact of methadone in reducing drug use, injecting and associated risks and deaths (Ward, Mattick and Hall 1999). For other treatments the research base is more sparse. For some clinicians, adverse findings may be seen as threatening the very existence of methadone as a treatment option. Recently, concerns regarding the cardiac effects of methadone were seen by clinicians as exposing methadone to a potential backlash that could reduce its availability. In fact, this risk is minimal but must be effectively managed, as it would be in any other, less politicised, clinical area (MHRA 2006). This example demonstrates the paranoia felt by clinicians, who fear that progress in harm reduction could be threatened by political agendas, exposing drug users to increased risk.

2007 UK National Treatment Guideline

The National Institute of Health and Clinical Excellence (NICE) commissioned systematic reviews of the evidence to inform this guidance (NICE 2007a–d). However, the 2007 UK National Treatment Guideline must still be seen as a document reflecting the opinions of an expert group. The 'level' of evidence appraised is not defined. In response to this acknowledged weakness, the guideline states: 'It is now more appropriate to stop asking whether treatment for drug misuse is effective and instead ask how treatment can be improved and how it can be tailored to the needs of different patients' (NTA 2007, p.13).

The guideline gives a benchmark against which clinicians' practice is measured, and clinical judgement in the face of individual patient need is emphasised. The 1999 guideline has been shown to have altered practice positively (Strang and Sheridan 2003). Building on this, the 2007 guideline emphasises the need for structured clinical processes – reflecting concerns that some doctors may see treatment as a simple process to introduce users to lifelong methadone. Sections on clinical governance and psychological interventions emphasise a new emphasis in which 'treatment' is seen holistically and not simply as a narrow medical harm-reduction intervention.

Effective treatment reduces harm and deaths. Research implies that those in treatment are more likely to have periods of sustained improvement in social functioning than those who aren't. Different treatments are associated with differing degrees of long-term 'cure' as well as negative outcomes – but it must be acknowledged that the evidence base is currently not robust enough to unpack the many variables that could be impacting on these outcomes.

Drivers for change

There are key factors driving a review of management of substance misuse. These include:

- *Numbers and costs* – The last ten years has seen increasing numbers in treatment with associated costs soaring (Scottish Government 2008).

- *Perceptions of treatment quality* – There has been an apparent improvement in evidence-based practice – though at times the analysis of 'quality' may be challenged. Access to 'treatment' may be seen as simply access to methadone, with services judged as delivering quality based on speed of access to that drug (NTA 2007). The 'dose relationship' with effectiveness is often taken as a proxy for good practice, enticing practitioners to enforce excessive methadone doses. These issues are readily resolved by a person-centred approach to care ensuring rapid access to the appropriate treatment to meet assessed need. Unfortunately it may not be uncommon for services to adopt a lowest common denominator approach when faced with high demand. Although this may improve numbers in contact with services and harm reduction, there is a need to better demonstrate the impact of treatment on users and society through measurement of clinical outcomes (SACDM 2007).

- *Implications of broadening 'harm-reduction'* – Other aspects of treatment can further complicate the discussion. Criminal justice and BBV-prevention approaches adopt a risk-averse position from a community-safety perspective with the needs of the individual less prominent. Concerns over the safety of children can drive treatment services to lower the threshold for treatment – prescribing first, assessing need later.

- *Lack of outcome measurement* – There is little measurement of outcomes. In England, audits of services have emphasised process measures (numbers attending or methadone doses) to demonstrate effectiveness. When in place, outcome measurement currently emphasises harm reduction with few aspirational outcomes (return to mainstream society, employment or parental responsibility) assessed (NTA 2007). Services having short- to medium-term harm-reduction effects cannot easily demonstrate long-term rehabilitative effects. Society's concerns about substance use are often at odds with professional statements of treatment effectiveness (SACDM 2007).

If we are to continue to have access to effective harm-reduction interventions and use these as a springboard to improved social functioning, there is a need to convince society that clinicians' claims are valid. The evidence base must improve.

The Great Debate

In this context treatment for drug misuse has come under scrutiny. Treatment professionals are criticised for delivering only medical 'harm-reduction' treatments, apparently without considering abstinence-orientated options. This criticism becomes stronger as public (and media) perception grows that harm-reduction and replacement prescribing does not work. Strong evidence bases do not seem to influence this view. Those responsible for strategic planning of drug services have been challenged in national media. The whole approach of 'harm reduction' has been brought into question. A common response from those involved in the delivery of interventions has been to react defensively with a rejection of approaches not focused on harm reduction. Abstinence-orientated treatments with long-standing support from clinicians – such as detoxification – have been presented as hazardous and even unethical (Ashton 2008).

Solutions

Recovery

In association with this circular debate there has been a resurgence of interest in achieving more aspirational outcomes for those experiencing drug problems. The term 'recovery' has long been associated with substance use (Day 1868) but has become unfashionable in a world dominated by harm reduction partly due to its close association with the Minnesota model. For some it seems impossible to separate recovery and abstinence. However, some organisations have challenged this 'either-or' view of harm reduction and abstinence – instead recognising the value of a continuum of recovery within which both approaches are valid (UN 2008).

In 2007 leading US clinicians met to develop a consensus view of recovery (Betty Ford Consensus Panel 2007). This consensus, delivered by a US organisation, closely aligned with abstinence, received little attention in the UK. In 2008 the UK Drug Policy Commission led a similar process (UKDPC 2008). The resulting consensus definition – delivered by British professionals and service users with a broad range of perspectives – offers an opportunity to bridge the fundamentalist harm-reduction and abstentionist extremes and place the service user at the centre of their treatment.

Measuring outcomes

Simultaneously, the Scottish Government published a strategy, building on reviews of services, users' views and clinical advice to position recovery central to treatment (SACDM 2007, 2008; Scottish Government 2008). In order to demonstrate the impact of all elements of the care continuum this has led to the development of an outcomes framework to guide service delivery, based on the impact of all interventions (SACDM 2009). This approach has encouraged agreement. A strategy from a minority government was unanimously accepted by the Scottish Parliament – though public political statements still suggest a lack of consensus or understanding of the issues (Ashton 2008).

Across the UK there is acknowledgement of the huge progress made through harm reduction, but also a recognition that services should be more responsive to individual need and be more aspirational in terms of outcomes for people. Strategic approaches are now emphasising this next step – but challenges still require to be overcome if this is to become an operational reality.

Conclusions

Substance misuse remains a complex field in which objective analysis of evidence is challenging. It is subject to heated debate by clinicians and is strongly influenced by socio-political perspectives. For clinicians dealing with a range of long-lasting presenting problems, embedded in deprivation and associated with serious morbidity and mortality, the ethos of harm reduction is appealing. It allows clinicians to engage those who were previously beyond reach and has a clear impact on mortality and morbidity. The evidence base is strong but has limitations.

Harm reduction has the potential to make the focus of treatment the good of society rather than the individual's progress. For service users, society, and its political leaders, the view is commonly expressed that clinicians have a limited view of what treatment aims to achieve, and a distorted view of the real impact of the treatments they offer. Until now these opposing perspectives have appeared irreconcilable.

'Recovery' brings an opportunity for resolution. It requires the effectiveness of treatment to be described in terms of an individual's progress along a continuum of care from harm reduction to abstinence. While the impact on society is a factor to be considered, focusing on the user's needs and delivering the most appropriate evidence-based treatment to address their circumstances remains the goal of treatment. This clearly echoes national treatment guidance which requires robust clinical processes. The users' communities are also crucial and require support to reduce exclusion and build their own therapeutic potential.

Moving to the measurement of impact through recording of outcomes is a key element of this change. Irrational opposition to harm reduction is more difficult when services can demonstrate their effectiveness. Likewise, spurious claims of success can be challenged and services modified to deliver ever better outcomes.

Scotland's current strategic approach can be seen as an example of successful engagement with this debate. The minority Scottish Government has driven forward an approach that has credibility. Acknowledging the evidence base and clinical opinion, they have developed a consensus across the political divide, gaining unanimous support for their strategy and funding plans; they have redesigned local delivery arrangements to improve both the crossing of organisational boundaries and community capacity to deal with substance misuse; valid outcome measurement has become the focus of performance management.

For the clinician the environment this creates offers a great opportunity to meet the needs of those experiencing problems with substance use.

Does drug treatment in Scotland work?

Neil McKeganey

Introduction

If there is one statement that sums up the view of drug treatment in the UK over the last ten to fifteen years it must surely be the claim that 'treatment works'. The belief on the part of government and others that treatment does indeed work resulted in record funding for drug-treatment services in the UK and record numbers of drug users in contact with drug-treatment services. In the six-year period from 2001 to 2007 there was a 70 per cent increase in the numbers of drug users in treatment in England from 118,500 in 2001 to 202,000 in 2007. Funding for drug-abuse treatment similarly rose from around £390m in 2002 to around £800m in 2007 (NTA 2008). In Scotland an estimated £115m is spent annually on drug and alcohol treatment and care (Audit Scotland 2009). The perception in Scotland that treatment works was evident most recently in an announcement from Fergus Ewing (minister with responsibility for drug issues) of additional funding for drug-treatment services in Aberdeen. Recognising that at a time of financial austerity some critics may question the appropriateness of allocating additional public funds for drug-abuse treatment, the Minister was quoted as saying:

> Some may query the spending on drugs treatment, when there are so many other demands for money. To that argument I would say that evidence has shown that for every £1 invested in treatment £9.50 is saved in reduced costs to the Scottish economy and society. (Reported in *The Scotsman* newspaper, 20 Jan 2009)

But just how effective are drug-abuse treatment services at facilitating addicts' recovery? To answer that question it is helpful to look at some of the data from the Drug Outcome Research in Scotland study.

The Drug Outcome Research in Scotland study (DORIS)

The DORIS study is the largest evaluation of drug-abuse treatment services ever undertaken in Scotland and involves re-interviewing a large sample of drug users in contact with drug-treatment services. This study design has been applied in a number of other major drug-treatment evaluation studies in both the UK and the US (Anglin, Hser and Grella 1997; Gossop, Marsden and Stewart 2001; Gossop, Marsden, *et al.* 2001; Gossop *et al.* 2005). At the outset of this study 1007 drug users were recruited from 33 different drug-treatment agencies spread across urban and rural locations in Scotland. The sample size for the DORIS study represented around one in twelve of all drug users starting a new episode of drug-abuse treatment in 2001. Respondents were interviewed at the start of their treatment and thereafter at eight months, 16 months, and 33 months. Just under half (45%, $N = 448$) of the drug users interviewed were receiving drug treatment within a prison setting, with the remainder receiving community or residential rehabilitation treatment. Sixty-nine per cent of the DORIS sample was male, 31 per cent female; the mean age was 28 years (range 16 to 53 years; median 27 years); 99 per cent were white; and 88 per cent of DORIS respondents had used heroin in the last three months. At the 33-month follow-up (DORIS 4) 695 of the original sample were successfully re-interviewed. After excluding the 38 deaths in the cohort, this is a follow-up rate of 70 per cent. Analysis of the DORIS 4 interviewees showed that the final sample differed from the DORIS 1 sample (interviewed on recruitment) in only two ways – those drug users who were homeless at DORIS 1 and those who were in prison at DORIS 1 were slightly less likely to be included in the final 33-month DORIS 4 interview.

Previous publications from the DORIS study have focused on such topics as the number of drug-related deaths in Scotland (Bloor *et al.* 2008), the aspirations of drug users seeking drug treatment within Scotland (McKeganey *et al.* 2004), the effectiveness of drug-treatment services within Scotland (McKeganey *et al.* 2006), sexual and physical abuse amongst drug users seeking drug treatment within Scotland (McKeganey *et al.* 2005), the effectiveness of prison-based drug-treatment services in Scotland (McIntosh and Saville 2006), the impact of methadone prescribing on addict behaviour (Bloor *et al.* 2008), the health and treatment needs of Scottish drug users (Neale 2004; Neale, Robertson and Saville 2005), drug users' risks of non-fatal overdose (Neale and Robertson 2005); drug use and violence (Neale, Bloor and Weir 2005) and what drug users think of drug-treatment services in Scotland (Morris and Gannon 2008).

Drug users on the road to recovery

In the following series of figures drug users' progress from the point of their recruitment into the DORIS study to their final follow-up interview at 33 months (DORIS 4) is summarised. The data in these figures give a good indication of the degree to which drug-treatment services in Scotland are successfully combining both abstinence and harm-reduction goals and moving addicts towards a drug-free status.

On the basis of Figure 4.1 it is immediately apparent that there is a marked reduction in the percentage of DORIS respondents reporting recent use of heroin (last three months) from 87 per cent at baseline to 53 per cent at DORIS 4, 33 months later. However, what is equally striking is the fact that the greatest reduction in heroin use occurs during the first eight-month period from DORIS 1 at baseline to DORIS 2. Thereafter there is a noticeable plateauing effect such that at DORIS 4, the 33-month follow-up point, more than half of the sample still report using heroin within the previous three months.

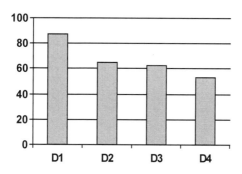

FIGURE 4.1 PERCENTAGE OF DORIS RESPONDENTS USING HEROIN IN THE PREVIOUS THREE MONTHS

Figure 4.2 summarises the data in relation to the reduction in the overall measure of drug dependency on the part of the DORIS sample over the course of their 33-month follow-up. The Severity-of-Dependence Scale was developed by Gossop and colleagues and used in their National Treatment Outcome Research Study which evaluated drug treatment services in England (Gossop *et al.* 1995). In Figure 4.2 we have summarised the reduction in dependency on the part of the DORIS sample across the 33 months of the study from DORIS 1 to DORIS 4. The greatest reduction in the extent of drug dependency on the part of the DORIS sample occurred from the first interview to the second interview eight months after starting treatment. Thereafter there are only relatively small further reductions in the overall level of drug dependency on the part of the DORIS sample.

In Figure 4.3 the data in relation to needle-sharing behaviour across the DORIS cohort is summarised. At DORIS 1 24 per cent of drug users reported recently using injecting equipment that had been previously used by someone else. By DORIS 4 that proportion had more than halved to 10 per cent.

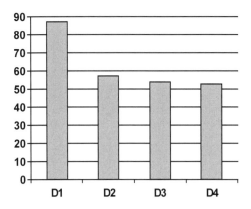

FIGURE 4.2 SEVERITY-OF-DEPENDENCE SCORE FOR DORIS RESPONDENTS

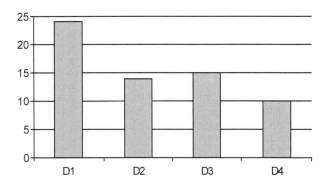

FIGURE 4.3 PERCENTAGE OF NEEDLE SHARING AMONG DORIS RESPONDENTS INTERVIEWED ON ALL FOUR SWEEPS (N = 668)

The substantial reduction in needle sharing on the part of drug users in contact with drug-treatment services in Scotland is probably indicative of the attention that this behaviour receives from drug-treatment staff focused on reducing drug-related risk behaviour and harm. Impressive as the reduction in needle sharing is amongst the DORIS cohort, an even greater reduction was evident in relation to self-harming behaviour amongst respondents. The data on this are summarised in Figure 4.4.

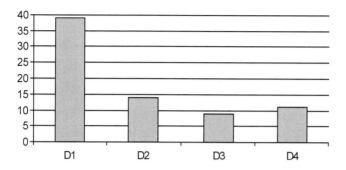

FIGURE 4.4 PERCENTAGE OF SELF-HARMING BEHAVIOURS AMONG DORIS RESPONDENTS INTERVIEWED ON ALL FOUR SWEEPS (N = 668)

At the outset of the DORIS study 39 per cent of respondents reported having self-harmed. By the time of the DORIS 4 follow-up 33 months later the proportion of respondents reporting self-harming in the period since their last interview had reduced to 11 per cent, although there had been a small increase from the DORIS 3 to DORIS 4 interview.

Much less impressive is the data on the level of alcohol consumption amongst DORIS respondents. The information on this is summarised in Figure 4.5. At the outset of the DORIS study 15 per cent of respondents reported drinking alcohol at an unsafe level. By the time of their DORIS 2 interview eight months later, that proportion had increased to 19 per cent and reduced only to 18 per cent by the time of the DORIS 4 interview. On

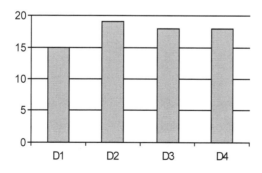

FIGURE 4.5 PERCENTAGE OF UNSAFE DRINKING AMONG DORIS RESPONDENTS INTERVIEWED ON ALL FOUR SWEEPS (N=668)

this basis one would have to say that drug-treatment services in Scotland were having very little impact on drug users' alcohol consumption. Concerning as this may be, it is notable that in some parts of Scotland in excess of 60 per cent of drug users are thought to be hepatitis C positive – a condition for which the current health advice is for the individual to avoid alcohol consumption altogether.

In Figure 4.6 we look at the proportion of DORIS respondents who were able to access paid employment following their contact with drug-treatment services. This is an important dimension with regard to individuals' sustained recovery from dependent drug use. McIntosh and McKeganey (2002), for example, in their qualitative study of the process of recovery from dependent drug use, identified the importance of addicts building up a non-addict identity. A key element of the process of developing a non-addict identity, as McIntosh and McKeganey were able to show, was drug users' involvement in a range of non-addict activities. Employment in these terms was seen to be very important in enabling addicts to develop a positive sense of self that was not tied to their involvement with illegal drugs. One of the ways in which employment helped in this context was the opportunity it provided of building up a new set of relationships and friendships that were not in any way focused upon illegal drug use. Although employment is an important part of the process of recovery from dependent drug use, in fact there was very little evidence within the DORIS data-set that drug-treatment services were having a positive impact in getting addicts into work. Indeed there was some indication that the provision of drug treatment in Scotland had reduced rather than enhanced an individual's likelihood of gaining paid employment. At the outset of

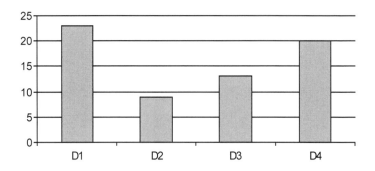

FIGURE 4.6 PERCENTAGE OF PAID EMPLOYMENT AMONG DORIS RESPONDENTS INTERVIEWED ON ALL FOUR SWEEPS (N = 668)

the DORIS study 23 per cent of drug users were in paid employment; by DORIS 2 interview eight months after recruitment into the study, only 9 per cent of drug users were in paid employment. By the time of their DORIS 4 interview some 33 months after having been recruited into the study the proportion of drug users in employment was still lower than had been the case at the outset of the study.

Finally in Figure 4.7 we look at the reductions in acquisitive crime associated with drug abuse treatment in Scotland. At the outset to the DORIS study 66 per cent of drug users reported having committed an acquisitive crime in the preceding three months. This reduced to 48 per cent by DORIS 2 interview eight months following their recruitment into the study, and reduced to 37 per cent by the time of their DORIS 4 interviews 33 months after their recruitment into the study.

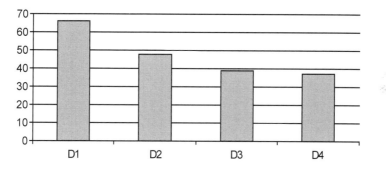

FIGURE 4.7 PERCENTAGE OF DORIS RESPONDENTS INTERVIEWED ON ALL FOUR SWEEPS (N = 668) REPORTING HAVING COMMITTED AN ACQUISITIVE CRIME IN THE PREVIOUS THREE MONTHS

Discussion: Implications and Big Questions?

These data show very clearly that contact with drug-abuse treatment services in Scotland is assocated with positive improvements in some areas of individuals' lives. Most notably in the reduction in needle and syringe sharing, in the level of self-harming, in the severity of dependence and in the recent use of heroin. However, in the face of substantial contact with drug-treatment services in Scotland more than half of the DORIS cohort are still using heroin, fewer are in employment than was the case at the outset of their treatment, there are continuing high levels of unsafe drinking, and more than a third of drug users are continuing to commit acquisitive crime. In addition to the patchy improvements in individuals' circumstances there is also a clear sense that the initial momentum towards recovery (which is evident in the first few months following contacting drug treatment services) starts to diminish by the time of the DORIS 3 interview at 16 months. It is evident then that the drug users within the DORIS study are a long way from the vision of recovery as set out within the current Scottish drug misuse strategy, which is defined as a process 'through which an individual is enabled to move on from their problem drug use, towards a drug-free life as an active and contributing member of society' (Scottish Government 2008, p.23).

It is beyond the scope of this chapter to try to explain why so few drug users are achieving the desired drug-free state even following long-term contact with drug-treatment services in Scotland. Part of the explanation may be that for the last ten to fifteen years workers within those services have been more focused on the harm-reduction goals of stabilising drug users, and on reducing their risk behaviour in the face of their continuing drug use, than with actually enabling individuals to become drug-free. The expertise associated with assisting and facilitating addicts' recovery (defined as becoming drug-free) may simply not be widely available within drug-treatment services in Scotland at the present time.

There may also be a degree to which the emphasis that has been placed on increasing the numbers of drug users in treatment in Scotland has in itself reduced the capacity of drug-treatment services to work intensively with clients in enabling them to become drug-free. Fergus Ewing, addressing drug-treatment services in Glasgow in 2008, commented:

> One simple statistic that I have is that the number of people in contact with services has almost doubled – let me say again that the number of people in contact with services has almost doubled and that is something to take great pride in, and we want to see that success continues.

Increasing the numbers of drug users in contact with drug-treatment services is only a cause for celebration if one assumes that any and all such contact is beneficial. If, as an alternative, one asks the question of whether the capacity of drug treatment services to deliver high-quality, recovery-focused work with their clients may be influenced by the numbers of drug users in treatment, then a different question needs to be raised. That question is whether there is an optimal number of clients with whom drug-treatment services can deliver high-quality effective treatment, and above which the quality of care and treatment starts to diminish? In their ethnographic research into the process of recovery from dependent drug use McIntosh and McKegany described how addicts who had sucessfully managed to overcome their dependency had created a new non-addict identity for themselves (McIntosh and McKeganey 2002). The process through which ex-addicts had been able to construct a new non-addict identity involved:

- building up contacts with individuals who were not using drugs and were unaware of their prior drug use

- becoming involved in non-drug-related activities

- redefining their drug use from something that was seen as positive and pleasurable to something that was seen as negative and harmful

- reflecting back on the impact of their drug use on their own life and the lives of others around them.

The process of building up a new non-addict identity was then an emotionally intensive and often long-term process. It was also a process that was often 'resource heavy' – individuals may need to be relocated to other areas where they were not known as an addict, and they may need support over an extended period of time. Recovery, in these terms, may not be a process that is amenable to dealing with large numbers of addicts.

If drug-treatment services are going to increase the proportion of their clients who become drug-free, they may need to become much better at differentiating between those clients for whom abstinence is an achievable goal and those for whom stabilisation in the face of their continuing drug use may be a more appropriate goal. In addition they may need to become much clearer about the fact that recovery from dependent drug use is a shared responsibilty, with obligations falling to both the staff of drug-treatment services and their clients. The commitment within Scotland to ensuring that drug-treatment services are indeed working towards addicts becoming drug-free may result in major changes in the way in which drug-treatment services are operating, entailing a much tighter specification on the responsiblities and obligations placed upon the clients of those services. Indeed within a climate of tighter financial conditions more generally within both the public and private sectors, such a shift in responsibility may become almost unavoidable.

References

Advisory Council on the Misuse of Drugs (1982) *Treatment and Rehabilitation*. London: HMSO.

Advisory Council on the Misuse of Drugs (1984) *Prevention*. London: HMSO.

Advisory Council on the Misuse of Drugs (1988) *AIDS and Drug Misuse Part 1*. London: HMSO.

Advisory Council on the Misuse of Drugs (1989) *AIDS and Drug Misuse Part 2*. London: HMSO.

Anglin, M., Hser, Y. and Grella, C. (1997) 'Drug addiction and treatment careers among clients in the Drug Abuse Treatment Outcome Study.' *Psychology of Addictive Behaviors 11*, 308–323.

Ashton, M. (2008) 'The new abstentionists.' *Druglink* special insert, Dec/Jan.

Audit Scotland (2009) *Drug and Alcohol Services in Scotland*. Audit Scotland.

Betty Ford Consensus Panel (2007) 'What is recovery? A working definition from the Betty Ford Institute.' *Journal of Substance Abuse Treatment 33*, 221–228.

Bloor, M., Gannon, M., Jackson, G., Leyland, A.H. and McKeganey, N. (2008) 'Contribution of problem drug users' deaths to excess, mortality in Scotland: Secondary analysis of cohort study.' *BMJ 337*, 478.

Day, H. (1868) *The Opium Habit with Suggestions as to the Remedy*. New York: Harper and *Brothers*.

Department of Health, Scottish Home and Health Department, Welsh Office (1991) *Drug Misuse and Dependence Guidelines on Clinical Management*. London: HMSO.

Department of Health, Scottish Home and Health Department, Welsh Office (1999) *Drug Misuse and Dependence Guidelines on Clinical Management*. London: HMSO.

Department of Health (England) and the devolved administrations (2007) *Drug Misuse and Dependence: UK Guidelines on Clinical Management*. London: Department of Health (England), the Scottish Government, Welsh Assembly Government and Northern Ireland Executive.

Downes, D. (1988) *Contrasts in Tolerance: Post War Penal Policy in the Netherlands and England and Wales*. Oxford: Clarendon Press.

Farrell, M. and Marsden, J. (2003) *Drug-related Mortality among Newly Released Offenders 1998–2000*. Home Office Online Report 40/05. Available at www.homeoffice.gov.uk/rds/pdfs05/rdsolr4005.pdf, accessed on 24 June 2009.

Gossop, M., Darke, S., Griffiths, P., Hando, J., Powis, B., Hall, W. and Strang, J. (1995) 'The Severity of Dependence Scale (SDS): Psychometric properties of the SDS in English and Australian samples of heroin, cocaine and amphetamine users.' *Addiction 90*, 607–614.

Gossop, M., Marsden, J. and Stewart, D. (1998) *NTORS at One Year. The National Treatment Outcome Research Study. Changes in Substance Use, Health and Criminal Behaviour One Year after Intake*. London: Department of Health.

Gossop, M., Marsden, J. and Stewart, D. (2001) *NTORS after Five Years. Changes in Substance Use, Health and Criminal Behaviour Five Years after Intake*. London: National Addiction Centre.

Gossop, M., Marsden, J., Stewart, D. and Treacy, S. (2001) 'Outcomes after methadone maintenance and methadone reduction treatments: Two year follow-up results from the National Treatment Outcome Research Study.' *Drug and Alcohol Dependence 62*, 255–264.

Gossop, M., Trakada, K., Stewart, D. and Witton, J. (2005) 'Reductions in criminal convictions after addiction treatment: five–year follow-up.' *Drug and Alcohol Dependence 79*, 295–302.

McIntosh M. and McKeganey, N. (2002) *Beating the Dragon: The Recovery from Dependent Drug Use*. New York: Pearson.

McIntosh, J. and Saville, E. (2006) 'The challenges associated with drug treatment in prison.' *Probation Journal: The Journal of Community and Criminal Justice 53*, 3, 230–247.

McKeganey, N.P., Bloor, M., Robertson, M., Neale, J. and MacDougall, J. (2006) 'Abstinence and drug abuse treatment: Results from the Drug Outcome Research in Scotland study.' *Drugs: Education, Prevention* and *Policy 13*, 6, 537–550.

McKeganey, N., Morris, Z., Neale, J. and Robertson, M. (2004) 'What are drug users looking for when they contact drug services: Abstinence or harm reduction?' *Drugs: Education, Prevention and Policy 11*, 5, 423–435.

McKeganey, N., Neale, J. and Robertson, M., (2005) 'Physical and sexual abuse among drug users contacting drug treatment services in Scotland.' *Drugs: Education, Prevention and Policy 12*, 3, 223–232.

Medicines and Healthcare Products Regulatory Agency (2006) *Current Problems in Pharmacovigilance* 31. London: MHRA.

Morris, Z.S. and Gannon, M. (2008) 'Drug misuse treatment services in Scotland: Predicting outcomes.' *International Journal for Quality in Health Care 20*, 271–276.

National Treatment Agency (2008) *Annual Report*. London: National Treatment Agency for Substance Misuse.

Neale, J. (2004) 'Measuring the health of Scottish drug users.' *Health and Social Care in the Community 12*, 3, 202–211.

Neale, J., Bloor, M. and Weir, C. (2005) 'Problem drug users and assault.' *International Journal of Drug Policy 16*, 393–402.

Neale, J., Roberston, M. and Saville, E. (2005) 'Understanding the treatment needs of drug users in prison.' *Probation Journal: The Journal of Community and Criminal Justice 52*, 3, 243–257.

Neale, J. and Robertson, M. (2005) 'Recent life problems and non-fatal overdose amongst heroin users entering treatment.' *Addiction 100*, 2, 168–175.

NICE (2007a) *Drug Misuse: Opioid Detoxification*. NICE clinical guideline 52. London: National Institute for Health and Clinical Excellence.

NICE (2007b) *Drug Misuse: Psychosocial Interventions*. NICE clinical guideline 51. London: National Institute for Health and Clinical Excellence.

NICE (2007c) *Methadone and Buprenorphine for the Management of Opioid Dependence*. NICE technology appraisal 114. London: National Institute for Health and Clinical Excellence.

NICE (2007d) *Naltrexone for the Management of Opioid Dependence*. NICE technology appraisal 115. London: National Institute for Health and Clinical Excellence.

NTA (2007) The NTA's 2006 National Prescribing Audit. London: National Treatment Agency for Substance Misuse.

Royal College of Psychiatrists (1987) *Drug Scenes*. London: Gaskell.

SACDM (2007) *Reducing Harm and Promoting Recovery: A Report on Methadone Treatment for Substance Misuse in Scotland*. Edinburgh: Scottish Government.

SACDM (2008) *Essential Care: A Report on the Approach Required to Maximise Opportunity for Recovery from Problem Substance Use in Scotland*. Edinburgh: Scottish Government.

SACDM (2009) *Delivering Better Outcomes. An Outcomes Toolkit*. Edinburgh: Scottish Government.

Scottish Government (2008) *The Road to Recovery: A New Approach to Tackling Scotland's Drug Problem*. Edinburgh: Scottish Government.

Scottish Home and Health Department (1986) *HIV Infection in Scotland: Report of the Scottish Committee on HIV Infection and Intravenous Drug Use*. Edinburgh: Scottish Office.

Stark, C., Kidd, B. and Sykes, R. (eds) (1999) *Illegal Drug Use in the United Kingdom: Prevention, Treatment and Enforcement*. Aldershot: Ashgate.

Strang, J. and Sheridan, J. (2003) 'Effect of national guidelines on prescribing of methadone: Analysis of NHS prescription data, England 1990–2001.' *British Medical Journal 327*, 321–322.

UK Drug Policy Commission (2008) *The UK Drug Policy Commission Recovery Consensus Group. A Vision of Recovery*. London: UKDPC.

United Nations Office on Drugs and Crime (2008) *Reducing the Adverse Health and Social Consequences of Drug Abuse: A Comprehensive Approach*. Available at www.unodc.org/documents/prevention/Reducing-adverse-consequences-drug-abuse.pdf, accessed 22 October 2009.

Ward, J., Mattick, R. and Hall, W. (eds) (1999) *Methadone Maintenance Treatment and Other Opioid Replacement Therapies*. Amsterdam: Harwood Academic Publishers.

CHAPTER 5

Employment and Problem Drug Use

The role of employment in recovery from problem drug use

Joanne Neale and Peter A. Kemp

Introduction

This article examines the role that employment can play in helping people to recover from problem drug use. It looks at the links between drug taking and employment, policy and practice, the barriers to employment faced by problem drug users, and ways of enabling people who have a drug problem to move closer to paid work. We begin by clarifying our use of the terms 'employment', 'problem drug use' and 'recovery'.

'Employment' typically refers to paid work, which may be full-time or part-time and involve a permanent or temporary contract. In its broadest sense, however, employment may also be defined to include voluntary, sheltered or therapeutic work, as well as education and training. These activities may all help to enhance the 'employability' of people wishing to enter the labour market and are therefore likely to be relevant to recovery from problem drug use.[1] By 'problem drug use', we refer to the consumption of heroin, crack cocaine or any other drug for which treatment is needed, and any illicit drug injection. While the meaning of 'recovery' is complex

---

1   Although employment might technically include unpaid caring duties, paid illegal activities and cash-in-hand work, these will not be considered here.

and contested, the UK Drug Policy Commission Recovery Consensus Group's definition is suitable for current purposes:

> The process of recovery from problematic substance use is characterised by voluntarily-sustained control over substance use which maximises health and well-being and participation in the rights, roles and responsibilities of society. (UK Drug Policy Commission Recovery Consensus Group 2008)

The links between problem drug use and employment

It is widely recognised that drug users experience high levels of non-employment.[2] For example, the British Crime Survey has shown that people using hard drugs, such as heroin and crack cocaine, are significantly more likely to be unemployed than those who are not (MacDonald and Pudney 2000). In Scotland, a large-scale survey of individuals seeking drug treatment in 2001/02 found that only 4 per cent were in paid employment at the time of their interview (Kemp and Neale 2005). Meanwhile, more recent data from the Scottish Drug Misuse Database have shown that 14 per cent of individuals seeking drug treatment were in paid or unpaid employment (including full-time education and training) and 67 per cent were unemployed (Information Services Division 2007).

These figures are reinforced by estimates of the number of problem drug users claiming out-of-work social security benefits. According to research commissioned by the UK Department for Work and Pensions (DWP), there were approximately 267,000 problem drug users claiming at least one of four key benefits – Incapacity Benefit, Income Support, Jobseeker's Allowance and Disability Living Allowance – in England in 2006. This represents 6.6 per cent of all working-age individuals receiving those benefits, yet problem drug users comprise only 1.1 per cent of the total working-age population of England (Hay and Bauld 2008).

Establishing exactly why drug users experience such high levels of unemployment is not straightforward. The reasons will vary between individuals, with changes also occurring over time and in different social and economic contexts (South et al. 2001). Unemployment may prompt involvement in a drug-based lifestyle, but may also be a consequence of it.

---

2   'Non-employment' includes both unemployment and economic inactivity. 'Unemployed' people are not in work but are both available for and actively seeking work. 'Economically inactive' people are not in work but also neither available for nor actively seeking work.

People who cannot secure employment and a work-based identity may be attracted to the sense of purpose and income generated by drug dealing (Allen 1999). Equally, those bored by having no work may take drugs to pass away the time (Neale 1998). Conversely, the effects of regular drug use on physical and mental health can reduce fitness for work or work performance, ultimately resulting in job loss (Kandel and Yamaguchi 1987).[3]

Despite uncertainties regarding cause and effect, the evidence suggests that being in paid work can help people to recover from addiction (Klee, McLean and Yavorsky 2002; South et al. 2001; Wolkstein and Spiller 1998). For example, employment stability is associated with reduced drug use (Shepard and Reif 2004), less depression (Zanis, Metzger and McLellan 1994) and reduced criminality (Siddall and Conway 1988). It has also been shown to improve post-treatment community functioning and community reintegration (Comerford 1999; Room 1998). In other words, employment seems to have an important therapeutic value for drug users (South et al. 2001).

The mechanisms by which paid employment can help people to move towards being drug-free have also been well-documented (Biernacki 1986; Cebulla, Smith and Sutton 2004; Luchansky et al. 2000; McIntosh, Bloor and Robertson 2008; McIntosh and McKeganey 2001). Besides increasing financial independence, work can engender a sense of responsibility and encourage individuals to feel that they have a stake in society (Phillips and South 1992; South et al. 2001). Confidence and self-esteem can be boosted, so enabling a sense of self and identity, which can in turn help to protect against relapse. The routine of daily work can assist recovering drug users to fill their time constructively, distract them from the physical and emotional symptoms of withdrawal and enable them to develop meaningful relationships with non-drug users. This can distance them from drug-using networks and facilitate their reintegration into mainstream society (Cebulla et al. 2004; McIntosh et al. 2008).

Policy and practice

In recent years, policy makers and practitioners have increasingly recognised that paid work – preceded as necessary by education, training and other related forms of support – is an important goal for those experiencing

---

3   Of course, drug taking and unemployment may both be caused by other factors, such as poor health, homelessness, family problems, and a chaotic lifestyle.

drug problems. This is particularly evident within the 2008 drug strategies for England, Scotland and Wales. For example, the English strategy states:

> While we have been successful at fast-tracking people into treatment, we need to focus more upon treatment outcomes, with a greater proportion free from their dependence and being re-integrated into society, coming off benefits and getting back to work. (Home Office 2008, p.4)

Meanwhile, the Scottish strategy strongly emphasises that community drug-treatment services need to deliver packages of support relating to family, social and financial issues, alongside preparing individuals for education, training and employment (Scottish Government 2008). Indeed, a stated priority is to enable more people to recover 'so that they can live longer, healthier lives, realising their potential and making a positive contribution to society and the economy' (Scottish Government 2008, p.8). This, it is recognised, will require action to improve the employment aspirations of recovering drug users and ongoing support from treatment and care services to enable them to move towards employment (Scottish Government 2008, p.27).

Until relatively recently, there were very few services actively working with drug users to increase their employability, but this has now changed. A quick search of the DrugScope helpfinder website (http://drugscope.soutron.com/helpfinder.asp), conducted by the present authors in November 2008, identified 98 drug projects providing employment advice in England and Wales. In addition, important statutory services and employability frameworks have been developed to facilitate drug users' entry to the labour market. These have included Progress2work (a cross-departmental initiative coordinated by Jobcentre Plus) and, in Scotland, the New Futures Fund, Workforce Plus, and the Fairer Scotland Fund.

A rare sense that politicians, policy makers, service providers and researchers might for once all be singing from the same song sheet does not, however, quite tell the full story. The Ministerial Foreword to the Scottish Drug Strategy informs us that problem drug users cost the taxpayer an estimated £2.6bn per year in Scotland. Furthermore, improving access to employment and training for problem drug users will 'revitalise some of the nation's most deprived communities' and 'allow significant public investment to be redirected' (presumably to more worthy causes). Chapter One of the strategy then states:

> In most cases the individuals [people with a drug problem]
> will be in receipt of benefits from the Government, which
> has implications for the public purse, as well as impacting
> on Scotland's labour productivity and, in turn, its sustainable
> economic growth. (Scottish Government 2008, p.3)

This emphasis on the financial burden of unemployed problem drug users is also evident in the English drug strategy, which proclaims:

> ...we do not think it is right for the taxpayer to help sustain
> drug habits when individuals could be getting treatment to
> overcome barriers to employment. So we will explore the case
> for introducing a new regime which provides more tailored
> and personalised support than that which is currently provided
> by the existing Incapacity Benefit or Jobseeker Allowance
> regimes. In return for benefit payments, claimants will have
> a responsibility to move successfully through treatment into
> employment. (Home Office 2008, p.5)

In other words, if drug users do not accept their 'responsibility' to find paid work, they may find that their social security benefits are reduced or withdrawn altogether. The notion that employment might be good for health, well-being and recovery thus seems to have been overtaken by the fact that getting drug users into work and off state benefits is good for taxpayers and the public purse. Moreover, it is unclear whether those currently making policy feel that drug users need to be coerced into work, or think that employment strategies must be couched in punitive terms in order to make them palatable to the general public, or genuinely believe that having more drug users in work will boost the economy (by keeping wage rates, and hence inflation, down).

Such uncertainty of motive is also evident in the recent DWP Green Paper *No One Written Off: Reforming Welfare to Reward Responsibility* (Department for Work and Pensions 2008a). This document notes that there is compelling evidence of the benefits of work for people's well-being and life chances, and expresses a desire to reduce social exclusion by improving the employment prospects of individuals facing the greatest disadvantage. Again, however, there is evidence of coercion, compulsion and benefit conditionality. For example, it is proposed that drug users claiming benefits should be required to declare their heroin or crack cocaine use to benefits workers, seek drug treatment and move successfully through treatment and into employment if they want to avoid having their benefits reduced (cf. Department for Work and Pensions 2008b). This is despite no known evidence of the effectiveness of such measures; and creates fears that service users' privacy will be compromised, therapeutic relationships will be undermined and crime will increase as drug users commit income-generating offences in order to replace lost welfare benefits.

Employment goals and barriers

Of course, the need for coercive measures to move drug users into employment would only be necessary if those who took drugs did not actually want to work. Whilst there are undoubtedly work-shy drug users, just as there are work-shy individuals in any population group, many of those who take drugs see employment as an important goal and consider it to be central to their efforts to rebuild daily routines and a steady life (Cebulla et al. 2004; McIntosh and McKeganey 2001; Neale 2002). Despite this, problem drug users tend to have fairly modest employment aspirations. For example, many anticipate gaining unskilled or semi-skilled manual work or want to undertake vocational training (Cebulla et al. 2004; Klee et al. 2002). There is also some evidence that they prefer a 'recovery first/work second' approach (Cebulla et al. 2004) and see full-time employment as a long-term, rather than a short-term, aim (Neale 1998).

When seen in the context of the many factors that can hinder or prevent drug users from obtaining paid work, one might argue that drug users have a more realistic understanding of their own employability than do many politicians and policy makers. The barriers to employment encountered by drug users have now been well-documented and are both personal and structural (Cebulla et al. 2004; Kemp and Neale 2005; Klee et al. 2002; Leukefeld et al. 2007; Neale et al. 2007). At the personal level, problem drug users commonly have limited or no qualifications, poor employment histories, and criminal records, all of which tend to make them unattractive to potential employers. In addition, they frequently experience chronic mental and physical ill-health and have insecure housing circumstances. These might be compounded by limited interpersonal skills, complex personal needs, lack of confidence and chaotic lifestyles.

At a more structural level, drug users often encounter negative attitudes from employers[4] (Klee et al. 2002; Scott and Sillars 2003) and job centre staff (Neale et al. 2007). They may also believe (often incorrectly) that they

---

4   In particular, employers can be reluctant to recruit drug users because they are concerned about risks associated with the management of drug use, risks to the reputation of their business and risks to other employees or customers (UK Drug Policy Commission 2008).

will be caught in the unemployment trap, whereby securing a job actually results in a reduction in their income because certain welfare benefits are lost. For drug users living in rural areas, limited public transport can be a further barrier to working since jobs are concentrated in urban centres (Leukefeld *et al.* 2007). In addition, some treatment programmes, including methadone substitution, inhibit employment because drug users are required to attend services on a daily basis (Neale 1998; Radcliffe and Stevens 2008). Finally, since drug users are likely to be at a competitive disadvantage relative to many other people looking for work, they may find themselves in temporary or insecure work and so at increased risk of losing their job in times of recession.

Conclusion: Combining aspiration with realism

This article has argued that the relationship between unemployment and problem drug use is complex, but for a whole range of reasons paid work is good for recovery. That said, drug users commonly encounter many barriers when they attempt to secure a job. Certainly, paid work will be achievable for some individuals. Nonetheless, others may struggle, and probably fail, to meet the demands of full-time paid employment (Kemp and Neale 2005; Perkins 2007). Policy and practice must therefore encourage individuals to have labour market aspirations and to fulfil their work potential. Yet, we need to avoid setting already vulnerable individuals up to fail by giving them overly ambitious goals and by not providing appropriate support to help them along the way.

Research now strongly indicates that problem drug users are more likely to secure a job if they have a staged (re-)introduction to the labour market (Cebulla *et al.* 2004). The exact nature of this will need to be tailored to the circumstances of particular individuals. However, many drug users will need support to improve their self-worth and confidence, and assistance with literacy, numeracy, communication, time management and other life skills (Cebulla *et al.* 2004; Kemp and Neale 2005; McIntosh *et al.* 2008). They might also benefit from formal education and training, employment 'taster days', work trials, voluntary work, 'mini-jobs' and intermediate employment. Although the latter tend to be less valued than full-time paid work, they can help people to become more 'job ready' and, when accomplished successfully, can demonstrate an ability to hold down a job (Kemp and Neale 2005).

In order to counter structural barriers to employment, we must also improve the attitudes of employers and their staff across the public, private and voluntary sectors. Training and education on drug issues could help individuals to feel more confident about working with drug users (Kemp and Neale 2005). In addition, the anxieties of some employers and service managers might be allayed if local drug action teams, drug service providers and employment service staff offered support in recruiting and retaining drug users (e.g. by helping them to develop appropriate policies or by providing advice should problems arise) (Scott and Sillars 2003; UK Drug Policy Commission 2008). Likewise, financial incentives (such as a government scheme to meet part of the minimum wage for a set period) could help to offset some of the additional costs of employing people with high support needs (UK Drug Policy Commission 2008).

Certainly, the employability of many drug users is undermined not only by their addiction, but also by the myriad other life problems they commonly face. We do not know whether unemployment causes drug use, drug use causes unemployment or unemployment and drug use are both caused by other factors. Equally, we are a long way from being able to predict which individuals will successfully secure jobs despite having difficult life circumstances. In the absence of such knowledge, a coordinated multi-agency approach that is realistic for individual clients and tackles their addiction, unemployment and other problems in tandem seems the most promising way forward. This will require a substantial investment of resources and recognition that it may take many months (and more than one attempt) for some individuals to become fully 'job ready'. Yet, as the new drug strategies are so quick to point out, there will certainly be benefits (to both drug users and society more generally) if we successfully enable more individuals currently experiencing drug problems to enter and remain in paid work.

Employment projects: Examples in practice

Bernadette Monaghan

Introduction

In the foregoing discussion, Neale and Kemp have highlighted significant points that need to be considered in the preparation of individuals for paid employment. These include:

- moving people forward, towards paid employment

- defining employment as voluntary, sheltered or therapeutic work, as well as education and training

- engendering a sense of responsibility and encouragement of individuals to feel that they have a stake in society

- linking treatment and core services to those of employment services

- recognising the role employment plays in rebuilding daily routines and a steady life

- understanding that employment may be a long-term aim

- providing an introduction or re-introduction into the labour market

- recognising the importance of the multi-agency approach in moving individuals forward in their search for normality and stability which employment may bring.

Neale and Kemp also indicate that the journey to recovery through employment is not easy, and that a number of statutory services and employability frameworks have been developed to assist drug users' entering into the labour market.

The following examples from a national voluntary organisation give some testament to how the use of employability frameworks and multi-agency work may assist in recovery through employment.

Apex is a national voluntary organisation that has been working since 1987 to give its clients – (ex-)offenders and young people at risk – the skills employers want. Its services are tailored to individual need, identified through an initial employability assessment, and then cross-referenced with a comprehensive range of training programmes, for both individual and group work, in five broad areas:

- Addressing criminality (including conviction relevance and disclosure).
- Employability.
- Life skills/behaviours.
- Money matters.
- Health and well-being.

A range of services is provided from 22 local units and in six prisons across Scotland. These include:

- *Employment and guidance*: in partnership with Criminal Justice Social Work, for those on probation or Community Service Orders

- *Supervised Attendance Orders*: as an alternative to custody for fine default and as a first sentence option available to the courts in Glasgow and Ayrshire

- *Progress 2 Work*: a Jobcentre Plus initiative of which Apex is the largest provider in Scotland; working in partnership with Phoenix Futures who provide addiction services, this initiative aims to progress ex-drug users and those who have obtained a measure of control over their habit, into employment

- *New Futures*: in partnership with Scottish Enterprise, aimed at addressing the employability needs of vulnerable and disadvantaged young people up to age 25

- *Contracts with local enterprise companies*: such as *Get Ready for Work*, aimed at young people who need assistance with life skills and employability

- *Prison-based services*: involving pre-release preparation work and aftercare support on release.

Apex argues that there is a significant relationship between poor educational attainment and crime. Most of their clients have a background of school exclusion and truancy and little or no formal qualifications. In turn, their expectations of themselves and of life in general are very poor. One of the benefits they gain from working with Apex is an increase in self-esteem and self-confidence, and the belief in themselves that they can make positive changes in their lifestyle and behaviour, and that other options are open to them, regardless of their past.

A substance misuser may fit into any of the many services that Apex provides; but Progress 2 Work (P2W) is the most obviously appropriate, and this will be the focus of what follows.

Apex Progress 2 Work services

Apex is the largest provider of P2W services in Scotland. Services are delivered through individual projects in Highland, Aberdeen (in partnership with Aberdeen Foyer), Tayside (in partnership with the Scottish Council for Voluntary Organisations), Fife, Forth Valley, Paisley, Borders, Edinburgh City (in partnership with Phoenix Futures), Lanarkshire and Ayrshire, Dumfries and Galloway. Some examples of these are described below.

Between 1 January and 31 December 2008, Apex P2W services worked with 1401 service users, of whom 178 obtained jobs, 388 progressed to further work related training and 76 accessed further education. As a provider, Apex is required to monitor and evidence that job outcomes are sustained for a period of 13 weeks. Of those who gained employment, 70 achieved this outcome, as well as 149 of the service users who took up further training.

These services are aimed at progressing into employment those who have achieved a measure of control over their drug habit. The following factors are essential if this client group are to engage with the programme and move on in their lives:

- to be stable either on a methadone programme or clean from drugs
- to be ready to move on with their lives
- to be open to ideas for progression and ready to accept assistance
- to build up a professional relationship with their Apex worker
- sound partnership working between their Apex worker and other agencies who are providing services to the individual
- aftercare support for those who do progress to employment.

Barriers to employment for this client group include:

- employers' lack of understanding of methadone and what can and cannot be achieved while on this programme

- the present economic climate

- inappropriate referrals where clients are not ready to progress to employment and change their lives

- lack of openness and partnership working with other agencies involved

- in some cases clients being 'held' on high methadone dosages for many years

- lack of aftercare support for the client

- the inability, in most cases, to work with and support the employer in as open and honest a way as the organisation would like.

P2W in Fife

In Fife, Apex Scotland is the Progress 2 Work and Progress 2 Work Link Up provider. It has offered Jobcentre Plus (JC+) staff the opportunity to 'buddy' a P2W/Link Up adviser for a half day. It was considered that this would give JC+ staff a good insight into the services being provided to their clients and would highlight the support they can access through Progress 2 Work and Link Up programmes at Apex Scotland. This knowledge would assist with the identification and referrals of clients who could benefit from the service.

Apex Scotland arranged sessions where staff could observe an initial referral appointment as well as a caseload interview to gain a broader understanding of the vast and varied work carried out within the organisation. Jobcentre Plus staff welcomed this opportunity and approximately 30 Jobcentre advisers from across Fife registered an interest and have now taken part in this process. The process was carried out over a four-month period. In the second phase of this programme, Apex Scotland's employment development advisers shadow Jobcentre staff in their various roles to give Apex a better understanding of the processes and targets that the JC+ staff face on a daily basis.

Apex Scotland also works directly with the Criminal Justice Service in Fife and has encouraged new social work staff to shadow appointments with the employment development adviser. This ensures that new and existing staff are well informed of the contents of the service and the suitability of prospective clients.

Successful case study

J (53) lives with his partner and two young children and is a former heroin user. He referred himself to Apex Progress 2 Work. His employment development adviser helped him seek the appropriate help to address his drug habit. He worked very closely with his adviser and also the Community Alcohol and Drug Team.

After a year, he became a volunteer with a local drugs project which meant that he was around more people like himself who had issues with alcohol and drugs. He did not find it easy, but persevered and eventually gained and sustained a full-time position. J said it was the best thing he ever did and intends to set a good example for his two young children.

SMART Recovery

SMART Recovery UK (Self Management and Recovery Training) is an organisation that provides a network of meetings to help people gain independence from addictive behaviours (substances or activities). The meetings are run by volunteers who have first-hand experience of addiction. The organisation helps to get meetings running, and also offers online support and guidance until there is a face-to-face meeting organised (see www.smartrecovery.co.uk). Apex has used this approach in setting up such meetings in Highlands.

SMART Recovery uses a four-point programme to teach individuals important skills and give them tools to help in their recovery. It is designed to provide participants with skills to work on any addictive behaviour. Addictive behaviour is defined as more than alcohol and drugs – it may include sex, relationships and behaviours as part of a criminal lifestyle, such as violence.

Each meeting focuses on the following areas:

- *Enhancing and maintaining motivation* – How ready someone is to change. It also shows clients how to look at the benefits and costs of their addictive behaviour.

- *Coping with urges* – This is about recognising and understanding the urges to use or participate in negative behaviour and how to manage these urges.

- *Problem solving* – Dealing with common upsets such as anger and rage, fear and anxiety, and loneliness and sadness.

- *Lifestyle balance* – This point teaches clients how to have a lifestyle that is healthy and balanced. They will also learn skills that will help prevent relapse. These skills include how to recognise triggers and high-risk situations and to improve social support networks.

The Delta Project

Another example of the SMART model in action is Apex's Delta Project. Individuals engaged in this programme have gone through some form of treatment and rehabilitation. The SMART intervention offered to service users aims to address and support them in relapse prevention. In 2008, 26 service users started on the course, 17 progressed to Progress 2 Work and 12 engaged with the Delta programme.

In partnership with the Scottish Prison Service and the Drug Treatment and Testing Order (DTTO) team in Inverness, the Delta project has provided this person-centred intervention to service users since 2007. SMART groups are held in an informal way with the added experience of professionally trained facilitators to offer specialist support to participants. The facilitator's role is to focus the discussion on how to abstain from addictive substances or behaviour, to introduce members to SMART tools and techniques and to give everyone who wants it the opportunity to express their views.

Successful case studies

Client A is a 46-year-old male who has over 53 convictions spanning a period of 19 years. He admits that these offences, mainly theft and fraud, were committed to support his drug addiction over the years. He served many sentences of imprisonment over this time and was introduced to the SMART 'Inside Out' programme during one of his latter sentences. He was referred to Apex from the DTTO team on his release and started attending the Apex SMART group. He attended the group weekly during his order, rarely missed a session, and helped to co-facilitate meetings. His offending behaviour ceased, and due to his methadone programme he is now stable and looking to move on in his recovery. He continues to offer support to his peers and to attend Apex to do Learn Direct courses, acupuncture for relaxation and relapse prevention, and has done several STRADA courses to continue to develop his skills. He now has a better idea of what he wishes to do with his future and has even been offered a voluntary position to help support other people who have addiction/homelessness issues.

Client A has recently been offered the opportunity to attend the ITALL (numeracy and literacy) training to take place within Apex so he can volunteer to support adults with literacy and numeracy issues in the near future.

Client B is a 56-year-old male who was referred to the Delta Project with an alcohol addiction problem. He presented as an extremely professional literate male who in the past had run several of his own businesses, which he had lost due to his alcohol addiction and eventual bankruptcy. His only conviction was for fraud. Because of his depression, he lacked the confidence and self-esteem to apply for positions of employment.

He started attending SMART as part of his action plan to help deal with his dependency and behavioural issues with regard to his alcohol use. He made extremely good progress in a few months although he did have a brief relapse. He maintained contact with his employment development adviser over this short relapse period and resumed attending SMART a month later. He stated that he found the support of the group sessions invaluable in teaching him new skills and ways to cope with his problems. He began to do some Learn Direct courses to update his computer skills and updated his CV with a view to looking for employment.

Think Again

The Think Again programme, a 'one-off' initiative run by Apex Scotland in partnership with Napier University, is a ten-week personal development programme aimed at addressing the barriers faced by ex-offenders, mostly in their 20s and 30s, who have drug-misuse issues, supporting them towards employment, education, training or voluntary work.

A major part of the programme focuses on self-esteem, motivation and assertiveness training along with learning and skills development, where the students take part in activities such as art work, creative writing, photography and web design.

A large part of the programme also involves group work through outdoor activities and problem solving. It also covers job-seeking skills and issues such as conviction relevance and disclosure of previous convictions to employers.

Participation in the programme is entirely voluntary. Participants often hear about the programme through prison education, job centres or social workers in Edinburgh and the Lothians.

The course has been running for eight years now and has met with considerable success. One former student gained an honours degree, and many have accessed further education through Jewel and Esk College. Confidence building is central, and each course ends with a 'graduation ceremony' at which each student is asked to speak about their experience of the programme. Over the four Think Again courses delivered last year, 50 out of 63 students completed the programme, 21 went on to college, one to full-time employment, one to further training and three have gone into voluntary work.

Successful case study

'From a young age I began to experiment with drugs and alcohol and, after my mum passed away, I became addicted. Getting involved in a life of crime ultimately led to me being imprisoned. Whilst in prison I was given the opportunity to tackle my addictions and a range of other issues. However, upon my release, I found it really difficult to adjust to life outside and my confidence was at an all-time low. Thanks to my probation officer I found out about the course and, for the first time in my life, I was ready to believe that I had the potential to achieve...

...to date I have passed all my exams and each successful step gives me the motivation to keep going and reach my full potential. I can't lie and say it has been easy, and at times I have struggled, but the support I have received has been phenomenal. I have begun to turn my life around for the better and now I know that I've got what it takes.'

Conclusion

A number of different initiatives have been described, involving different partnerships between Apex and other agencies, and using different models or methods designed according to the service users' needs. All have a similar aim of helping those at various stages of substance misuse towards employability. Work is a means of feeling useful and gaining inclusion, and thus of building up self-confidence and self-belief – necessary ingredients for overcoming addictions.

References

Allen, D. (1999) 'Outside society: drugs and social exclusion.' *Druglink*, July/August, 16–18.

Biernacki, P. (1986) *Pathways from Heroin Addiction: Recovery Without Treatment.* Philadelphia: Temple University Press.

Cebulla, A., Smith, N. and Sutton, L. (2004) 'Returning to normality: Substance users' work histories and perceptions of work during and after recovery.' *British Journal of Social Work 34*, 1045–1054.

Comerford, A.W. (1999) 'Work dysfunction and addiction: Common roots.' *Journal of Substance Abuse Treatment 16*, 247–253.

Department for Work and Pensions (2008a) *No One Written Off: Reforming Welfare to Reward Responsibility.* Welfare Reform Green Paper. London: Department for Work and Pensions.

Department for Work and Pensions (2008b) *Raising Expectations and Increasing Support: Reforming Welfare for the Future.* Welfare Reform White Paper. London: Department for Work and Pensions.

Hay, G. and Bauld, L. (2008) *Population Estimates of Problematic Drug Users in England who Access DWP Benefits: A Feasibility Study.* Department for Work and Pensions Working Paper No 46. London: Department for Work and Pensions.

Home Office (2008) *Drugs: Protecting Families and Communities. The 2008 Drug Strategy.* London: Home Office.

Information Services Division (2007) *Drug Misuse Statistics Scotland 2007.* Edinburgh: Common Services Agency.

Kandel, D.B. and Yamaguchi, K. (1987) 'Job mobility and drug use: An event history analysis.' *American Journal of Sociology 92*, 4, 836–878.

Kemp, P. and Neale, J. (2005) 'Employability and problem drug users.' *Critical Social Policy 25*, 28–46.

Klee, H., McLean, I. and Yavorsky, C. (2002) *Employing Drug Users.* York: Joseph Rowntree Foundation and York Publishing Services.

Leukefeld, C., Webster, J.M., Staton-Tindall, M. and Duvall, J. (2007) Employment and work among drug court clients: 12-month outcomes. *Substance Use and Misuse 42*, 1109–1126.

Luchansky, B., Brown, M., Longhi, D., Stark, K. and Krupski, A. (2000) 'Chemical dependency treatment and employment outcomes: Results from the "ADATSA" program in Washington State.' *Drug and Alcohol Dependence 60*, 151–159.

MacDonald, Z. and Pudney, S. (2000) 'Illicit drug use, unemployment and occupational attainment.' *Journal of Health Economics 19*, 1089–1115.

McIntosh, J. and McKeganey, N. (2001) *Beating the Dragon: The Recovery from Dependent Drug Use.* London: Prentice Hall.

McIntosh, J., Bloor, M.J. and Robertson, M. (2008) 'Drug treatment and the achievement of paid employment.' *Addiction Research and Theory 16*, 1, 37–45.

Neale, J. (1998) 'Drug users aren't working.' *Druglink*, March/April, 21–22.

Neale, J. (2002) *Drug Users in Society.* Basingstoke: Palgrave.

Neale, J., Godfrey, C., Parrott, S., Sheard, L. and Tompkins, L. (2007) *Barriers to the Effective Treatment of Injecting Drug Users.* Final Report submitted to the Department of Health.

Perkins, D. (2007) 'Improving employment participation for welfare recipients facing personal barriers.' *Social Policy and Society 7*, 1, 13–26.

Phillips, C. and South, N. (1992) 'A sense of worth: drug users as community volunteers.' *Druglink*, September/October, 8–10.

Radcliffe, P. and Stevens, A. (2008) 'Are drug treatment services only for "thieving junkie scumbags"? Drug users and the management of stigmatised identities.' *Social Science and Medicine 67*, 1065–1073.

Room, J. (1998) 'Work and identity in substance abuse recovery.' *Journal of Substance Abuse Treatment 15*, 65–74.

Scott, G. and Sillars, K. (2003) *Employers' Attitudes to Hard-to-employ Groups: Executive Summary.* Report prepared for Westworking Partnership. Glasgow: Glasgow Caledonian University and Scottish Poverty Information Unit.

Scottish Government (2008) *The Road to Recovery: A New Approach to Tackling Scotland's Drug Problem.* Edinburgh: Scottish Government.

Shepard, D.S. and Reif, S. (2004) 'The value of vocational rehabilitation in substance user treatment: A cost-effectiveness framework.' *Substance Use and Misuse 39*, 13–14, 2581–2609.

Siddall, J.W. and Conway, J. (1988) 'Interactional variables associated with retention and success in residential drug treatment.' *Substance Use and Misuse 23*, 12, 1241–1254.

South, N., Akhtar, S., Nightingale, R. and Stewart, M. (2001) 'Idle hands.' *Drug and Alcohol Findings 6*, 24–30.

UK Drug Policy Commission (2008) *Working Towards Recovery. Getting Problem Drug Users into Jobs.* London: UK Drug Policy Commission.

UK Drug Policy Commission Recovery Consensus Group (2008) *A Vision of Recovery.* Available at www.ukdpc.org.uk/resources/A%20Vision%20of%20Recovery.pdf, accessed on 25 June 2009.

Wolkstein, E. and Spiller, H. (1998) 'Providing vocational services to clients in substance abuse rehabilitation.' *Directions in Rehabilitation Counseling 9*, 65–77.

Zanis, D.A., Metzger, D.S. and McLellan, T. (1994) 'Factors associated with employment among methadone patients.' *Journal of Substance Abuse Treatment 11*, 443–447.

CHAPTER 6

Children Affected by Parental Drug and Alcohol Misuse

Hidden harm: Working with serious parental drug misuse

Donald Forrester

Parental misuse of drugs is an enormous social problem. Around 350,000 children have a parent with a serious drug problem, and about half of these children do not live with that parent (Advisory Council on the Misuse of Drugs 2003). For those who still live with the parent, evidence suggests a greatly increased likelihood that they will experience abuse and neglect, and live in poverty, and that they are more likely to do poorly at school, become involved in crime and to develop drug or alcohol problems themselves (Brisby, Baker and Hedderwick 1997; Forrester and Harwin 2006, 2008, 2009; Velleman and Orford 1999). The accounts of neglect and emotional harm given by these children make for harrowing reading (e.g. Barnard 2007). If the impacts of parental drug misuse were public, there would be a national outcry. Most people have no idea about the conditions that children such as these live in – the bare, dirty, dark flats and houses, the unpredictable behaviour of the parents, violence and neglect – because it generally happens in the privacy of family homes and is concentrated amongst the poorest and most deprived families and neighbourhoods, it is a social problem that has received little coverage and even fewer resources. This has to change.

This article is not, however, about the nature or impact of parental substance misuse, as these questions have been addressed in depth elsewhere (e.g. Forrester and Harwin 2009; Kroll and Taylor 2002). It is rather about the ways in which change needs to occur if we are to help these children, and the nature of the revolution required to bring those changes about. Parental drug misuse is the issue used here to illustrate and demonstrate the nature of the changes that are needed.

So, as Lenin said in a different context 'What is to be done?' The answers may in part be surprising, because the core of the argument is that there is little about parental drug misuse that requires specialist services. Rather, the failure of our current provision to deal with this issue is due to our misunderstanding and mismanagement of children's services in general for decades. As a result, children's services are struggling to cope adequately with a range of serious family difficulties. Outcomes for children whose parents have serious drug problems would improve if there were better services for all very vulnerable children; and services that would work better for parental drug misuse would work better across the board.

Key issues in working with parental drug misuse

Good practice with parental drug misuse is good practice, full stop

So many families are affected by parental substance misuse that it is not possible to be a good child and family social worker – or any other professional working with children and their families – if you are not competent to work with drug and alcohol misuse. However, at a more profound level the key challenges in working with parental drug misuse are essentially the same as those involved in effective child protection or safeguarding work across the board.

Effective risk assessment and difficult judgements

Predicting the likelihood of future harm to a child with complete accuracy is impossible – both in theory and in practice. The best assessment schemas that researchers have come up with still fail to identify some children at risk of harm and include many others who are not actually harmed; and professional experts do not tend to be any better (Forrester and Harwin 2009; Forrester and Pitcairn 2008). Social workers are therefore literally being asked to do an impossible job. Furthermore throughout the work there is a need to make incredibly difficult and important judgements.

Social workers (in particular) have to decide whether children can remain at home or whether court proceedings need to be started; but at the less extreme end there are a host of subtle and complex balancing judgements between the rights of parents and the needs of children. For instance, a parent may have reduced their misuse but there is a high likelihood of future relapse. Should the case remain open indefinitely? Or the parent may well address their substance misuse, but to do so would take months of intensive input. Can a young child wait in the (by no means certain) hope that a parent will succeed in changing?

The key issue here is not so much telling professionals what the 'right' decision is (as this will vary from child to child) as it is deciding what the best way of supporting wise decision making is. There are conceptual resources that may be helpful (such as an awareness of risk and resilience factors), but the key to effective risk assessment is likely to be well-educated professionals, who are given the time and space to reflect critically on the decisions that they are making, and have regular and high-quality supervision that challenges and supports them (Forrester and Harwin 2009; Forrester and Pitcairn 2008).

Engaging parents and promoting change

The key challenge that social workers and other professionals identify repeatedly in working with parental drug or alcohol misuse is being faced with parental denial or minimisation (Kroll and Taylor 2002; Forrester and Harwin 2006, 2008). In addition, parents can be hostile and threatening (and sometimes actually violent) or passive and uncommunicative. Yet these are understandable responses to the situation that parents find themselves in. Dealing effectively with these issues requires communication skills of the highest order. Developing these requires extensive training, ongoing supervision and a focus on actual practice (e.g. through reflection on taped or videoed sessions).

These key elements of effective practice with parental drug misuse are in fact key elements of effective practice full stop. In fact, beyond a basic understanding of the nature of different substances, the nature of use, misuse and 'addiction' and the psycho-social factors involved in substance misuse, there is little specific information that the practitioner needs. Instead, what they require is a system that allows them to work in a thoughtful and considered way with these complex issues.

Shortcomings of current provision in children's services

The reforms of the last 15 years or so have been little short of an unmitigated disaster. All were brought in with good intentions: nobody deliberately set out to make what was already a poor system even worse. Yet that has been the net effect. And children's services' inability to respond to parental drug or alcohol misuse is – I would argue – simply a manifestation of this broad systemic failure rather than a particular problem that should be considered in its own right.

In a nutshell, these are some of the key problems with recent reforms of children's services:

- The government has systematically tried to move away from 'child protection' toward 'family support', without recognising that families with serious problems – such as significant parental drug misuse – require highly skilled interventions backed up by statutory powers. In fact, there has been too much focus on what should or should not be defined as 'child protection' and not enough on how we work with families with serious problems who do not voluntarily engage in supportive services (see Platt 2006, 2008).

- A closely related issue is the perception that care is a bad thing for children. In the first place, this is untrue as a matter of fact (Forrester 2008; Forrester *et al.* 2009). Most children's welfare improves once they enter care, and therefore recent attempts to reduce the use of care appear misguided. However, at a more profound level this is a reflection of the fact that the system attempts to polarise care and family support as if they were alternatives. In fact, for many children who enter care permanent alternative families are not an appropriate option. For these children, care should be seen as a form of family support – whether for some weeks or for a large proportion of childhood. This is particularly appropriate for many children living with serious parental drug misuse. Once children have formed strong attachments with their parents it may not be appropriate to find them permanent alternative care; and yet living at home may be damaging for them.

- There have been attempts to 'proceduralise' and 'bureaucratise' practice. As a result, it now appears that around 70 to 80 per cent of social workers' time is spent at a computer, with no signs that this is producing real improvements in even the collection or analysis of information, and a strong sense that it is leading to an erosion of the core business of social work – helping parents and children.

- A closely related problem has been an obsession with a centralised form of management, involving performance indicators, league tables and other forms of measurement of processes rather than outcomes. There is no evidence that most of these measure anything meaningful.

- Inspection regimes have grown out of all proportion to their ability to tell government anything meaningful or reliable about the realities of practice. Unlike Ofsted inspections of schools, it is not possible to garner either objective measures of outcomes or direct observations of practice through Ofsted inspections of social services. As a result the inspection regime focuses on paperwork and performance indicators. It does not produce evidence that would be – for instance – publishable in an academic journal. To be publishable, evidence needs to be both reliable and valid, and inspections are neither. The worst recent example of this was the glowing report of the inspectors into Haringey Social Services shortly after the death of Baby Peter.

- There has been a strong government focus on systems change, and in particular more integrated working; yet there is little or no evidence that different systems or greater integration actually makes a difference (Galvani and Forrester 2009). In fact, what is striking is that the features found to be important in integrated services are also key elements of any good service, and they typically involve good management, a clear vision for the service, and support and time for staff to do their job.

- There is a massive under-investment in social work and social care research. The government spends around £1600 per year on research for each person in the health service. In social work and social care the figure is around £24 (Marsh and Fisher 2005). Is it any wonder that we have such limited evidence within children's services – and that we have virtually no evidence on what works in child and family fieldwork?

Yet these problems are not solely those of the government. Social work as a profession has failed to articulate a convincing alternative to the managerial vision enforced by central government. So what is to be done?

Changing social work practice

The key to an effective response to parental substance misuse – and across children's services – requires a re-professionalisation of social work with a focus on developing and delivering 'evidence-based' interventions There should be a number of elements to this. However, the most important change is a shift in focus. The focus must be on:

- What do workers do when they meet children and parents?
- What is it about what they do that makes a difference?

In essence, policy makers, managers, academics and social work as a profession have lost a focus on the nature of practice. A vivid indication of this is the parlous state of social work research on what happens when workers meet clients. In a recent review of evidence from the last 25 years we were only able to find one UK study based on a single interview that systematically analysed what happened in a social work interview, and none that analysed what worked and what did not work (Forrester *et al.* 2008). As pointed out in a recent Social Care Institute for Excellence review this means that the bulk of social work training in communication skills focuses on teaching basic counselling skills (SCIE 2004). When social workers then go into practice and discover that social work is very different from counselling, they are left with few conceptual or empirical resources.

This neglect of what happens in practice is reflected in both training and supervision. Social work qualifying training emphasises portfolios of 'evidence', or reflective commentaries on their work. There is limited direct observation of practice. These problems are replicated at post-qualifying level, where the focus tends to be on the completion of academic assignments rather than applying the skills of academic analysis and research to actual practice as captured on tape or video. The situation is even more concerning once social workers qualify. The provision of supervision is variable, and where it does happen it increasingly focuses on managerial tasks (such as ensuring forms are completed) rather than providing either a reflective space to consider the complexities of the job or a way of systematically developing skilled practice through direct observation.

All of these examples point to the ways in which social work has lost its focus on direct practice. In contrast, it is worth considering the example of Motivational Interviewing (MI) – an evidence-based approach that has developed in the substance misuse field based on systematic reflection on direct practice experiences. MI is an example of what can be achieved when practitioners, academics and policy makers come together to focus on how professionals should talk with individuals about problem behaviours (such as alcohol or drug difficulties), and evaluating what practice works (and what does not).

It is hard to think of a better book about how to help people with behaviour problems than Miller and Rollnick's introduction to MI (Miller and Rollnick 2002).

MI is an exemplar of what can be achieved when there is systematic reflection on practice and outcomes that brings together practitioners and researchers. The key point here is not that MI 'works'. Often it does, sometimes it does not, and there are complex reasons why one or the other is more likely to be the case. Crucially, we cannot simply import MI into a completely different context and then assume that it will 'work'; MI was developed for the challenges of clients with alcohol issues, and using it in a child protection situation would be very different. The key point is therefore that systematically reflecting on and researching practice makes a difference, whatever the client group. It produces a clearer description of practice and it provides evidence about what does (and does not) work.

A summary of necessary changes

A theme of this article has been that at present the entire focus of policy is not on practice; and that it will not be possible to transform practice until we revolutionise the systems within which we deliver practice. To encourage practitioners and researchers to work together on practice and its outcomes we need a twin focus on *professional excellence* and *evidence-based practice.*

First, social work as a profession needs to be reformed so that there is a career progression to consultant social worker level that allows individuals to remain in practice. Consultant social workers – expected to deliver the highest standards of practice and to support newer workers and students to become experts – are the key individuals if we are to transform the profession. They should not be appointed on the basis of experience alone, but on their demonstrated ability to deliver effective evidence-based interventions.

Second, closely related to the above, there needs to be a focus on developing good practice through direct observation and feedback. This should be at the heart of social work courses, post-qualifying training and ongoing development of practice.

Third, there needs to be a commitment to evidence-based practice – that is, working in ways that have been found to tend to work. This requires a very significant investment in evaluative social work research in order to find out what works. It is hard to overstate the importance of the lack of such an evidence base.

Fourth, research suggests that individuals in supportive working environments, with regular and high-quality supervision, who are given the space and time to work effectively, make a positive difference (Glisson and Hemmelgarn 1998). This – rather than level of integration or the computer system they use – is what makes a difference to children and families. Of course, creating such environments is much harder than legislating for new structures. A local or national politician or a senior manager can relatively easily create a new structure, and thus provide the illusion of purposeful change, but it is much harder to create the supportive environments that are at the heart of effective services. Yet ultimately this is a more important creator of positive outcomes for children and their families than changed structures without changed cultures.

Conclusion

This article has argued that effective work with families affected by parental drug misuse is synonymous with effective work in general. It has tried to outline what the ingredients of effective practice are, and the changes to the policy framework that are required in order to help individuals work in effective ways. Underlying all is a belief that we can only improve the outcomes for children living with parental drug misuse if we are prepared to invest in highly professional and evidence-based services, which can then be aimed at working with the families with the most serious problems. Doing so would allow us to focus on the key issue in improving practice and outcomes for these families, namely what workers do when they meet parents and children. It really is as simple – and as complicated – as that.

The role of training in changing the lives of children affected by parental substance misuse

Joyce Nicholson

In 2003 the publication of *Getting Our Priorities Right – Good Practice Guidance for Working with Children and Families Affected by Substance Misuse* (Scottish Executive 2003) and of *Hidden Harm – Responding to the Needs of Children of Problem Drug Users* (Advisory Council on the Misuse of Drugs 2003) gave recognition to the significant challenges faced by both children living in families where problematic substance misuse is evident, and the services charged with ensuring their welfare and protection. Reflecting the findings of reviews of child protection practice, both documents underline the need for a cultural shift in working practices, strategically and operationally, in the interaction between drug and alcohol misuse and child welfare and protection.

In order to implement the guidance to improve the identification, assessment and service development for children affected by parental substance misuse, Drug and Alcohol Teams and Child Protection Committees were asked in *Getting Our Priorities Right* to:

> work together to ensure that all relevant local interests agree a framework of common policies and protocols based on this guidance for work with families in which parents have substance misuse problems. (Scottish Executive 2003, p.63)

Mirroring the recommendations of numerous inquiries (Lord Laming 2003; Reder and Duncan 1999; Sinclair and Bullock 2002) into instances of fatal or serious child abuse, training is seen as central to the process of implementing change:

> Training is an important lever in developing good practice and improvements in collaborative working between agencies, with greater emphasis on the connections between substance misuse and poor outcomes for children. Training should underpin the implementation of protocols for joint working at all levels to make this guidance operational. (Scottish Executive 2003, p.65)

The scope of this agenda is recognised in *Hidden Harm* (2007):

There is a need for large-scale training and workforce development, to equip mainstream children's and adult services to identify and respond appropriately to the needs of this group of children.

In order to implement the practice required by both *Getting Our Priorities Right* and *Hidden Harm*, a number of local authorities in Scotland sought to establish multi-agency protocols. These protocols were commissioned by Drug and Alcohol Action Teams and Child Protection Committees from Joy Barlow, Head of STRADA (Scottish Training on Drugs and Alcohol), and were separately designed for each local authority. Development of the protocols was followed by substantial training and implementation work, delivered by specialist STRADA trainers seconded to specific geographical areas. This work is now carried forward under the 'Children Affected by Parental Substance Misuse' agenda in Scotland's new drugs strategy.

This article will describe some key issues in local protocol implementation; and the role of training as a tool in changing cultures, thereby shifting operational practice. The importance of including and involving the voices of children and their families and the role of reflective practice will be considered alongside the challenges and opportunities in multi-agency practice.

First steps

Sometimes professionals are seen as working 'in silos' – with good intentions but with the focus just on their own client group – often neglecting the needs and impact on the whole family. The welfare and protection of children requires:

- better communication and collaboration between and within agencies
- shared responsibilities across agencies for the identification of, and response, to the needs and risks of children
- earlier intervention
- clear multi-agency assessments
- ongoing information sharing
- a clear understanding of roles and responsibilities of all involved.

Agencies are required to engage with families where there are a highly complex range of issues and difficulties and where intervention is sometimes not welcomed.

Certainly the need for cultural change – a shift in both thinking and action in the roles and responsibilities of agencies involved with families with addiction issues, has been evidenced (Scottish Executive 2003). The movement towards a universally shared responsibility for safeguarding children requires all individuals and whole organisations to take on ownership, to recognise 'it is my job' and to accept a role in the jigsaw. This is a significant challenge to both service providers and to service users. Such shifts in working practices can be threatening and overwhelming in an environment that is undoubtedly demanding. It is then not difficult to understand that there may be reluctance and resistance to adopt new processes, changes to working practice and shifts in responsibilities.

Training has often been seen as central to practice change in child welfare and protection work: for example, Reder and Duncan (2004) in their review of the Victoria Climbié inquiry consider training and education to be the 'cornerstone' in improving practice. Training should aim to 'arm practitioners with knowledge, skills and the capacity to think'.

Local protocols and implementation strategies provide a crucial context for training. Without support for the process in the working environment by strategic managers, training will not necessarily enhance child-centred practice. As Horwath (2001) argues, 'training cannot be delivered in a vacuum. Effective training depends on the continual dialogue between operational managers and trainers, ensuring that training is used appropriately rather than as a panacea to cure all ills' (p.33).

A clear multi-agency implementation strategy should be in place before training commences. All agencies need to develop a shared ownership of the protocol. It is important that agencies are involved in, and consulted about, the local changes being developed, and that managers expected to make decisions about referrals are given clear pathways to discuss and review operational issues. Operational systems (e.g. on how to share recording and monitoring information) need to be put in place prior to the commencement of the training; and the changes to practice should be reflected in supervision systems across agencies. Multi-agency steering groups, with links to wider planning structures in children and adult services, can address systems in each individual agency, at the interface between agencies, address challenges and report changes in practice and outcomes for children and families.

Training delivery

The training delivered on the protocols has been structured into 'briefing' sessions, and a skills-focused, practice-based workshop. Both are on a multi-agency basis.

The briefings aim to familiarise participants with the local Protocol on Children and Families Affected by Substance Misuse; and give them a working knowledge of it sufficient to implement *Getting Our Priorities Right*. Also to make participants more aware of aspects affecting the welfare and safety of children growing up in families where substance misuse is problematic. The briefing sessions describe:

- an overview of the policy context
- the impact on children of parental substance misuse
- the impact of substance misuse on parenting capacity
- resilience factors
- the processes, roles and responsibilities set out in the protocols.

The workshop is targeted across a range of agencies including substance misuse teams, social work staff, health staff, including midwives and health visitors, voluntary sector staff, education staff and family centres. Workshops aim to increase awareness and understanding of the impact of parental substance misuse on children; and to develop practice-based skills in relation to the protocols. They do this by:

- discussing existing practice issues
- problem-solving based on live practice, providing opportunities for reflection on practice and providing an understanding of different professional perspectives.

The practice-based workshops thus explore the complex relationships between substance misuse and parenting capacity, through reflection on knowledge, attitudes and values.

Practice-based skills are developed in:

- identification of needs, assessment, care planning and reviewing
- risks and protective factors
- the impact on child development of chronic neglect, and recognition of threshold issues in relation to this

- the range of needs and issues children face in living with substance misusing parents
- working with pregnant substance misusers.

Live case practice is used, and, crucially, hearing the voices of children and their family members. The child is placed at the centre of practice.

For many participants this will be the first training they have received on substance misuse, and it is important that time is spent responding to the differing levels of knowledge and confidence on this topic. Often participants come to the briefings and workshops with an expectation of gaining knowledge about drugs and effects, rather than the need to explore the interaction between substances, lifestyle and impact for children. Increasing knowledge about substances and their effects may increase worker confidence when interacting with substance users; but it will not aid in understanding the impact of substance use on children. Knowing what dose of methadone a parent is receiving does not clarify the level of care a child is receiving. It is important to explore the impact that styles and patterns of substance misuse may have on a child's development and emotional well-being, on parenting capacity, and on often co-occurring issues such as mental health and domestic violence.

Participants can become upset and distressed during the training and it is important to acknowledge that a significant number of participants will have had an experience of parental substance misuse themselves as children or are living with family members with substance misuse issues. There may also be participants who have alcohol and drug problems and are parents. It is therefore critical that safety in the group and support systems are put in place at the earliest opportunity, and trainers are equipped to respond to distress and disclosures appropriately.

For organisations to commit to a significant training programme is a huge investment financially and organisationally, and this does much to validate the protocols themselves.

'Light bulb' moments

The importance of offering multi-agency training cannot be overstated. Each participant brings a fresh perspective and knowledge to the training experience. Multi-agency training:

- increases knowledge and understanding
- improves relationships and communication

- clarifies roles and responsibilities
- can break down barriers and increase trust between professionals
- helps understanding of differences in thresholds for services, and issues surrounding confidentiality and information sharing.

It also provides opportunities to develop intra and inter-agency networks, recognition of expertise, and an understanding of the limitations and legal frameworks in which they work. It helps participants see through the lens from which other agencies view the world; and is an opportunity for participants to challenge each other in a safe environment.

The world view you hold as a practitioner in your field is critical and impacts on thresholds and interpretations of information. An example of this emerged in a recent multi-agency reflective case practice. The worker commented about a house with 40 catalogues from a high street shop in a pile on the living room table. Staff in the reflective case study group were asked to highlight what they were assuming about the parents' lifestyle. The drug worker thought the parents were drug dealing and using the catalogues as wraps; the criminal justice worker thought they might be shoplifting to order; a nursery worker assumed they were for art work and making collages; and a psychiatric nurse thought perhaps there was a compulsive disorder. However, on clarifying the situation no one had asked the parent why they had the catalogues. We must all continue to speculate on the reason for the catalogue collection. The meaning attached to the scenario will shape each professional assessment of the impact of parental behaviour and lifestyle on the child. Clarification is pivotal to challenging professionals' assumptions.

The training focus is on building child-centred practice – recognition of how situations are experienced by children and how it is best to support them. Parents who have substance misuse issues often have a complex array of problems and issues, and it is difficult to see the child in such a context of chaos, confusion and hostility when attempting to support change in parents' behaviours, lifestyles and parenting. The challenge is to hear the experience of children living with parental substance misuse, and to recognise the different thresholds professionals place on the family depending on their perspectives. Experience from workshops demonstrates a lack of understanding of the impact of alcohol on children's lives; often this is reflected in the participant's view of alcohol as culturally acceptable.

A pivotal aspect of the training is hearing the voices of children speaking about how their lives were affected by their parents' drug and alcohol use. It is unusual to hear, even in childcare and protection settings, the reality of the children's lives amongst the secrecy, isolation and defensive love for their parents. This is perhaps the biggest lever of all in terms of justifying the case for practice change and the need for joined-up working.

In some areas where the training has been delivered an important inclusion has been the involvement of local service users and family members in developing the material for the workshops. The material is a living document of the guilt, shame, hopes, aspirations and isolation felt by parents who misuse substances. If we are to help children we need to understand and support whole families. Parents are able to reflect on their situation when they are asked challenging and insightful questions by empathic professionals.

Space to reflect

All professionals should have the opportunity to reflect on their practice during supervision. As Brandon *et al.* (2008) suggest: 'Supervision helps practitioners to think, to explain and to understand. It also helps them to cope with the complex emotional demands of work with children and their families' (p.106). But this is often not the experience of practitioners. Despite the importance of reflecting on practice, practitioners rarely get an opportunity to reflect on attitudes and practice in a safe learning environment.

During the training, participants undertake a multi-agency case study which is an opportunity to reflect on practice. A volunteer presents a current case and the care plan, often a case which feels 'stuck'. It is an opportunity to discuss child-centred practice from different perspectives with different thresholds. The small group discusses the impact on the child from their different professional perspectives, and identifies strengths and resilience, protective factors, risks and needs from the perspective of the child. It is a supportive process helping the presenter to hear the views of other colleagues and accommodate their perspectives. This can be challenging. The worker is sometimes able to devise a new comprehensive care plan for the family, or receive affirmation of the care plan in place. The process has a supportive rather than a critical approach to practice.

Through the process of reflection, a number of participants have felt the need to leave the training and to take immediate action around the case they have presented. It highlights the importance of finding time to help staff reflect, and the power that bringing professionals together can have on shifting practice. The age-old issue around thresholds of risk is often raised within reflective practice, and it is an opportunity for all participants to challenge, reflect and often agree a common threshold of risk for children living with parental substance misuse.

The training is evaluated on many different levels – from reaction forms to focus groups and audits of practice. Training can be developed and refined from feedback given by focus groups. In reviewing how the training has impacted on practice, service users should be involved in the process. Auditing outcomes and pathways of referral and care are useful tools in reviewing the efficacy of the protocols in improving outcomes for children. The development of IT systems to support the recording of the work is critical.

Conclusion

If we are to see, hear and protect children affected by parental substance misuse, there is no quick fix. Implementing protocols to ensure that the needs of children are met requires significant investment and long-term commitment. Specialist training is an essential component of a wider implementation strategy.

> It is important that training in recognising and responding to parental substance misuse is integrated into mainstream workforce development programmes, for both children's and adult services. (Advisory Council on the Misuse of Drugs 2007, p.101)

In the last few years documents such as *Hidden Harm* and *Getting Our Priorities Right*, and subsequent training, have significantly changed how addiction staff think about children living in households with parents misusing substances. The road has been a difficult one for addiction and other adult-focused agencies, but protocols have meant they have to gather information, assess risk and work with colleagues to meet the needs of children. It is perhaps now more of a challenge for staff in childcare settings to understand the shifts they may need to make in having a meaningful engagement with the family as a whole.

Long-term work is needed to ensure the ownership of the processes and shifts in practice required. Training often raises lots of structural, resource and capacity issues that multi-agency groups must address

– otherwise it becomes a mere token to children who are on the cusp of invisibility. Practitioners need time to shift their practice and to embed new ways of working. Managers are crucial to this work. They need to provide the opportunity for workers to reflect critically on their practice – space to think. Each agency has a responsibility to ensure continuing staff and service development as an essential factor in ensuring that children affected by parental substance misuse remain visible.

References

Advisory Council on the Misuse of Drugs (2003) *Hidden Harm: Responding to the Needs of Children of Problem Drug Users.* London: Home Office.

Advisory Council on the Misuse of Drugs (2007) *Hidden Harm Three Years On: Realities, Challenges and Opportunities.* London: Home Office.

Barnard, M. (2007) *Drug Addiction and Families.* London: Jessica Kingsley Publishers.

Brandon, M., Belderson, P., Warren, C., Howe, D., Gardner, R., Dodsworth, J. and Black, J. (2008) 'Analysing Child Deaths and Serious Injury through Abuse and Neglect: What Can We Learn?' *A Biennial Analysis of Serious Case Reviews 2003–2005.* London: Department for Children, Schools and Families.

Brisby, T., Baker, S. and Hedderwick, T. (1997) *Under the Influence: Coping with Parents Who Drink Too Much.* A report on the needs of the children of problem drinkers. London: Alcohol Concern.

Forrester, D. (2008) 'Is the care system failing children?' *Political Quarterly 79*, 2, 206–211.

Forrester, D. and Harwin J. (2006) 'Parental substance misuse and child care social work: Findings from the first stage of a study of 100 families.' *Child and Family Social Work 11*, 4, 325–335.

Forrester, D. and Harwin, J. (2008) 'Outcomes for children whose parents misuse drugs or alcohol: a 2-year follow-up study.' *British Journal of Social Work 38*, 1518–1535.

Forrester, D. and Harwin, J. (2009) *Parents who misuse drugs or alcohol: Effective Interventions in Social Work and Child Protection.* Chichester: Wiley.

Forrester, D., Cocker, C., Goodman, K., Binnie, C. and Jensch, G. (2009) 'What is the impact of public care on children's welfare? A review of research findings and their policy implications.' *Journal of Social Policy 38*, 3, July, 439–456.

Forrester, D., Kershaw, S., Moss, H. and Hughes, L. (2008) 'Communication skills in child protection: How do social workers talk to parents?' *Child and Family Social Work 13*, 1, 41–51.

Forrester, D. and Pitcairn, R. (2008) *Evidence Based Practice: A User's Guide.* Available at www.ccinform. articles.

Galvani, S. and Forrester, D. (2009) 'What works in interagency working?' Cardiff: Welsh Assembly Government.

Glisson, C. and Hemmelgarn, A. (1998) 'The effects of organizational climate and interorganizational coordination on the quality and outcomes of children's service systems.' *Child Abuse and Neglect 22*, 5, 401–421.

Horwath, J. (2001) 'Child care practice innovations: Using a model of change to develop training strategies.' *Child Abuse Review 10*, 18–34.

Kroll, B. and Taylor, A. (2002) *Parental Substance Misuse and Child Welfare.* London: Jessica Kingsley Publishers.

Lord Laming (2003) *The Victoria Climbié Inquiry: Report of an Inquiry by Lord Laming.* London: The Stationery Office.

Marsh, P. and Fisher, M. (2005) *Developing the Evidence Base for Social Work and Social Care Practice.* London: Social Care Institute for Excellence.

Miller, W.R. and Rollnick, S. (2002) *Motivational Interviewing: Preparing People for Change* (2nd edition). New York: Guilford Press.

Platt, D. (2006) 'Investigation or initial assessment of child concerns? The impact of the refocusing initiative on social work practice.' *British Journal of Social Work 36*, 1, 267–281.

Platt, D. (2008) 'Care or control? The effects of investigations and initial assessments on the social worker-parent relationship.' *Journal of Social Work 22*, 3, 301–315.

Reder, P. and Duncan, S. (1999) *Lost Innocents: A Follow-up Study of Fatal Child Abuse*. London: Routledge.

Reder, P. and Duncan, S. (2004) 'Making the most of the Victoria Climbié Inquiry Report.' *Child Abuse Review 13*, 95–114.

Sinclair, R. and Bullock, R. (2002) *Learning from Past Experience – A Review of Serious Case Reviews*. London: Department of Health.

Scottish Executive (2003) *Getting Our Priorities Right: Good Practice Guidance for Working with Children and Families Affected by Substance Misuse*. Edinburgh: Scottish Executive.

Social Care Institute for Excellence (2004) *Teaching and Learning Communication Skills in Social Work Education*. Knowledge Review 6. London: SCIE.

Velleman, R. and Orford, J. (1999) *Risk and Resilience: Adults Who Were the Children of Problem Drinkers*. Amsterdam: OPA.

CHAPTER 7

We Are Family

The role of families

Vivienne Evans

Families are a crucial, yet frequently forgotten, element in drugs strategy and service provision; this article outlines some key issues, drawn from the current literature and the work of Adfam, a leading national organisation that is in touch with family members across England and Wales.

Adfam uses the term 'family' to mean anyone closely involved with, and affected by, someone else's substance misuse. We use the term 'substance misuse' because illegal and prescription drugs, and alcohol, can have an impact on an entire family, and on individual family members, including siblings, partners, grandparents and parents.

The scale of the problem

It is very difficult to estimate the number of people affected by someone else's substance misuse (Templeton *et al.* 2006). The 2008 UK national drug strategy, states that there are 332,000 problem drug users in England alone, but the numbers affected are far greater than this when account is taken of parents, partners, siblings, other family members and friends – all of whom often take on caring roles, and at the very least are affected in one way or another. According to the *Hidden Harm* report (Advisory Council of the Misuse of Drugs 2003), problematic drug use has an impact on up to 350,000 children in the UK. Figures relating to alcohol use inflate this figure even further: for example the 7.1 million 'hazardous and harmful' drinkers, 1.1 million dependent drinkers and 1.3 million children affected by parental alcohol misuse (Cabinet Office 2004; Department of Health 2007). Even more importantly, the families most in need are the ones who avoid ever disclosing their circumstances and have no contact with treatment or support services; these people are likely to be outside the scope of official figures. Though the total number of people affected is difficult to estimate with great confidence (some scholars, and the national charity Adfam, claim it is approximately 7 million), there can be no doubt that a startling number of people require help and support.

The impact of drug use on the family

Having a drug user in the family can have a devastating impact on family life, arousing complex emotions, fracturing family values, promoting family dysfunction and causing mental and physical ill-health. This impact is not confined to the nuclear family unit, it also affects social networks and communities (Copello, Velleman and Templeton 2005). Moreover, substance misuse rarely occurs in isolation, but with other co-existing problems including, but not limited to, mental health problems, isolation, deprivation, unemployment and domestic abuse. Although not the focus of this chapter, children and young people can suffer, with familial substance misuse making a negative impact upon schoolwork, development, health, conduct, friendships and family harmony (Barnard 2006; Barnard and McKeganey 2004; Velleman and Templeton 2007).

Adfam's evidence base of consultations with families reveals that their emotional ill-health tends to stem from their feelings of anger, betrayal, guilt, shame and isolation. Families report frustration with their own lack of understanding of the situation, their feeling that the drug user has somehow betrayed their trust and care, and sometimes their relief if and when the drug user is imprisoned. They also report feeling powerless to deal with a situation that has brought chaos to their family structure, values and cohesion.

Parents in particular report feeling responsible for the drug user's habit and behaviour, believing they have failed in their role, and even guilty when they do positive things for other family members. These feelings are often compounded by the need to demonstrate strength and control in keeping the family together, whilst believing that they could have prevented all this happening in the first place. In these situations family members often neglect their own needs.

Shame and isolation are common reactions to drug misuse by a family member. Many find that they are unable to speak about the situation to wider family, friends, neighbours or colleagues, and become unable to participate in normal social activities. Grandparents caring for grandchildren whose parents are drug users report that they become isolated from their peer group because their new life circumstances are so different.

The advantages of involving families

There are compelling reasons for supporting families and carers, both for their own benefit and that of substance users and treatment services. Evidence outlines the advantages of acknowledging families as a factor in engaging a drug user in treatment, in retaining them in the treatment process, and in improving treatment outcomes and overall recovery (Copello *et al.* 2005; Liddle 2004; Szapocznik *et al.* 1988). If families are involved:

- support for the drug user is increased
- the family's understanding of drugs, and drug treatment is improved
- a common goal for the treatment agency, user and family is created, for example a realistic expectation of treatment outcomes.

There are also advantages and benefits for the family unit because:

- families can be helped to recognise their own needs and seek help for themselves
- communication within the family can be improved
- isolation and anxiety can be reduced
- family problems can be identified and addressed.

We can also make a range of assumptions about the strategic and financial benefits of families supporting drugs users, including:

- Family support costs for services are non-existent or very low – they are an unpaid workforce. However, unpaid is not necessarily without cost – families often suffer loss of earnings, debt and loss of employment through caring for a drug user.
- Families are in abundant supply.
- There is high availability and flexibility of family support – 24 hours a day, seven days a week.
- Families are not subject to some of the restrictions that apply to formal organisations and can concentrate on service delivery.
- Families can offer a long-term commitment.

- Family members and other carers are a good means to reach people who are not in treatment.

- Families have specialist knowledge of the individual drug user.

- Families usually have a high degree of investment in the individual and are motivated towards a successful outcome.

- Families are an untapped resource of a range of skills and have easy access to the individual.

But family members can only provide this support if their own needs are recognised and they receive support in their own right. Supporting carers both helps carers themselves and improves support for drug users. This has important implications for practice.

Implications for practice

Since families have a range of needs, so they will require a variety of responses, services and support. Copello *et al.* (2005) have identified three types of intervention for families affected by substance misuse:

- interventions that work with family members to promote the entry and engagement of drug/alcohol users into treatment; for example, community reinforcement and family training

- joint interventions of family members and relatives using drugs and/or alcohol in the treatment of the user; for example, behavioural couples therapy and social behaviour and network therapy

- services that respond to the needs of families in their own right; for example, Families Anonymous and local support groups that form part of Adfam's network. (These are the subject of the next section.)

Services that respond to the needs of family members in their own right

These services currently are largely provided by the voluntary sector, often by a committed family member with personal experience of the problem, who is driven by a desire to help others in the same situation. The models of support tend to be informal, unstructured and based on the principles of self-help. Geographically, these vary from area to area and are by no means universal or standardised. In some areas, there are well-developed and sophisticated services for families; in others, provision may be limited to an able and willing volunteer with a mobile phone.

Adfam campaigns for the need to drive up both the number of services and to develop these services as well-organised and structured responses to the needs of families. To this end, Adfam has produced a good practice guide (*We Count Too*, 2004), for work with family members affected by someone else's drug use. The guide was informed by the views, experiences and practice of family members themselves, who identified the following 'menu' of support:

- *Information* – Obtaining the right information is a crucial first step in seeking support. Families are often confused and lacking in knowledge about substances and treatment options. Information can offer a gateway to a wealth of other services or provide simple solutions to issues that the family member can deal with on their own. Families need to acquire the key knowledge, skills and confidence to understand and cope with their situation.

- *Telephone helplines* – Telephone helplines provide a dedicated, confidential service. As well as providing information about drugs, drug services and other family support services, the helpline worker also supports the caller to talk about his/her experiences, feelings and worries.

- *One-to-one support* – This kind of service provides support to family members on an individual basis. The service is focused on helping the family member to identify and meet his/her immediate needs, and on developing the confidence, knowledge and skills to start to plan how to take more control of his/her life in the future. One-to-one support services may be provided at a central base, or at a range of outreach settings, including the family member's home.

- *Support groups* – This type of support provides a self-help or facilitated group for family members. It provides group members with opportunities to share their experiences with, and learn from, others in a similar situation. The focus of the group is on learning to 'help yourself' rather than continually focusing on the needs of the drug user.

- *Support to help family members work together* – This kind of intervention enables family members to focus on the family as a whole, rather than on the needs of individual members, to work together to deal with the consequences of having a family member who is a drug user.

- *Services that provide respite* – Receiving quality family support is perceived by many family members to be a form of respite in itself, and some services have branched out to offer weekend breaks, activity days, training, acupuncture and aromatherapy.

- *Services for specific groups* – There are some family members who have specific needs. Even if the organisation is not able to provide a specialist service itself, it can be aware of and liaise with other services that can provide information and support. These include services for grandparents, partners, children and siblings, families who have a family member going through the court system or in prison and family members bereaved by drug use.

Standards for working with families

Adfam has developed a set of quality standards to help organisations to provide quality services based on the needs of family members themselves.

There are *Essential Requirements* – the organisational processes that are necessary in order to deliver quality services – which all family support services should aim to achieve:

- Family members affected by drug use are actively involved in the organisation.

- The service works in partnership with other relevant local organisations and services.

- The service is clear about its principles, aims and focus and how these will be achieved and monitored.

- The service has in place policies, procedures and protocols covering, for example, legal responsibilities, confidentiality and information sharing.

- All service staff are appropriately trained and supported.

There are also seven basic *Quality Standards* for family services to work towards:

- The service should be confidential and safe.

- It should offer choices of support.

- It should present itself as an inclusive service, and be accessible.
- It should support family members to care for their own needs.
- Its approach should be non-judgemental and caring.
- There should be clear boundaries.
- It should be informed and informing.

Continuing challenges

Families affected by substance misuse have finally caught the attention of policy makers. The UK government's 2008 drugs strategy (HM Government 2008) provides a clear lead, and an action plan, to cut the number of families 'devastated by drug use'; while the National Carers' Strategy (Department of Health 2008), and the NICE clinical guidelines on opiod detoxification and psychosocial interventions all refer to the need to include families in treatment.

Despite continued reference in government documents, challenges remain. Access to resources for support for families will be via local budgets. Experience suggests that, unless specific targets or ring-fenced budgets are allocated for the purpose of providing services for families, or a local champion acts as an advocate, services for families will not become a reality. Where they do exist, prejudice and stigma act as major barriers in accessing those services – families often suffer from a self-inflicted exclusion derived from the fear of being judged.

The prevention of substance misuse amongst young people tends to be the focus of much of recent policy initiatives. This is to be welcomed, but it excludes the imperative to address the needs of family members who are not parents of young people. Many individuals accessing local services are caring for sons or daughters who are now adults. This in itself poses another challenge. Current language which uses the term 'carer' can be confusing. Many family members do not perceive themselves as carers, having distanced themselves from the substance user, but they continue to experience distress as a result of former contact and occasional involvement.

The need to involve families in a user's treatment can be misleading. Many substance users are not in treatment, or a family member may be providing the treatment for them – a home detox for example. It is estimated that only 6 per cent of hazardous and dependent drinkers access treatment. Relying on evidence of the positive impact of a family member on a user's treatment outcomes is limiting – it neglects the case for providing support for the family member in their own right. In addition, not all drug users wish to involve their families in treatment, either because they no longer have any contact with their family, because they believe their family would desire different treatment outcomes (e.g. abstinence, rather than maintenance) or because they wish their drug use to remain a secret from their family. But the consequences for families, and sometimes perhaps the root cause of the drug problem, remain.

Services still exist which exclude the family member from the treatment process, believing them to be an intrusion and a hindrance, rather than a help. In Adfam's consultation, *Families in Focus 2003*, families reported anger and confusion about their exclusion from participation in the treatment provided to their family member.

There are also particular groups known to find it difficult to access support, including black and minority ethnic communities, people with disabilities, men, and lesbian, gay, bisexual and transgender people. People in rural communities can also find it difficult to access services. We need evidence to inform service provision for these groups.

Ways forward

The provision of specialist services for families affected by substance misuse may be an unrealistic, highly aspirational goal. What may be more realistic is to accept that many families affected in this way have multi-dimensional problems, for example mental health or domestic violence, and to ensure that mainstream services can cater for their particular needs around substance misuse. This requires investment in workforce development and cross-agency working, together with creative commissioning.

More research is needed to inform the development of services. We do not have an accurate picture of the number of families across the UK affected in this way. Nor do we know the cost savings to health and to social services made possible by families' care and support for substance users, or the expenditure on dealing with their own physical, social and emotional needs. Intelligence on these issues would acknowledge these families' needs and advance the argument for service provision.

We also need greater levels of support for kinship carers – those family members who take full-time care of a young relative due to parental substance misuse. Evidence of their existence is widening as children grow up in families where substance misuse is inter-generational.

Acknowledgement

The author wishes to thank Oliver French from Adfam for his help with this chapter.

Making family a part of the treatment

Maurizio Coletti

Relationships between family organization and drug use

Nowhere, in cases linked to an individual's biological, psychological and social health, has the urgent necessity to involve the family been so recognized as in cases of drug use and abuse.

Ever since drug abuse has become a modern problem, it has been and continues to be most prevalent among children in their late teens and young adults. This means that, apart from the family's social organization (which can vary greatly among different cultures), we are primarily dealing with the delicate and difficult period some authors refer to as 'young adulthood'; a period of change in the development of an individual on the course to becoming an adult. According to Jay Haley (1976), adolescence can be a rather problematic crossroad during which a child and his/her parents must face a period of crisis and proceed toward a restructuring of their relationship. According to other authors (e.g. McGoldrick and Carter 1982), in cases where the families fail to meet these challenges, or in some cases refuse to, the child is generally not considered qualified to meet the responsibilities of an adult.

Epidemiological studies show that a large percentage of drug use and abuse begins and takes root in this developmental phase. In Italy, for example, the average age during which people first use opiates, cocaine, cannabis and synthetic drugs, and the age where they begin to use these habitually both fall between the ages of 15 and 24 (2007 Annual Report on Drugs to the Italian Parliament).

Research has focused more and more intensely on the relationship between problematic drug use and family. The study of the organization and function of a drug addict's family has been the subject of many studies, among which that of Shelder and Block (1990) is quite notable. In a longitudinal study spanning 15 years, 101 young people were studied between the ages of three and eighteen. Upon reaching the latter age, the participants' propensity towards alcohol and drug consumption was then compared with all past observations regarding their development and their families. The purpose of this study was to trace back all possible events or predictive factors that could predispose a person to drug consumption. Researchers reported that at 18 years of age roughly 20 percent displayed a propensity towards the use, and gave other information regarding the behaviours and personalities of these subjects. It seems reasonable to conclude that these young adults will be the ones most likely to have continued contact with drugs throughout their lives, possibly to the point of drug use, abuse or addiction. Data regarding families, and the mother/child and father/child relationships, while showing, curiously enough, no substantiating indication on the father figure, point to specific behaviours on the mother's side in relation to the child. These mothers, having undergone certain tests regularly throughout the length of the study, showed themselves to be 'frigid, critical, overbearing and insensitive to their children's needs'. Generally where these 'user' subjects were shown to be 'relatively insecure, emotionally disturbed and incapable of forming healthy relationships', researchers found them to have received 'inadequate nurturing from their families'.[1]

It is worth observing analogous efforts conducted during the same time period and with convergent results. In the United States, Minuchin (1967) developed a model of interpretation and intervention in cases of social problems, based on his work among families in the slums of Philadelphia. He noted that there existed certain consistencies among the family structures of marginalized families in the area, and that these repetitive

---

1   It is highly noteworthy how another section of the sample, roughly 25 percent, at the end of the study displayed an attitude of complete refusal towards consumption of any substances, enough to earn the title 'abstinents'. Characteristics of personality and, especially, family structure and upbringing were virtually identical as those of the 'users'. Among the sample, the remaining 55 percent was composed of subjects more balanced both from individual and familial points of view, whose relationships regarding substance use were both sporadic and brief. Researchers named this group 'experimenters', asserting that adolescence and young adulthood both are characterized by an attitude of exploration towards the outside world, which may even 'touch' psychotropic drugs, but soon after distances itself.

characteristics played a large functioning role in the behaviours of the adolescents living in these homes; young African-Americans and Puerto Ricans, in particular, made frequent use of psychotropics, among other typical delinquent behaviour. Minuchin studied the families' structure and organization, and hypothesized the possibility of intervention precisely at this level, tackling therapeutically the most evident elements of these family structures, such as the excessive centralization of the mother, the contrastingly peripheral role of the father (often absent altogether) and the presence of a precocious, gifted sibling, whom he referred to as the 'parental child'. Picking up where Salvador Minuchin left off, Stanton and Todd (1982) described the organization and functioning of a drug addict's 'typical' family, characterized by a strong, 'central' mother, who typically shares a close bond with the user child, a 'peripheral' father, seldom present in regular family life, usually in conflict with his wife and drug-using child, who nevertheless plays a relevant role in the entire family dynamic. Stanton and Todd described other siblings of the user who sometimes play the role of the 'good son/daughter', the successful, wise child, who plays a supportive role to the mother. From a therapeutically strategic point of view, Stanton and Todd insist on a flexible organization that allows for a therapy free of these fixed, familial rules, which very often cause drug addicts to preemptively distance themselves from therapy programs.

Cancrini (1982) hypothesized a classification of drug addictions where the interpreted relationship between the family's organization and the drug abuse plays a major role. The symptom is considered functional to a certain organization of the family system. The behaviour of drug addicts often hinders the family's growth, especially as members enter key developmental phases. A study on the families of drug addicts has been conducted by Cirillo *et al.* (1996), who have studied roughly more than 100 cases of drug addiction in various contexts, both under public service programs and within private treatment facilities. These studies, in conclusion, tend to identify three different types of juvenile addiction:

- addiction related to neurotic-based family system
- addiction related to psychotic-based family system
- addiction related to multi-problematic family system.

Finally, one of the arguments for considering family as part of the treatment comes from the direct and daily clinical experience with addicted patients. Very often, a drug addiction will be signaled to a clinic by a relative of the drug addict, claiming to 'first off' seek help for themselves, but most importantly, for the drug addict. In this case, professionals and treatment centers can consider the patient's family as part of the problem (if they feel it stands in the way of treatment) or as a resource (if they feel the inclusion of the family can be advantageous for the treatment).

Working with families and integrated treatments

Working with the families of drug addicts has shown the relative and only partial utility of the traditional settings used in family therapy (periodic sessions, co-therapy, progressive phases of family intervention using classic tools). Rather, it is more useful to include family in different forms of integrated treatments. If it is acceptable to divide the principal approaches to treatment into:

- pharmaceutical interventions
- residential and semi-residential interventions
- psychosocial interventions

it is possible to foresee the inclusion of work with the family in each of these treatment groups. In medical treatments, in fact, family support shows itself to be greatly useful, especially:

- when patients must increase motivation upon entering treatment, pressure from their relatives can be decisive in convincing them; in this case, regular sessions with the whole family (even without the patient, if he/she is 'unwilling') can be very useful
- when the patient is in treatment and displays difficulty in taking his/her medication with the necessary consistency; here, too, it is important to meet with the whole family, to monitor both the treatment's progress and the reactions and situations that might arise
- when the medical treatment is in its final phase (especially in cases of detoxification); here, relatives can play a crucial role in helping to prevent relapses and supporting the patient through the period of societal reinsertion.

Generally, family support during a medical treatment is considered to be a great advantage and prevents patients from becoming depressed or losing interest in themselves.

For residential treatments, co-operation with families has always been considered crucial. Here, too, relatives can be integrated in the treatment either before commencing community therapy (or a day program), with the purpose of preparing both patient and family and to create and raise motivation to treatment, and during the residential or semi-residential phase, which allows for an intensive study of past family history and of the meaning of addiction symptoms, to further the development of the family and its individual components. In the final phase of residential treatment, family co-operation can prepare the patient for his or her re-entry into society following the treatment, where regular work with the family can be helpful in the post-cure period, and be useful in managing eventual relapses.

In the tradition of therapeutic communities it is common to include family members through groups. The latter are commonly conducted by volunteers, not professionals, often parents of ex-addicts. They consist of a form of self-help, which is rather useful, and do not exclude working with family members one-on-one or in groups.

Outpatient treatments (psychosocial) are, naturally, those capable of reaping the most benefit from working systematically with families. It is important to understand how each member of the family reacts to the patient's symptomatic behaviour, to find the meaning of the behaviour, and help the family system support the patient throughout therapy, rather than hinder him/her.

In cases of addiction such as gambling, internet, or others, the advantage of including family in the treatments remains just as evident.

Notes on therapy tactics

Working with families can often be difficult for a professional. If a person is used to working with individuals, he/she will notice that in sessions spent with families, everything happens very quickly and it is necessary to have a certain kind of experience to govern such sessions.

Even simply gathering an entire family can be challenging in some cases; very often, parents will not want to participate out of fear of being blamed for the problem at hand. Therefore, it is absolutely necessary to avoid doing so: meetings with families must be motivated by the need to gather more information, to help those involved face such a difficult situation and to sustain, as much as possible, a given treatment.

The placing of guilt, is therefore counterproductive and should be avoided and contested. Each member must feel that they are being respected, encouraged and listened to. An even worse problem arises from blaming family members, forcing them to think 'This might be my fault, it must be. Now tell me what to do.' This attitude is highly negative and can hinder productive therapy.

Often there are times of tension and intense conflict. Such tension is most easily found in sessions prior to starting a treatment for drug use and abuse. In this phase, verbal abuse and accusations are frequently exchanged not only among the family and the patient, but often among spouses, too. The therapist must never take part in these conflicts and must maintain his or her role as an expert.

Frequently, professionals will come across families centered mainly around the mother, while the father remains a peripheral figure. This has been confirmed by the studies and clinical experiences above mentioned. Very often there exist strong tensions and differences, which may manifest as strong tension and differing opinions concerning the intervention. In most of these cases, the parents will ask for an alliance with the therapist, demanding his or her confirmation in what they say, and will often criticize the partner. The professional should not take this risk and must avoid 'taking sides'.

Another very common situation has to do with the manipulative and lying nature of an addicted patient: parents are often able to 'sniff out' a lie, but not able to engage this with a proper attitude. Naturally, they complain about this to the therapist and implore him/her to support them and act as judge. The therapist must not take part in seeking out the patient's lies, and must not feel him/herself to be the target of these lies. His/her role must be to support the family as a whole, to identify possibilities for improvement and to facilitate the elimination of dysfunctional behaviours; not to decide who is right or wrong.

When siblings are involved, they will sometimes play the role of the 'model' or 'parental' child. It is crucial to attempt to include them in the therapy and to allow them, too, to free themselves from these roles within the family, as they are often stuck in these 'improper' supportive roles.

One last observation regarding family therapy has to do with the haste with which families demand radical and definitive solutions or 'magic bullets'. Here, the therapist's responsibility, though difficult, is to avoid offering predetermined solutions, and to recognize the distress that lies behind such haste, without giving in to it.

Of course, there are no existing, rigid protocols in working with families. However, in the past decade, a methodology known as MDFT (multi-dimensional family therapy) has established itself both in the United States and Europe.

Multi-dimensional family therapy is an approach to research and treatment for adolescents struggling with substance abuse. MDFT began roughly 20 years ago with the work of Howard Liddle and his group, and consists of an organic effort to incorporate traditional elements of family therapy (strategic and structural approaches) with fundamental principles of developmental psychology and evidence-based interventions specifically dealing with substance abuse (Liddle, Dakof and Diamond 1991). As a research-based approach, MDFT has received many national recognitions in the United States from the major agencies in charge of drug-addiction research, such as the Center For Substance Abuse Treatment (CSAT) and the National Institute of Drug Abuse (NIDA) and as been certified as a model program by the Substance Abuse and Mental Health Services Administration (SAMHSA). As a family treatment, it is notably established and highly valuable.

Conclusions

Working with the families of drug addicts is both possible and advantageous. Including relatives in the treatments of addictions makes these treatments more effective and complete. On the other hand, excluding them from the outset can often be a grave error, especially when working with adolescent drug users. Involving the whole family in the search for a more functional family dynamic, most notably in the post-cure, lowers the rate of relapse.

Family is therefore a valuable resource for an effective treatment.

References

Advisory Council on the Misuse of Drugs (2003) *Hidden Harm: Responding to the Needs of Children of Problem Drug Users*. London: Home Office.

Barnard, M.A. (2006) *Drug Addiction and Families*. London: Jessica Kingsley Publishers.

Barnard, M.A. and McKeganey, N.P. (2004) 'The impact of parental problem drug use on children: What is the problem and what is being done to help?' *Addiction 99*, 5, 552–559.

Cabinet Office (2004) *Alcohol Harm Reduction Strategy for England*. London: Prime Minister's Strategy Unit.

Cancrini, L. (1982) *Quei temerari sulle macchine volanti*. Roma: NIS.

Cirillo, S., Berrini, R. and Cambiaso, G. (1996) *La Famiglia del Tossicodipendente*. Milano: Raffaello Cortina Editore.

Copello, A., Velleman, R. and Templeton, L. (2005) 'Family interventions in the treatment of alcohol and drug problems.' *Drug and Alcohol Review 24*, 369–385.

Department of Health (2008) *Carers at the Heart of 21st Century Families and Communities: A Caring System on Your Side, a Life of Your Own*. London: Department of Health.

Department of Health, Home Office, Department for Education and Skills, and Department for Culture, Media and Sport (2007) *Safe. Sensible. Social. The Next Steps in the National Alcohol Strategy*. London: Department of Health.

Haley, J. (1996) *Leaving Home: The Therapy of Disturbed Young People* (2nd edition). New York: Brunner/ Routledge.

HM Government (2008) *Drugs: Protecting Families and Communities. The 2008 Strategy*. London: Home Office.

Liddle, H. (2004) 'Family-based therapies for adolescent alcohol and drug use: Research contributions and future research needs.' *Addiction 99*, 76–92.

Liddle, H.A., Dakof, G.A. and Diamond, G. (1991) 'Adolescent Substance Abuse: Multidimensional Family Therapy in Action.' In E. Kaufman and P.N. Kaufman (eds) *Family Therapy of Drug and Alcohol Abuse* (pp.120–171). Boston: Alyn & Bacon.

McGoldrick, M. and Carter, E. (eds) (1980) *The Family Life Cycle: A Framework for Family Therapy*. New York: Gardner Press.

Minuchin, S. (1974) *Families and Family Therapy*. Cambridge, MA: Harvard University Press.

Minuchin S, Montalvo, B., Guerney, B.G., Rosman, B.L. and Schumer, F. (1967) *Families of the Slums*. New York: Basic Books.

NICE (2007a) *Drug Misuse: Opioid Detoxification*. NICE Clinical Guideline 52. London: National Institute for Health and Clinical Excellence, 2007.

NICE (2007b) *Drug Misuse: Psychosocial Interventions*. NICE Clinical Guideline 51. London: National Institute for Health and Clinical Excellence.

Shedler, J. and Block, J. (1990) 'Adolescent drug use and psychological health: A longitudinal inquiry.' *American Psychologist 45*, 612–630.

Stanton, D. and Todd, T.C. (1982) *The Family of Drug Abuse and Treatment*. New York: Guilford.

Szapocznik, J., Perez-Vidal, A., Brickman, A.L., *et al.* (1988) 'Engaging adolescent drug abusers and their families in treatment: A strategic structural systems approach.' *Journal of Consulting and Clinical Psychology 56*, 552–557.

Templeton, L., Zohhadi, Z., Galvani, S. and Velleman, R. (2006) *'Looking Beyond Risk': Parental Substance Misuse: Scoping Study*. Edinburgh: Scottish Executive.

Velleman, R. and Templeton, L. (2007) 'Understanding and modifying the effect of parents' substance misuse on children.' *Advances in Psychiatric Treatment 13*, 79–89.

CHAPTER 8

Drugs and Crime

Toby Seddon

Introduction

> The greatest cause of crime, as all law-abiding people know,
> is drugs. (Nick Hawkins MP, House of Commons debate, 18
> October 2004)

Like many things that are apparently obvious and understood by all,
the drugs–crime link turns out to be less straightforward than we might
imagine – a 'puzzle inside an enigma' as Simpson (2003) nicely puts it.
There is a vast international research literature here, that I cannot hope to
summarise fully in this short chapter. In any case, others have already done
a good job of reviewing this body of work – in particular Seddon (2000),
Stevens, Trace and Bewley-Taylor (2005) and Bennett and Holloway
(2005), although there are innumerable other reviews. My more modest
goal in this chapter will be to set out some of the key findings and ideas
and to signpost where to go for more detail. Along the way, I will also
alert readers to some critical conceptual and theoretical issues that are
easily missed when we are navigating our way through the dense thickets
of the research evidence in this area. I am presenting, in other words, a
small-scale map of the overall terrain, rather than a detailed description of
every twist and turn on the ground.

A brief historical detour

Let me begin with an assertion: there is nothing inevitable, natural or timeless about the drugs–crime link. What do I mean by this? Simply that historically this link has not always been evident. A typical heroin user in Britain in the 1930s, for example, was most likely to be a middle-class professional with no involvement in crime at all. As recently as the early 1970s, Home Office research found that a clear majority of opiate users had no criminal history, and even amongst the minority with convictions many of these related to drug possession offences only (Mott 1975). In Britain, the close connection between drugs and crime that seems so obvious today only really emerged in the early 1980s. In other places, the history is a little different. In North America, for example, the link seems to have developed several decades earlier. The classic book *The Road to H* by Isidor Chein and colleagues described the clustering together of heroin use, crime and poverty in 1950s New York City (Chein *et al.* 1964). But even there, a few decades earlier, no such connections or patterns would have been apparent.

So what does this tell us? I think that two critical points follow from this. First, one of the most fundamental matters we should be addressing is how to explain this historicity. In other words, why do strong drugs–crime connections emerge at particular times and in particular places (and not at others)? Regrettably, this is a research agenda that has been largely ignored (for a couple of exceptions, see Pearson and Patel 1998; Seddon 2006). Most research and policy in this field proceeds as if the link is indeed universal and timeless. Second, in assuming that there are 'truths' to be found about the nature of the drugs–crime link which transcend time and place, a particular style of research has come to dominate. This takes the individual as the unit of analysis and follows what I would term a quasi-epidemiological approach. A good example of this tendency is the proliferation of large-scale arrestee surveys in Britain and elsewhere. It seems to me that reliance on such studies to advance understanding of the drugs–crime link is fundamentally misconceived. A nice comparison that illustrates this point is with the post-war epidemiological research on smoking and lung cancer conducted by Richard Doll and colleagues. Here, the creation and utilisation of large data-sets drawn from multiple studies in different settings was entirely appropriate, as the connection with cancer was based on some intrinsic properties of cigarette smoking. In contrast, the historicity of the drugs–crime link demonstrates that it is a connection of a fundamentally different kind. Put simply, there is nothing intrinsic to drug-taking that links it with crime.

Definitional issues

I have perhaps already got ahead of myself. I have been talking about the 'drugs–crime link' and 'drug–crime connections' as if these are uncontested terms. In fact, this is very far from the case. But rather than directly going over this well-trodden ground – and interested readers are referred to Hammersley (2008, Chapters 2–4) for a thorough tour of these issues – I will instead make three important points that go to the heart of the matter of definitions.

First, in describing drug–crime connections, *specificity* is essential. There is no blanket link between the broad categories of 'drugs' and 'crime'. Rather, what we are typically talking about are associations between particular drug-taking practices and particular forms of criminality – for example, between frequent heroin injecting and prolific shoplifting.

Second, these specific links also have to be clearly *located in time and space*. The current crime of choice for crack cocaine users in Baltimore is not necessarily the same as for their counterparts in Sydney, Berlin or Cape Town. As well as varying by place, these connections also change over time. In England, for example, local heroin outbreaks in the 1980s were associated with rapid rises in domestic burglary and theft from vehicles (see Parker and Newcombe 1987). Today, this is much less the case – the most common crime committed by heroin users is shoplifting.

Third, different drug–crime connections can be seen at *different levels of the global drug economy*. Let me take the example of heroin. I have already mentioned the connection that can be seen today in Britain between heavy heroin use and shoplifting. But this is a link at the consumer end of the market only. If we go back up the chain to opium cultivation in Afghanistan, which is currently the source of almost all of Britain's heroin, we see a rather different heroin–crime link. Here, the connections are with organised crime groups, warlords, terrorism and money laundering (UNODC 2009). Similarly, the trafficking of opiates from Afghanistan to Western Europe through the 'Balkan Route' has had a major impact on organised crime structures and levels of corruption of officials in those transit countries (UNODC 2008).

So, in terms of definitional matters, it is clearly essential to be more rigorous and precise in defining exactly what we are talking about when we use concepts like the 'drugs–crime link'. An extremely wide range of phenomena are potentially describable by the term, from shoplifting heroin users in Sheffield to warlords controlling heroin labs in Afghanistan.

Case study: Heroin, crack and crime in Britain today

I want to focus down now on a particular sector in my map of drug–crime connections that is of current policy and research significance. The links between use of heroin and/or crack cocaine and involvement in income-generating property crime, such as theft, have become a major focus in contemporary British drug policy. But what do we know about the nature and extent of these links?

In the most basic terms, the evidence for a strong association between the two is clear. If we take samples of offenders, we find very elevated levels of heroin and crack use. For example, research on arrestees in England and Wales has found rates of recent heroin use that are around ten times higher than in the general adult population (Boreham *et al.* 2006; Holloway, Bennett and Lower 2004). Similarly, if we look at samples of heroin and crack users, levels of involvement in property crime are also high (Harocopos *et al.* 2003; Jones *et al.* 2007). Further, there is evidence that heavier and more frequent use of heroin or crack is associated with higher rates of property offending (Best *et al.* 2001; Hammersley *et al.* 1989). Drilling down a little further, we find that these links are most marked within the 25–34 age group (Boreham *et al.* 2006) and that the most common offence type is shoplifting, followed by handling stolen goods and then drug selling (Jones *et al.* 2007). So the association or correlation is certainly well established.

At this point, we come to what is undoubtedly one of the thorniest but most important questions in this field: how can we explain these drug-crime connections? But unravelling the causal relationships has proved to be exceptionally difficult. For full reviews of this area, see Seddon (2000) and Bennett and Holloway (2005). There are basically three hypotheses:

1. *Drugs cause crime.* Dependent heroin and crack users, with little or no legitimate income, are driven to commit property crime to generate money to buy drugs – 'stealing to fund their habit'. This is sometimes called the 'economic necessity' model.

2. *Crime leads to drug use.* Drugs like heroin and crack are commodities that circulate in local criminal economies. Their consumption is part of patterns of leisure funded by success in crime.

3.   *Drugs and crime are both linked to common factors/processes.* Heroin and crack use and involvement in property crime are not directly related but rather both are connected to a common causal factor. A variety of common causes have been suggested from low self-control to poverty.

For all three hypotheses there is both supporting and counter evidence and, frustratingly for many, we are perhaps no nearer to resolving the matter than we were 25 years ago when researchers like Geoffrey Pearson and Howard Parker conducted their pioneering studies of young heroin users in northern England. So what are we to make of this lack of progress? Are the causal connections simply ungraspable? Or do we need to rethink how we are approaching the question? A clue to the answer lies, I think, in the earlier discussion of historicity. Rather than focusing on these three hypotheses, the most important research agenda in my view is to conduct detailed studies of local patterns of drug–crime connections with the aim of explaining how and why they have emerged and unfolded in particular ways and in that specific time and place. Only in this way can we properly get to grips with the causal processes. An outstanding example of this type of approach is the study by Pearson and Patel (1998) of heroin use amongst young Pakistanis in Bradford in West Yorkshire. Although not directly concerned with crime, its rich and sophisticated account of how heroin, poverty and ethnicity came to be closely intertwined in this particular corner of 1990s England offers a rare level of insight. I think it is through research of this kind that the causal conundrums about the drugs–crime link will begin to be solved, rather than the type of large-scale surveys of arrestees that have dominated British research endeavours over the last ten years to only modest explanatory effect.

Conclusions

When we look up and down the levels of the world drug economy, from production through to consumption, it is tempting to conclude that the connections between drugs and crime are ultimately rooted in a global drug prohibition regime which uses the criminal law to regulate commodities like heroin and cocaine. This view is certainly one of the centrepieces of the arguments of drug law reformers (e.g. TDPF 2009). And undoubtedly such claims have some force – prohibition very significantly shapes the context in which these connections have emerged and unfolded. But this argument is hard to sustain. We might note, for example, that there is a voluminous literature on the links between alcohol and crime; and that cigarette smuggling by organised crime groups is a major problem in many regions of the world. But even more telling is a historical perspective – in Britain, for instance, heroin was first prohibited in 1920, yet the close heroin–crime link that I described above only emerged 60 years later in the early 1980s. We are left again with a puzzle.

I think part of the solution to this puzzle is to be found in an idea that has become ubiquitous in the social sciences in recent years: *globalisation*. As I have argued elsewhere, the global drug economy has been transformed by the acceleration of globalising forces in the post-war period and especially since the 1970s, as capital, commodities and people flow around the world with increasing rapidity (Seddon 2006, 2008). Paradoxically, rather than effacing the importance and meaning of the 'local', globalisation has had a profound impact on localities, shaping new patterns of inequalities and deprivation. And it is precisely these localised concentrations of poverty that have provided fertile soil for the growth of strong drug–crime connections (Seddon 2006). The study of young Pakistanis by Pearson and Patel (1998) that I have already referred to is so insightful partly because it attempts to engage with the particular global–local dynamic in Bradford in the 1990s, as they explored 'what might be the implications for the Bradford drug scene of the fact that Pakistan is situated in a geopolitical region that constitutes one of the world's major areas of opium production' (p.213). Such questions lie at the heart of the 'puzzle inside an enigma' (Simpson 2003) that is the relationship between drugs and crime in the early 21st century.

References

Bennett, T. and Holloway, K. (2005) *Understanding Drugs, Alcohol and Crime*. Maidenhead: Open University Press.

Best, D., Sidwell, C., Gossop, M., Harris, J. and Strang, J. (2001) 'Crime and expenditure amongst polydrug users seeking treatment: The connection between prescribed methadone and crack use, and criminal involvement.' *British Journal of Criminology 41*, 119–126.

Boreham, R., Fuller, E., Hills, A. and Pudney, S. (2006) *The Arrestee Survey Annual Report: Oct 2003–Sept 2004*. Home Office Statistical Bulletin 04/06. London: Home Office.

Chein, I., Ferard, D., Lee, R. and Rosenfeld, F. (1964) *The Road to H: Narcotics, Delinquency and Social Policy*. London: Tavistock.

Hammersley, R. (2008) *Drugs and Crime: Theories and Practices*. Cambridge: Polity Press.

Hammersley, R., Forsyth, A., Morrison, V. and Davies, J. (1989) 'The relationship between crime and opioid use.' *British Journal of Addiction 84*, 1029–1044.

Harocopos, A., Dennis, D., Turnbull, P., Parsons, J., Hough, M. (2003) *On the Rocks: A Follow-up Study of Crack Users in London*. London: Criminal Policy Research Unit, South Bank University.

Holloway, K., Bennett, T. and Lower, C. (2004) *Trends in Drug Use and Offending: The Results of the NEW-ADAM Programme 1999–2002.* Research Findings 219. London: Home Office.

Jones, A., Weston, S., Moody, A., Millar, T., Dollin, L., Anderson, T. and Donmall, M. (2007) *The Drug Treatment Outcomes Research Study (DTORS): Baseline Report.* Research Report 3. London: Home Office.

Mott, J. (1975) 'The criminal histories of male non-medical opiate users in the United Kingdom.' *Bulletin on Narcotics 4,* 41–48.

Parker, H. and Newcombe, R. (1987) 'Heroin use and acquisitive crime in an English community.' *British Journal of Sociology 38,* 3, 331–350.

Pearson, G. and Patel, K. (1998) 'Drugs, deprivation and ethnicity: Outreach among Asian drug users in a northern English city.' *Journal of Drug Issues 28,* 1, 199–224.

Seddon, T. (2000) 'Explaining the drug–crime link: Theoretical, policy and research issues.' *Journal of Social Policy 29,* 1, 95–107.

Seddon, T. (2006) 'Drugs, crime and social exclusion: Social context and social theory in British drugs-crime research.' *British Journal of Criminology 46,* 680–703.

Seddon, T. (2008) 'Drugs, the informal economy and globalisation.' *International Journal of Social Economics 35,* 10, 717–728.

Simpson, M. (2003) 'The relationship between drug use and crime: A puzzle inside an enigma.' *International Journal of Drug Policy 14,* 307–319.

Stevens, A., Trace, M. and Bewley-Taylor, D. (2005) *Reducing Drug Related Crime: An Overview of the Global Evidence.* Beckley Foundation Drug Policy Programme Report Five.

Transform Drug Policy Foundation (TDPF) (2009) *A Comparison of the Cost-Effectiveness of the Prohibition and Regulation of Drugs.* Bristol: Transform.

United Nations Office on Drugs and Crime (UNODC) (2008) *Crime and Its Impact on the Balkans.* Vienna: UNODC.

United Nations Office on Drugs and Crime (UNODC) (2009) *Annual Report 2009.* Vienna: UNODC.

PART IV

Prevention

CHAPTER 9

Redefining Drug Prevention

Harry Sumnall and Lisa Jones

What is prevention?

Traditionally, drug prevention has been seen as those interventions which are designed to prevent the onset, delay the initiation, promote cessation, and reduce the harms associated with substance use, including illegal drugs, alcohol and tobacco. Desired messages and outcomes of substance education and intervention for young people have largely centred on promoting abstention from and cessation of substance use. Indeed, in a public consultation, the Chief Medical Officer of England has recommended that children aged under 15 years should not consume alcohol (CMO 2009). The prevention framework classifies interventions into three categories:

- *Universal* – targeting entire populations without any prior screening for substance abuse risk.

- *Selective* – targeting specific sub-populations whose risk of use is significantly higher than average.

- *Indicated* – targeted at individuals who are exhibiting indicators that are highly correlated with a risk of developing substance use later in their life or additionally early signs of problematic substance use (but not clinical criteria for dependence).

This classification replaces previous concepts of primary, secondary and tertiary prevention (Mrazek and Haggerty 1994). The new classification is important as it allows targeting of populations by assumptions of risk for substance use, rather than by imposing the overall objectives of a prevention programme on undifferentiated groups. This also means that coordinated prevention strategies can include a range of different interventions and activities. Of increasing interest is the notion of *environmental prevention*, whereby prevention strategies are aimed at altering the immediate cultural, social, physical and economic environments in which people make their choices about drug use.[1] Relevant approaches are diverse and include school drugs policies, tobacco bans, transport provision, and event licensing.

Whilst substance-use prevalence in under-18s has generally fallen in the UK since 2001, Class A drug use (including cocaine) has remained stable at around 5 per cent, and around 10 per cent of 11- to 15-year-olds report cannabis use in the previous year (e.g. Fuller *et al.* 2008). For example, in one Scottish survey around 5 per cent of 13-year-olds and 22 per cent of 15-year-olds reported recent use of cannabis (Currie *et al.* 2008). At the more problematic end of the substance-use spectrum around 24,000 under-18s in England presented at specialist drug-treatment services in 2007/08 (NTA 2009) (mostly for cannabis and alcohol use; comparable data is not available for Scotland). The continued use of illicit substances by young people has led to strong criticism of current prevention approaches, particularly those delivered in educational settings and through the mass media. In their review of current provision the UK Drug Policy Commission concluded:

> There is little international or UK evidence to suggest that drug education and prevention have had any significant impact on drug use. The international literature consistently indicates that most school-based prevention efforts do little to reduce initiation. Even those programmes that are delivered effectively seem to have very little impact on future drug use. (Reuter and Stevens 2007, p.10)

Similarly, referring to school-based prevention, the Advisory Council on the Misuse of Drugs (ACMD), an independent expert body that advises the government on drug-related issues in the UK, reported: 'Most schools in the UK provide drug prevention programmes. Research indicates that these probably have little impact on future drug use' (ACMD 2006, p.6).

---

1   See the European Monitoring Centre for Drugs and Drug Addiction pages on drug prevention for a full description of all these prevention approaches (www.emcdda. europa.eu/themes/prevention/environmental-strategies).

However, upon closer examination of the factors that drive substance use and the biographies of those young people who decide to use them, expectations of a drug-free lifestyle can appear simplistic, and may not adequately fulfil the priorities of key policies such as *Every Child Matters*. Substance use results from a complex interaction of biological, environmental, socio-cultural (including norms and familial/social relationships) and psychological factors (Frisher *et al.* 2007). Drug involvement is highly individualised and it is often difficult to predict who might be susceptible to use drugs or develop use disorders. However, early initiation of substance use does tend to cluster with other high-risk or problematic behaviours, such as early sexual initiation, mental illness, involvement in crime, poor educational attainment, and self-harm, and personality traits such as impulsivity and externalisation. This has led some researchers to argue that substance use is one of many varied manifestations of 'problem behaviour proneness' (see Glantz and Hartel 1999 for an interesting and accessible overview). This theory suggests that there may be a set of common underlying causes for these behaviours. Whilst the evidence is not unequivocal, it is plausible that different problematic behaviours are at least partially determined by different specific factors. For practitioners, substance use may be an easily identifiable indicator of a range of developmental and biographical problems, and this means that substance use should not be considered in isolation.

The question of whether a prevention campaign has reduced substance use or not, may not therefore be the right question to ask. It is important that both researchers and practitioners understand how interventions work, and understand that it is unlikely that there will be direct effects of an intervention on substance-use behaviour (Donaldson 2002). The essence of all good health education is to change the antecedent factors that lead to behaviour, not the behaviour itself. So, too, effective prevention does not attempt to change substance-use behaviour directly, it tries to change the way that people think about the behaviour, alter the social environment that influences the behaviour, or provide skills that reduce the risk for occurrence of the behaviour (Hansen and McNeal 1996). Outside of the influence of the individual, but usually the focus of policy, is the structure and quality of the environment in which the behaviour takes place.

Another important point to consider, although often overlooked, is that the majority of young people do not suffer adversely from their substance use (consequences of legal proscription not withstanding) (e.g. Wagner and Anthony 2007). This is not to dismiss the experiences of those young people who display more problematic patterns of use or who find that use begins to impact negatively on their life; but some authors have even argued, albeit controversially, that substance experimentation in adolescence is part of normal psychological development (Shedler and Block 1990). This suggestion is supported by national surveys, such as the British Crime Survey, that indicate low continuation rates for all types of substances (i.e. far fewer people report use in the previous month or year than in their lifetime). Whilst there are no general trends across substances, many individuals seem to discontinue use in their mid to late twenties, coinciding with dedication to career and family, or if they no longer desire the effects that drugs produce (Chen and Kandel 1998; Sumnall et al. 2005). Substance-use experimentation should therefore not be seen as an automatic predictor of future problems.

Contemporary thinking on prevention is also driven by a wider, more comprehensive understanding of risk and protective factors; which not only has implications for the evaluation of effectiveness of prevention but also for how interventions are designed and delivered. This means that rather than traditional models of reliance upon information (i.e. changing knowledge, attitudes, and behaviours) or of social influence (i.e. promoting drug resistance skills), modern prevention recognises and incorporates multiple modifiers of risk-taking behaviour (Advisory Group on Drug and Alcohol Education 2008). In practice, our definition of prevention should be expanded to include those interventions that promote health and healthy, informed choices; reduce vulnerabilities and risk behaviours; and increase inclusion and social/health equity. Reducing substance use and associated harms is of course still a priority, but interventions that achieve the aforementioned outcomes may be associated with longer-term benefits for health and social function.

The Advisory Group on Drug and Alcohol Education (2008) has made a number of recommendations:

- that practitioners focus universal education and information on sustaining the choices of the majority of young people who do not take illegal drugs

- that they increase protective interventions with young people vulnerable to drug misuse

- and, where necessary, increase access for young people in targeted groups to harm minimisation information and education.

A key part of these recommendations was the use of vulnerability matrices and the Common Assessment Framework (CAF) for the screening and identification of young people at risk. This reflects National Institute for

Health and Clinical Excellence (NICE) public health guidance (2007a), which recommends that health, social and education professionals should become familiar with appropriate mechanisms of identification, support and referral for those at risk of substance use. However, guidance is often lacking on *what* prevention activity should be done with young people once they have been identified as at risk.

Evidence and guidance on substance-use prevention
Universal approaches
Universal substance-use education is typically delivered in schools through the educational curriculum and in the community through the mass media, such as leaflets, internet and television broadcasts. Effective components of universal drug education for delivery in schools are outlined in Table 9.1.

TABLE 9.1 CHARACTERISTICS OF EFFECTIVE COMPONENTS OF UNIVERSAL
DRUG EDUCATION FOR DELIVERY IN SCHOOLS (ADAPTED FROM
DUSENBURY AND FALCO 1995)

Characteristic	Description
Are research driven	based on evidence of effectiveness
Are developmentally appropriate	information and materials designed for skills and knowledge level of young people
Have a broad skills base	help young people to address influences, make better-informed decisions etc.
Include social resistance skills	help with the acquisition of life skills (e.g. how to resist unwanted pressure)
Include normative education	showing young people that drug use is not as widespread as they might think
Use interactive teaching styles	pupil participation techniques
Include teacher training and support	to help ensure that teachers have the skills, awareness and knowledge to credibly lead lessons
Have adequate lesson coverage	sufficient classroom time to cover topics and follow-up
Are culturally sensitive	for a range of diverse groups
Include added components (e.g. family, community, media etc.)	multi-component programmes are more effective than school-based ones alone
Are rigorously evaluated	to identify evidence of what works

Despite criticism of educational approaches to prevention, schools have an important role to play as they offer an efficient means of targeting young people. Schools have also been identified as an important protective factor against substance use (Lloyd *et al.* 2000), and action to improve school ethos and support for student engagement can have positive effects on student substance use (Fletcher, Bonell and Hargreaves 2008). School-based intervention programmes have been shown to delay the onset of substance use by non-users for a short time, and temporarily reduce use by some current users (Canning *et al.* 2004; McGrath *et al.* 2006). Programmes based on promoting life skills have been shown most consistently to reduce some aspects of substance use in schools, indicating that there is a fairly good evidence base to support programmes based on the social influences model (Faggiano *et al.* 2005; Jones *et al.* 2007; Thomas and Perera 2006). However, there is conflicting evidence about the long-term effects of these programmes. Findings are also mixed with regard to the effectiveness of peer-led education (Canning *et al.* 2004; McGrath *et al.* 2006), and it has been suggested that the peer educator may benefit most from the experience. However, one peer-led intervention for smoking prevention delivered outside the classroom achieved a sustained reduction in the uptake of regular smoking in adolescents up to two years after delivery (Campbell *et al.* 2008).

In their 2007 guidance, NICE recommended that alcohol education should be embedded in the national science and PSHE education curricula (including that for alternative provision such as pupil referral units and secure units) (NICE 2007b). Lessons should aim to:

- increase knowledge of the potential damage alcohol use can cause – physically, mentally and socially (including the legal consequences)

- provide the opportunity to explore attitudes to, and perceptions of, alcohol use

- help develop decision making, assertiveness, coping and verbal/ non-verbal skills and help develop self-esteem

- and increase awareness of how the media, advertisements, role models and the views of parents, peers and society can influence alcohol consumption.

Pupils identified as drinking harmfully should be offered brief one-to-one advice, and offered a follow-up consultation and/or referral to a range of external services if appropriate. The research evidence that was reviewed to support this guidance found that programmes that combine classroom-based intervention with components promoting parental participation, and focusing on wider problem behaviours appear to have more consistent effects on alcohol use (Jones *et al.* 2007). Examples from the international literature demonstrated that moderately intensive family-based interventions can reduce risk factors for substance use in young people. For example, the US Strengthening Families Programme (which provides guidance to parents on family management skills, communication, academic support, and parent–child relationships) has been shown to delay the initiation of alcohol and cannabis use (Spoth *et al.* 2002). Researchers at Oxford Brookes University are planning to undertake a large-scale evaluation of this programme in England in the near future (Foxcroft, personal communication).

MASS-MEDIA INTERVENTIONS

Mass-media interventions use a range of methods to communicate a message. This can include local, regional or national television, radio and newspapers, the internet, and leaflets and booklets. Increasingly media campaigns are associated with social marketing techniques, which utilise imagery and phrases specifically aimed at target groups (e.g. young people) typically to increase their positive health behaviours. Both national organisations and local services in the UK routinely develop such interventions, but often with little evidence of how each campaign will specifically affect targeted outcomes. There are suggestions that the successes of social marketing campaigns are, in part, determined by the domain and substance targeted. Evidence from the US, for example, indicates that social marketing interventions have positive short-term effects on alcohol-related beliefs and attitudes, but little effect upon drinking behaviour (Haines and Spear 1996; Vicary and Karshin 2002). Some of the best known examples of mass media approaches in the UK include FRANK in England and Wales (www.talktofrank.com), and Scotland's Know the Score (www.knowthescore.info). Whilst these types of resources typically have high reach and can be judged to be successfully marketed, there is little evidence of any positive impact upon substance-use behaviours. For example, whilst 89 per cent of young people aged 11–21 recognised FRANK advertising, only 21 per cent of those pressured to use drugs would say 'no', and no data is currently available on drug use or other behavioural outcomes (Mitchell 2008). Similarly, evaluation of Scotland's Know the Score campaign on cocaine (Phillips and Kinver 2007) showed that whilst 30 per cent of 16- to 26-year-olds interviewed said that they were less likely to use cocaine after seeing the advertisements, 56 per cent reported that the campaign did not alter their intentions to use cocaine and 11 per cent reported that they were in fact more likely to use.

Part of this apparent lack of effectiveness may be due to poor evaluation. Evaluation studies of prevention in the UK tend to be based on short-term, crude and/or insensitive outcome measurements, such as stated intentions and self-reported knowledge rather than actual drug use and potential mediating and moderating factors. In the US, well-funded and implemented mass-media campaigns implemented at the state level and targeted at the general population in conjunction with tobacco control programmes have been associated with reduced smoking rates (Friend and Levy 2002). With reference to illegal substance use, however, there are indications that mass-media interventions are largely ineffective, and can sometimes be harmful (Sumnall and Bellis 2007). In the US, where prevention science is more advanced, comprehensive evaluations of the multi-million dollar National Youth Anti-Drug Media Campaign (1998–), and the Montana Meth Project (2005–) have shown that exposure to their messages, typically focusing on the negative effects of use, was associated with an increased belief that their peers used cannabis regularly (i.e. descriptive normalisation) (USGAO 2006), and increased acceptability of methamphetamine use (Erceg-Hurn 2008). In contrast, personally tailored information (which may still be classed as social marketing: Stead *et al.* 2006), or information targeted to a particular social or peer group, and delivered as a brief intervention, have positive short- to medium-term effects on drinking behaviours (Lewis and Neighbors 2006). Message framing, whereby equivalent outcome information is provided in terms of either gains or losses, has also been shown to be an effective strategy for promoting behaviour change across a wide range of health-related practices (Rothman *et al.* 2006). Gain-framed messages might highlight the benefits of engaging in a health protective behaviour or avoiding a risky behaviour, whereas loss-framed messages highlight the costs of not engaging in a health-protective behaviour or engaging in a risky behaviour. Individuals are generally more willing to pursue a risky course of action when considering losses, but tend to be more risk averse when considering gains.

NICE have, almost uniquely, published detailed guidance on mass-media-based smoking prevention (NICE 2008). Although directed towards England, it remains equally valid for Wales, Scotland and Northern Ireland. Similar guidance does not yet exist for alcohol and illegal drugs. The guidance recommends that mass-media interventions should be informed by the needs of the target audience (i.e. social marketing), but must also be combined with other prevention activities as part of a comprehensive tobacco-control strategy. Such strategies might encompass price and regulation policies, education programmes, smoking cessation support services and community (cessation) programmes. Importantly, mass-media campaigns should not be developed in conjunction with the tobacco industry (even through 'independent' funding), in order to limit ethical paradoxes and increase the acceptability of the intervention by young people. The evidence also suggests that the messages conveyed should elicit a strong, negative emotional reaction (in contrast to research on illegal drugs) while providing sources of further information and support; should portray tobacco as a deadly product; should use personal testimonials that children and young people can relate to; should be presented by celebrities to whom children and young people can relate; should empower children and young people to refuse offers of cigarettes; and should include graphic images portraying smoking's detrimental effect on health as well as appearance. These messages should be repeated in a number of ways and be regularly updated to keep the audience's attention.

Targeted prevention activities (i.e. selective and indicated prevention)

Research has indicated that certain populations are at greater risk of initiating drug use, more likely to experience adverse consequences, and less likely to access services than the general population (Edmonds *et al.* 2005; EMCDDA 2008). Groups at increased risk include young people who are offenders, those who are sexually exploited, looked after children, school excludees, black and minority ethnic youth, and those who have behavioural, mental health or social problems, or are in families with existing substance-use problems. Unlike in the US, prevention activity with young people in the UK who are deemed to be vulnerable or at heightened risk of using substances is usually delivered on a needs-led basis rather than according to a programmed approach. In addition to responding to individual needs, practice should be built upon a foundation of robust behaviour change and support models. Both NICE (www.nice.org.uk) and the National Treatment Agency (www.nta.nhs.uk) have issued guidance on drug prevention and specialist drug treatment for young people, and this is complemented by documents specifically supporting work with young offenders issued by the Youth Justice Board (www.yjb.gov.uk). Nevertheless, in an age of evidence-based practice, there is still little UK research that has investigated effective responses for the most vulnerable young people.

A wide-ranging systematic review of the effectiveness of community-based interventions for vulnerable and disadvantaged young people found that, despite a variety of approaches producing improvements in substance-use knowledge and attitudes, regardless of the type of population targeted, few interventions resulted in a reduction of substance-use behaviours in the longer term (Jones *et al.* 2006). Successful approaches with vulnerable populations tend to address a wide variety of risk factors and problem behaviours rather than having an exclusive substance-use focus. However, even for these types of approaches there is not a broad evidence base. This review identified that for young people exhibiting multiple risk factors, family focused work showed the most promise.

NICE recommends that the implementation of family-based programming is central to the five evidence-based recommendations made by NICE to support intervention with vulnerable populations (NICE 2007a). Local strategic partnerships are advised to develop and implement local needs-informed strategies to reduce substance misuse among vulnerable and disadvantaged people aged under 25, as part of a local area agreement.[2] Existing screening tools, such as the Common Assessment Framework, should be used to identify those using, or who are at risk of using, substances, and appropriate referrals made. Associated care plans should take account of the child or young person's needs and include review arrangements. Practitioners working with vulnerable young people, including those in the social care, youth and criminal justice sectors are advised to offer long-term (up to two years) family-based programmes of structured support, including Motivational Interviewing and parental skills training, and offer more intensive support (e.g. family therapy) to families who need it. Children who are persistently aggressive or disruptive and assessed to be at high risk of substance misuse should be offered long-term (one to two years) group-based behavioural therapy, focusing on coping mechanisms and relaxation techniques. The sessions should help to develop recipients' study and problem-solving skills, whilst parents should be offered stress management support and advice on how to set age appropriate rules, expectations and targets for their children. Finally, all young people considered problematic substance users (but not meeting criteria for dependence) should be offered Motivational Interviewing, encouraging them to discuss use of both legal and illegal substances to discuss the physical, social, psychological, educational and

2	Full guidance available from www.nice.org.uk/guidance/index.jsp?action=download&o=31939.

legal consequences of use; and to set goals to reduce or to stop their substance use.

Conclusion

This chapter has briefly explored modern understanding of the aims, objectives and limitations of substance-use prevention. Practitioners are urged to address substance-use issues as part of work within the wider biographies of young people. As has been discussed, although it is not possible to provide the practitioner with entirely evidence-based recommendations on the content of drug prevention, sensible guidance has been issued by national organisations. Although many types of intervention require specialist training, all workers can contribute to prevention objectives. After receiving suitable training, workers should be able to identify signs of drug misuse and identify those young people most at risk of harmful consequences. Through the use of locally adapted screening tools, appropriate referrals to specialist agencies can be made. Brief interventions incorporating motivational components have shown good promise in research. Although not all workers will be qualified to deliver such specialist interventions, motivational techniques can be incorporated into day-to-day interactions with young people to persuade them to assess their own behaviours and to consider the effects they may have on health and social function. Finally, it is important not to underestimate the limitations of the use of media and information provision in drug prevention. Whilst these approaches *can* be effective in raising awareness, providing information or as a source of advocacy, they should not be seen in isolation as an instrument for behaviour change.

References

ACMD (2006) *Pathways to Problems: Hazardous Use of Tobacco, Alcohol and Other Drugs by Young People in the UK and its Implications for Policy.* London: COI.

Advisory Group on Drug and Alcohol Education (2008) *Drug Education: An Entitlement for All.* A report to Government by the Advisory Group on Drug and Alcohol Education. London: Drug Education Forum.

Campbell, R., Starkey, F., Holliday, J., Audrey, S., Bloor, M., Parry-Langdon, N., Hughes, R. and Moore, L. (2008) 'An informal school-based peer-led intervention for smoking prevention in adolescence (ASSIST): A cluster randomised trial.' *Lancet 371,* 1595–1602.

Canning, U., Millward, L., Raj, T. and Warm, D. (2004) *Drug Use Prevention among Young People: A Review of Reviews.* London: Health Development Agency.

Chen, K. and Kandel, D.B. (1998) 'Predictors and cessation of marijuana use: An event history analysis.' *Drug and Alcohol Dependence 50,* 109–121.

Chief Medical Officer (2009) *Draft Guidance on the Consumption of Alcohol by Children and Young People from the Chief Medical Officers of England, Wales and Northern Ireland.* London: Department of Health.

Currie, C., Gabhainn, S.N., Godeau, E., Roberts, C. *et al.* (2008) 'Inequalities in young people's health: International Report from the HBSC 2005/06 survey.' *WHO Policy Series: Health Policy for Adolescents 5,* WHO Regional Office for Europe.

Donaldson, S.I. (2002) 'High-potential Mediators of Drug-Abuse Prevention Program Effects.' In W.D. Crano and M. Burgoon (eds) *Mass Media and Drug Prevention: Classic and Contemporary Theories and Research.* London: Lawrence Erlbaum Associates.

Dusenbury, L. and Falco, M. (1995) 'Eleven components of effective drug abuse prevention curricula.' *Journal of School Health 65,* 420–425.

Edmonds, K., Sumnall, H.R., McVeigh, J. and Bellis, M.A. (2005) *Drug Prevention Among Vulnerable Young People.* Liverpool: Centre for Public Health.

Erceg-Hurn, D.M. (2008) 'Drugs, money, and graphic ads: a critical review of the Montana Meth Project.' *Prevention Science 9,* 256–263.

European Monitoring Centre for Drugs and Drug Addiction (2008) *Drugs and Vulnerable Groups of Young People.* Lisbon: EMCDDA.

Faggiano, F., Vigna-Taglianti, F., Versino, E., Zambon, A., Borraccino, A. and Lemma, P. (2005) 'School-based prevention for illicit drugs use.' *Cochrane Database of Systematic Reviews,* Issue 2. Art. no. CD003020.

Fletcher, A. Bonell, C. and Hargreaves, J. (2008) 'School effects on young people's drug use: A systematic review of intervention and observational studies.' *Journal of Adolescent Health 42,* 3, 209–220.

Friend, K. and Levy, D.T. (2002) 'Reductions in smoking prevalence and cigarette consumption associated with mass-media campaigns.' *Health Education Research 17,* 1, 85–98.

Frisher, M., Crome, I., Macleod, J., Bloor, R. and Hickman, M. (2007) *Predictive Factors for Illicit Drug Use among Young People: A Literature Review.* Home Office online report 05/07.

Fuller, E., Clemens, S., Jotangia, D., Lynch, S., Nicholson, S. and Pigott, S. (2008) *Drug Use, Smoking and Drinking Among Young People in England in 2007.* London: National Centre for Social Research and NHS Informations Centre.

Glantz, M.D. and Hartel, C.R. (eds) (1999) *Drug Abuse: Origins and Interventions.* Washington, DC: American Psychological Association.

Haines, M. and Spear S.F. (1996) 'Changing the perception of the norm: A strategy to decrease binge drinking among college students.' *Journal of American College Health 45,* 134–140.

Hansen, W.B. and McNeal, R.B. (1996) 'The law of maximum expected potential effect: Constraints placed on program effectiveness by mediator relationships.' *Health Education Research 11,* 501–507.

Jones, L., James, M., Jefferson, T., Lushey, C., Morleo, M., Stokes, E., Sumnall, H., Witty, K. and Bellis, M.A. (2007) *A Review of the Effectiveness and Cost Effectiveness of Interventions Delivered in Primary and Secondary Schools to Prevent and/or Reduce Alcohol Use by Young People under 18 Years Old.* London: National Institute for Health and Clinical Excellence.

Jones, L., Sumnall, H., Witty, K., Wareing, M., McVeigh, J. and Bellis, M.A. (2006) *A Review of Community-based Interventions to Reduce Substance Misuse among Vulnerable and Disadvantaged Young People.* London: National Institute for Health and Clinical Excellence.

Lewis, M.A. and Neighbors, C. (2006) 'Social norms approaches using descriptive drinking norms education: A review of the research on personalized normative feedback.' *Journal of American College Health 54,* 213–218.

Lloyd, C., Joyce, R., Hurry, J. and Ashton, M. (2000) 'The effectiveness of primary school drug education.' *Drugs: Education, Prevention and Policy 7,* 109–126.

McGrath, Y., Sumnall, H., McVeigh, J. and Bellis, M.A. (2006) *Drug Misuse Prevention among Young People: A Review of Reviews.* Evidence Briefing Update. London: National Institute for Health and Clinical Excellence.

Mitchell, M. (2008) *FRANK Campaign: Performance and Development.* Available at http://drugs.homeoffice.gov.uk/publication-search/frank/frankpresentation, accessed on 23 June 2009.

Mrazek, P.J. and Haggerty, R.J. (1994) *Reducing Risks for Mental Disorders: Frontiers for Prevention Intervention Research.* Washington, DC: National Academy Press.

National Institute for Health and Clinical Excellence (NICE) (2007a) *Community-based Interventions to Reduce Substance Misuse among Vulnerable and Disadvantaged Children and Young People.* NICE Public Health Guidance 4. London: NICE.

National Institute for Health and Clinical Excellence (NICE) (2007b) *Interventions in Schools to Prevent and Reduce Alcohol Use among Children and Young People.* NICE Public Health Guidance 7. London: NICE.

National Institute for Health and Clinical Excellence (NICE) (2008) *Mass-media and Point-of-sales Measures to Prevent the Uptake of Smoking by Children and Young People.* NICE Public Health Guidance 14. London: NICE.

National Treatment Agency (NTA) (2009) *Getting to Grips with Substance Misuse among Young People: The Data for 2007/08.* London: NTA.

Phillips, R. and Kinver, A. (2007) *Know The Score: Cocaine Wave 4 – 2006/07 Post-Campaign Evaluation.* Edinburgh: Scottish Executive.

Reuter, P. and Stevens, A. (2007) An Analysis of UK Drug Policy. A monograph prepared for the UK Drug Policy Commission. London: UKDPC. Available at www.ukdpc.org.uk/docs/UKDPC%20drug%20policy%20review.pdf, accessed on 26 June 2009.

Rothman, A.J., Bartels, R.D., Wlaschin, J. and Salovey, P. (2006) 'The strategic use of gain- and loss-framed messages to promote health behavior: How theory can inform practice.' *Journal of Communication 56*, 202–220.

Shedler, J. and Block, J. (1990) 'Adolescent drug use and psychological health: A longitudinal inquiry.' *American Psychologist 45*, 612–630.

Spoth, R.L., Redmond, C., Trudeau, L. and Shin, C. (2002) 'Longitudinal substance initiation outcomes for a universal preventive intervention combining family and school programs.' *Psychology of Addictive Behaviors 16*, 129–134.

Stead, M., McDermott, L., Gordon, R., Angus, K. and Hastings, G. (2006) *A Review of the Effectiveness of Social Marketing: Alcohol, Tobacco, and Substance Misuse Interventions.* London: National Social Marketing Centre for Excellence.

Sumnall, H.R. and Bellis, M.A. (2007) 'Can health campaigns make people ill? The iatrogenic potential of population-based cannabis prevention.' *Journal of Epidemiology and Public Health 61*, 930–931.

Sumnall, H.R., Bellis, M.A., Lodwick, A., Bucke, T. and Vicente, J. (2005) *Analysis of Drug Profiles from EMCDD: A Databank on Surveys of Drug Use* (CT.03.P1.200). Lisbon: EMCDDA.

Thomas, R.E. and Perera, R. (2006) 'School-based programmes for preventing smoking.' *Cochrane Database of Systematic Reviews*, Issue 3. Art. no. CD001293.

United States Government Accountability Office (2006) ONCDP Media Campaign. Washington, DC: United States Government Accountability Office.

Wagner, F.A. and Anthony, J.C. (2007) 'Male-female differences in the risk of progression from first use to dependence upon cannabis, cocaine, and alcohol.' *Drug and Alcohol Dependence 86*, 191–198.

Vicary, J. and Karshin, C. (2002) 'College alcohol abuse: A review of the problems, issues and prevention approaches.' *Journal of Primary Prevention 22*, 299–331.

CHAPTER 10

Children, Young People and Prevention

Richard Ives

Awareness and use of drugs

What do children and young people know about drugs?

Children's awareness of drugs is high. Even nursery children are aware of cigarettes and how they are used. In the 1980s, when tobacco advertising was still permitted, interviews with Glasgow children showed that the majority of primary-school children were well aware of cigarette advertising, and many could identify cigarette brands in 'puzzle' advertisements which did not show brand names (Aitken *et al.* 1987). A study of New Zealand 8- to 9-year-olds reported that the majority had tried alcohol, and a quarter would have at least a sip or drink in a typical month (Casswell *et al.* 1985).

A Scottish study indicated considerable awareness of, and contact with, illegal drugs among young teenagers. More than half (51.6%) the school children from one Scottish city in this study (average age 13.3 years), had themselves been offered drugs, and rather more (57.8%) had been in situations where drugs were taken. A similar proportion (57.4%) had friends whom they reported as having personal experience of drugs. The study concluded that drugs are ubiquitous in young people's lives, whether or not they are themselves personally involved in their use (Barnard 1996).

How many children and young people have tried illegal drugs?

Information from annual school surveys conducted by the Department of Health (Annual Survey of Drinking, Drugs and Drug Use) show that, among children and young people aged 11 to 15 years, 17 per cent had used an illegal drug in the previous 12 months (Department of Health 2008). From the British Crime Survey, the figure for 16- to 24-year-olds is 24 per cent.

Drug use increases with age: among 11-year-olds, 3 per cent reported taking drugs in the last month compared with 17 per cent of 15-year-olds. The most common illegal drug tried is cannabis, but 4 per cent of 11- to 15-year-olds reported using a 'Class A' drug (this class includes heroin, cocaine, ecstasy and LSD) (National Statistics 2007). (Other research on the subject is quoted by Sumnall and Jones in Chapter 9.)

A survey of children aged 10 to 12 years in Glasgow and Newcastle found that around a third had been exposed to illegal drugs; fewer, less than 4 per cent, had used illegal drugs, but pre-teen drug use was significantly associated with frequent smoking and alcohol consumption. It was also associated with a range of problem behaviours, and with family difficulties (McKeganey et al. 2004). Evidence from national data confirms this association: for example, the National Statistics Report states that 'pupils who said they had truanted or been excluded were more likely to have taken drugs in the last month compared to those who had not truanted or been excluded' (National Statistics 2007).

Levels of drug use and drinking are higher in the UK than in most other European countries, and the 'drinking culture' follows the 'Northern European' pattern of binge drinking in heavy drinking sessions. There is considerable concern about the effects of early heavy drinking on the long-term health of young people.

Some young people smoke cigarettes and girls' smoking levels now exceed those of boys. However, levels of young people's smoking have decreased:

> There has been a long-term decline in the proportion of pupils who have tried smoking, from 53% in 1982 to 33% in 2007. In 2007, 6% of pupils said they smoked regularly (at least once a week). This is down from 9% in 2006, and at the lowest level ever measured by this survey. Girls (8%) are more likely than boys (5%) to be regular smokers. The proportion of regular

smokers increases with age, from 1% of 11-year-olds to 15% of 15-year-olds. (Health and Social Care Information Centre 2008)

It is sensible and realistic for parents to be concerned about substance misuse. But they sometimes think that *their* child will not take drugs. A 2008 survey for the *Observer* newspaper found that, although 27 per cent of those adults questioned had taken an illegal drug, only 13 per cent of those with children aged 12–35 thought their offspring had 'certainly' done so (Campbell and Hinsliff 2008).

Action on prevention

There is a widespread feeling that 'something must be done' to 'protect' children and young people from drugs. Some argue for complete liberalisation of the drugs laws, although far more people want tighter enforcement of the existing laws. But most people recognise that completely controlling the supply of drugs is impossible. And most people understand that young people are growing up in a 'drug-using society' and therefore the 'protection' given to them should include some knowledge about drugs, as well as skills for dealing with drug-related situations. Some parents are concerned about their children receiving early education about drugs, arguing that children's 'innocence' needs to be preserved. But while the government's guidelines on drug education recommend tackling the topic right from primary school, no educator believes that teaching about drugs in the early years should address illegal drugs directly – rather, it focuses on care for oneself and refusal skills (DfES 2004).

The government is the main funder of drug-prevention activities and campaigns, but many other agencies are involved. Drug prevention takes place in schools, but it also takes place in the community and in the home. Drug prevention is conducted through the mass media, through paper publications and the internet.

Involving parents

'Universal' prevention is targeted at everyone, and generally aims to stop people trying drugs, or at least to delay the onset of drug use. Most universal prevention focuses on children and young people; but it may also involve parents.

An example of UK substance misuse prevention was the campaign against volatile substance abuse (VSA – the misuse of glues, gases or aerosols) in the 1990s – a form of substance misuse at that time associated with younger teenagers. The campaign included TV advertisements aimed at parents, and a parents' booklet sent to households. While parents welcomed the booklet, few used it as the basis for discussion with their children, perhaps because they didn't know how to approach the subject and were afraid to raise it. There is insufficient evidence to say for certain whether this and other elements of VSA prevention campaigns in the UK were part of the reason for the dramatic fall in VSA-related deaths from a peak of 152 in 1990 to 48 in 2006 (Field-Smith *et al.* 2008). However, this reduction can be seen as a significant achievement of prevention activities involving government, and the voluntary and private sectors working in partnership.

The UK government's FRANK campaign has tried to address parents' fears in amusing advertisements, one showing a mother being arrested for trying to discuss drugs with her teenage son. The accompanying slogan, 'Drugs are illegal, talking about them isn't', was designed to reassure parents and encourage them to have conversations with their children.

Involving parents was also a theme of the largest-ever drug education trial in the UK, the Blueprint programme. This multi-dimensional school-based programme tested some of the best evidence-based approaches in a package designed to fit the realities of English schools, concluding (in relation to the parental involvement element):

> Recruiting parents of secondary school children to participate in drug education is challenging. Parents are hard to engage, particularly in areas of disadvantage. Recruiting parents to drug prevention activities may be a much longer-term process than expected... Parents appear not to like being asked to participate in groups and have a reluctance to take part in activities... In drug awareness sessions it would be helpful to include ways for parents to address the impact that their own purchase and consumption of drugs (including alcohol and tobacco) may have on their children. (Home Office 2007, p.3)

Any teacher will agree that the parents one most wants to involve, and about whose children there is more concern, are those least easy to engage.

Methods of drug prevention

Early attempts to prevent drug use by children and young people used shock tactics in the hope that fear would deter young people. This approach has been discredited by research, although not, unfortunately in the minds of many politicians and members of the public (Ashton 1999). Fear of drugs may well deter some young people from trying them, but these young people were probably never likely to try them in the first place. A risk of highlighting the dangers of drugs is of making them more attractive to those children and young people who are 'thrill-seekers' and like the idea of taking risks – those who were anyway more vulnerable to the attractions of drug use.

Also found to be ineffective was a 'rational' approach of 'tell them the facts and they will reach the right decisions' (the 'right decision' being not to take drugs). Unfortunately, some young people found the facts very intriguing, and their interest was stimulated; others who might have been deterred found it difficult to decline an actual offer of drugs. From this failure came Nancy Reagan's famous 'Just Say No' campaign, and the UK campaign including a storyline in *Grange Hill* (a children's TV series) with a cringe-making spin-off pop song.[1] But how were young people to say 'no' without the skills to do so? Skills development was therefore promoted, and this approach shows promise. But to be effective, it must go beyond skills to say 'no' – not least because drugs are 'pulled not pushed' – young people will typically seek out drugs (or at least hang around with people who might have access to them), rather than being offered them 'out of the blue'.

More recently, two main approaches have been used in UK schools (ACMD 2006):

- The *social influence approach* – This seeks to achieve 'psychological inoculation' and aims to encourage anti-drug use attitudes, counteract beliefs that using illegal drugs is normal, and develop the ability to resist offers of drugs.

- The *social competence* or *life skills approach* – This seeks to develop a broader range of personal and social skills in addition to tactics to refuse offers of drugs.

Using the mass media

Drug prevention work frequently involves the mass media to inform people about drugs, to alter their attitudes towards drugs (e.g. to discourage young people from trying drugs), and to help people to act on drugs issues (e.g. helping parents to have conversations with their children about drugs). It

---

1   The Grange Hill 'Just Say No' song can be found at http://uk.youtube.com/ watch?v=jCLsOjv_Efk.

may also incorporate broader messages, such as the benefits of a healthy lifestyle. Information about the availability of services (such as where to get help and advice) can also be provided.

Media campaigns can communicate simple messages that can be followed up with more complex messages in different contexts. However, many campaigns are ineffective and may be counterproductive (e.g. inappropriately raising awareness of drugs, or increasing parents' fears about their children using drugs). Caution is therefore required: campaigns must be well thought through, carefully targeted, and assessed to measure impact (including any unexpected or unwanted impact).

Different messages can (and should) be aimed at particular groups. Many 'official' channels of communication are seen as suspect by some young people – often those very young people (perhaps the more 'disaffected') who, being more likely to use drugs, are those that campaigns aim to reach ('targeted prevention').

The UK government launched the FRANK brand in 2003 as a 'credible, non-judgmental and reliable source of information about drugs and their effects'. FRANK would be: 'an anonymous friend – whether to a user, potential user, concerned friend or worried parent. FRANK was designed to…be synonymous with reliable drugs information and messages' (Home Office 2006, p.2).

The various campaigns under the FRANK brand have targeted different groups. Creative use has been made of the internet, which FRANK uses to address different messages to different audiences (www.talktofrank.com). But political control has meant compromise; and the reclassification of cannabis (returning to Class B in 2009 after a period as a Class C drug) has led to less credible messages about this drug – such as the poorly received 'Brain Warehouse' advertisements, which attempted to link cannabis smoking to significant brain impairment. More recently, the 'Pablo the Drugs Mule' advertisement aimed to raise awareness of the international criminal nature of the supply chains, as well as pointing out the health risks.

The FRANK website has materials for older teenagers, for adult drug users, and for parents, but it does not have suitable material for children and younger teenagers. And while it has several leaflets available for download, none of these are suitable for younger children – this is a surprising state of affairs.

However, regarding the effectiveness of the FRANK campaign and other mass media approaches, as Sumnall and Jones say in Chapter 9, 'there is little evidence of any positive impact upon substance-use behaviours'.

The challenges

Towards the end of the 20th century, much was learnt from the mistakes of drug prevention activities. The lessons include:

- Scaring doesn't work.
- Information alone is not enough.
- Drug-related skills are needed.
- Attitudes to drugs must be explored and developed.
- Parents should be involved in drug prevention.
- Interventions must be appropriately targeted.

It was also learnt that drug prevention needs to respond to what children and young people think about drugs and to the drug-related situations to which they are exposed. These change as they grow up, and as the world changes.

A more rational approach, combining a theoretical understanding of why young people might try – and continue to use – drugs, together with extensive evaluation, has developed confidence in certain preferred approaches – in particular, lifeskills and social influence approaches. The Cochrane Systematic Review of school-based drug education (Faggiano et al. 2005) has led to a large European study (EUDAP – European Drug Addiction Prevention Trial – www.eudap.net) of the school-based programme 'Unplugged', showing promising results.

Drug prevention faces challenges in the 21st century. There remain doubts about the effectiveness of prevention, and in particular the cost-effectiveness of universal prevention when compared to more targeted approaches. Prevention is a long-term investment and the benefits do not accrue directly to the services providing them (for example, schools do drug education, but the potential benefits of reduced drug use in adult life don't affect them much).

While tobacco use is declining, this dangerous substance is still used by far too many young people and may be, for some, a 'gateway' to the use of illegal drugs. Excessive alcohol use by young people is of great public concern, but government responses to it have been mixed. As the Children's Commissioner for England points out:

> By condemning anti-social behaviour in youths from drunkenness and yet extending the licensing hours, and allowing alcohol to be cheaper now than at any time in recent history, we are exposing children and young people to mixed messages

with respect to alcohol promotion. Why are the present laws against sale of alcohol to underage children not more rigorously enforced? (Aynsley-Green 2007, p.36)

Drug prevention is a complex challenge that must involve partnership between government and other stakeholders. A wide range of professionals must be engaged. Targeted prevention activities must reach vulnerable groups without stigmatising them. Prevention should aim to reduce the risk factors for drug misuse and promote those attributes that help to keep young people safe ('protective factors').

As the DfES has pointed out, addressing drugs issues in school should take place within the context of a whole-school approach that is 'supported by consistent messages from family and community' (DfES 2004, paragraph 2.4). It is therefore crucial – however difficult – to engage parents. The views of young people must be carefully considered and they must be engaged in the process through active participation, not only in schools, but also in community and youth-work-based initiatives.

Young people tend not to see 'drugs' as an issue to be addressed separately from other parts of their lives. They prefer holistic responses to the challenges and problems that they face. 'Things to do and places to go' (DfES 2006) are often their priority. Following their lead, drug prevention in the 21st century should cease to be an isolated activity, and become embedded in education and prevention that promotes healthy lifestyles and embraces the challenges of growing up in a complex civilisation.

References

Advisory Council on the Misuse of Drugs (2006) *Pathways to Problems: Hazardous Use of Tobacco, Alcohol and Other Drugs by Young People in the UK and Its Implications for Policy.* London: ACMD.

Aitken, P.P., Leathar, D.S., O'Hagan, F.J. and Squair, S.I. (1987) 'Children's awareness of cigarette advertisements and brand imagery.' *Addiction 82*, 6, 615–622.

Ashton, M. (1999) 'The dangers of warnings.' *Drug and Alcohol Findings 1*, 22–24.

Aynsley-Green, A. (2007) *Reflections on Children, Child Health and Society.* London: Nuffield Trust.

Barnard, M. (1996) 'Levels of drug use among a sample of Scottish schoolchildren.' *Drugs: Education, Prevention and Policy 3*, 1, 81–89.

Campbell, D. and Hinsliff, G. (2008) 'Public favours harder line on drugs.' *The Observer*, 16 November. Available at www.guardian.co.uk/society/2008/nov/16/drugs-policy, accessed 23 June 2009.

Casswell, S., Brasch, R., Gilmore, L. and Silva, P. (1985) 'Children's attitudes to alcohol and awareness of alcohol-related problems.' *Addiction 80*, 2, 191–194.

Department for Education and Skills (2004) *Drugs: Guidance for Schools.* London: DfES.

Department for Education and Skills (2006) *Youth Matters: Next Steps: Something to Do, Somewhere to Go, Someone to Talk to.* London: DfES.

Department of Health (2008) *Drug Use, Smoking and Drinking among Young People in England in 2007.* London: Department of Health.

Faggiano, F., Vigna-Taglianti, F., Versino, E., Zambon, A., Borraccino, A. and Lemma, P. (2005) 'School-based prevention for illicit drugs use.' *Cochrane Database of Systematic Reviews*, Issue 2. Art. no. CD003020.

Field-Smith, M.E., Butland, B.K., Ramsey, J.D. and Anderson, H.R. (2008) *Trends in Death Associated with Abuse of Volatile Substances 1971–2006*. St George's, University of London.

Health and Social Care Information Centre (2008) *Drug Use, Smoking and Drinking among Young People in England in 2007*. London: NHS Information Centre.

Home Office (2006) *Frank Review 2004–2006*. London: Home Office.

Home Office (2007) *Blueprint Drug Education Research Programme: Summary of Delivery Report and Practitioner Report Research Findings*. London: Home Office.

McKeganey, N., McIntosh, J., MacDonald, F., Gannon, M., Gilvarry, E., McArdle, P. and McCarthy, S. (2004) 'Preteen children and illegal drugs.' *Drugs: Education, Prevention and Policy 11*, 4, 315–327.

National Statistics (2007) *Statistics on Drug Misuse: England*. Available at www.statistics.gov.uk/hub/index.html, accessed 18 September 2009.

CHAPTER 11

The Impact of Social Exclusion and Poverty on Education and Prevention

Diverse communities – diverse needs: Delivering information on drugs and drug services to members of Black and minority ethnic communities

Jane Fountain

Background

The Department of Health's Black and minority ethnic drug misuse needs assessment project was conducted throughout England between 2001 and 2006. It employed the Centre for Ethnicity and Health's Community Engagement Model (Fountain, Patel and Buffin 2007) to train and support 179 community organisations to carry out the needs assessments among their own communities. A variety of strategies to recruit samples and of quantitative and qualitative data collection methods were utilised by the community organisations.

This article presents the results relating to drug information needs from 154 community organisations' reports, representing a total sample of 19,229 study participants (Table 11.1).

TABLE 11.1 STUDIES AND PARTICIPANTS IN THE DEPARTMENT OF HEALTH'S
BLACK AND MINORITY ETHNIC DRUG MISUSE NEEDS ASSESSMENT PROJECT
2001–2006

Ethnic group	Studies conducted by community organisations	Community members	Professionals working with the communities
South Asian (Bangladeshis, Pakistanis, Indians, Sri Lankans)	65	10,485 (including 0.4% of mixed South Asian and white heritage)	265
Black African	42	4657 (including 1% of mixed Black African and white heritage)	120
Black Caribbean	34	1863 (including 13% of mixed Black Caribbean and white heritage)	98
Kurdish, Turkish Cypriot and Turkish	9	1395 (including 0.3% of mixed Turkish and white heritage)	16
Chinese	3	202	15
Vietnamese	1	113	0
Totals	154	18,715	514

The project reported here was not intended to be a prevalence survey, but the results indicate that, overall, the illicit drugs used and the relative popularity of each is the same among the sample as among the population of England as a whole. However, it does not follow that Black and minority ethnic people can simply slot into existing drug information, advice and treatment services. Responses may have to be different in order that the barriers to drug service access that they face can be overcome.

One of these barriers is a lack of knowledge about drugs and drug services. This impedes access to drug services for all community members, including families who are trying to deal with the drug use of a member, and non-problematic drug users who would benefit from information about the substances they use and advice on harm-reduction strategies. The lack of knowledge also hinders access to treatment for problematic drug users, and means that, even if treatment is accessed, there is an unrealistic expectation of what can be achieved and the process by which it is achieved.

Delivering the message
Information about drugs

There was a strong correlation between age, gender and knowledge of drugs, with young men knowing more than other community members, but even this group's knowledge, including that of drug users, was limited. For example, several studies of the Black Caribbean communities probed their participants' knowledge of drugs in some depth and concluded that it is not as comprehensive as it might first appear:

> A key learning point…is the danger of assuming that young people have detailed knowledge of a drug's effects simply because they are able to state the name.

The provision of comprehensive information about the illicit drugs and their effects was recommended by all the study reports, although the reasons for wanting to acquire this knowledge differed. Many of the South Asians, Black Africans and Kurdish, Turkish Cypriot and Turkish people saw the primary aims of drug education as encouraging these communities to acknowledge drug use within them and to increase their confidence to discuss and address this. Thereby, they argued, the stigma and taboo surrounding drugs would begin to be lifted and those who needed help (for themselves or others) would be more likely to seek it.

The Black African sample were divided over the messages that should be transmitted to their communities about illicit drugs and about khat, which was reported to be used by some Somalis, Ethiopians and Eritreans in England, but which, at the time of writing, is not illegal in the UK. A majority thought that the sole message should be abstinence, because *'if our children are taking to drugs…then that will be the doom of the society'*. Few wanted it to include harm-reduction messages for drug users.

A harm-reduction approach to drug education was advocated by the majority of the Black Caribbean study participants, to allow them (especially young people) to make informed choices about their drug use. It was argued that if Black Caribbeans' knowledge of drugs was greater, their capacity for increasing family and community support for drug users would increase.

The study reports from Chinese and Vietnamese community organisations stressed the lack of knowledge these communities had about drugs and drug services. Many Chinese parents added that they wanted information about drugs so that they would be able to detect if their children were using them.

Information about drug services

The main reasons given for the need for drug information, advice and treatment services were because when a drug user and/or their family decide to seek help, they do not know where to obtain it nor what it entails. The South Asian, Black African, Black Caribbean and Chinese study reports particularly emphasised the need for explicit information about what drug services can achieve and how they achieve it.

The reports also stressed that information on drug services should include clear statements about confidentiality. Among South Asians, for instance, the link between the stigma of drug use, the importance of maintaining the respect of the family within the community and a lack of trust in the confidentiality of drug services was a recurrent theme throughout the study reports and cannot be over-emphasised as a barrier to drug service access.

Language

The first language of the Black Caribbean sample was English. Among the other study participants, English was reported to be unproblematic for most of the younger generations, but some members of the older generations were reported to find speaking and reading English problematic.

For example, the Black African sample originated from 30 different African countries and a third had been in the UK for less than five years. Between them, they had 40 first languages and, in some cases, those from the same African country did not all speak the same language. Although a majority spoke English, not all of them were fluent, especially older people, and fewer could read the language(s) they spoke.

A common recommendation from the study reports was therefore that information about drugs and drug services should be produced in written, visual and oral versions, in the languages and dialects of the local Black and minority ethnic communities.

Media

A very wide variety of media was recommended to transmit information on drugs and drug services. The majority of study reports stressed that, whatever the media, drug education for young people should be enjoyable.

In order to attract the target groups, attention to cultural appropriateness was emphasised, including language and that members of the target Black and minority ethnic community should feature in the media used.

The two most common recommendations were for oral and visual media in the relevant languages and dialects, as they do not require reading skills, and for media that can be used in private, because of the stigma attached to drug use. These included videos, DVDs, CDs, the relevant local and Black and minority ethnic community radio and television channels, and telephone helplines (including faith-based helplines). Suggested written media included community and local newspapers; community and religious newsletters; billboards and posters; leaflets; and the internet.

Many study reports recommended incorporating drug-related information into their communities' music, drama and sporting events. The South Asian and Black African reports also recommended that the existing method of verbal communication through the family, friends and community networks should be utilised to transmit information. Most of the Chinese and the Kurdish, Turkish Cypriot and Turkish study reports recommended workshops and seminars as the best way to transmit information about drugs and drug services to their communities.

Educators

'Expert' peers and outreach workers were most commonly recommended to educate Black and minority ethnic communities about drugs and drug services. Religious leaders, mentors and role models were also suggested.

There were different opinions regarding who could be defined as an 'expert'. Many – especially young people – thought that drug users and ex-users were the 'real' experts. Many others cited 'professionals' – drug workers, GPs, community organisation workers, community leaders, teachers, school counsellors and development workers. It was recognised, though, that many of these would need training before they could play an effective role in drug education.

Drug education delivered by peers was a popular recommendation, especially for young people, parents and women. The rationale was that peers would understand the culture of those they were educating and, in the case of young people, would be seen as a more credible source of information than adults.

A common recommendation was that members of the target communities were employed as highly proactive drug outreach workers to deliver drug education 'on the streets' especially in settings where drugs are used and young people congregate.

A majority of the study reports that were concerned with the Muslim and Christian communities wanted religious leaders to play a role in educating their congregations about drugs and drug services. However, many study participants thought that religious leaders, although respected, were too remote from the day-to-day lives of their community due to their total commitment to the observation of religious beliefs, and that they would not understand the issues surrounding drug use. Nevertheless, it was generally agreed that if religious leaders became involved in drug education, the stigma and taboo surrounding drug use would be lessened.

Many among the Black Caribbean sample did not envisage drug education for young people as a one-off event, but as an ongoing process involving mentors and positive role models. The value of youth workers and of the older generations of Black Caribbeans (after training) as educators and as mentors was stressed.

Some of the South Asian studies recommended that ex-drug users act as 'buddies' or mentors to drug users, particularly those who become estranged from their friends and family because of their drug use. They also thought that celebrities should be used to attract the attention of young people to issues surrounding drugs and drug services.

Recipients

Overall, the study reports provided a great deal of evidence to support their recommendation that every member of their communities should be targeted by drug education initiatives, so that families and a community can support each other and drug users within them.

All the studies reported that children and young people were in particular need of information about drugs and drug services because this generation is most likely to come into contact with drugs. Drug education for parents and carers was also a popular recommendation, so that they can talk confidently to their children about drugs and deal with the consequences of drug use. Many study participants (especially those from the South Asian, Black African and Chinese communities) wanted drug education to be delivered to parents and their children *'sitting together'* in order to promote *'a lively exchange of ideas'*. This, they stressed, would improve inter-generational communication on this issue while maintaining the traditional method of family involvement in solving problems.

Many of the study reports also recommended that initiatives should target drug users and those vulnerable to drug use. The latter group included, for example, newly arrived Black African asylum seekers (especially unaccompanied minors in care) and young Black Caribbeans who are (or are at risk of being) excluded from school or unemployed.

Many of the South Asian and the Kurdish, Turkish Cypriot and Turkish study participants thought that the women in their communities should be targeted, as they are the ones who have to deal with drug use in a family. It was thought that those women who lead *'sheltered lives'*, especially older Muslim women, were in particular need.

The South Asian study reports stressed that religious leaders and community elders needed drug education, so that they could advise community members and mobilise their support for drug education for their community. Most of the Black Caribbean reports recommended drug education for all workers from agencies that came into contact with members of the Black Caribbean communities (such as GPs, teachers, police and probation officers, youth workers, community workers, housing officers and community centre workers). It was argued that this would enable these workers to support drug users and those trying to deal with the drug use of friends and/or family members.

Delivery sites

The most popular recommendations on drug education delivery sites were that they should be community-based, familiar venues, especially community centres and schools. It was particularly stressed by the Chinese and by the Kurdish, Turkish Cypriot and Turkish samples that their community centres were well visited by the local population. However, the South Asian, Black African, Kurdish, Turkish Cypriot and Turkish study reports recognised that because of the stigma of drug use, many community members would not attend a public discussion of the issue. Suggestions for alternatives included, from many of the South Asian study reports, drop-in facilities that advertised themselves as giving advice on a variety of issues, so that those visiting them would not be identified as seeking information on drug-related issues. For young people, drug education delivered in schools (including religious and Saturday/supplementary schools) was a very popular recommendation, along with youth clubs and sports and leisure centres.

Other recommended locations comprised every place that community members might ever pass by, visit or congregate in, in addition to community centres and schools; these included the street, Black and minority ethnic shops and restaurants, libraries, places of worship, GP surgeries and health centres, community festivals, cinemas, pubs and nightclubs. For those women (particularly Muslims) for whom it is culturally unacceptable to mix with men, women-only venues or their homes were thought most appropriate. The studies dealing with khat use in some of the Black African communities recommended that information should be given to men in the mafrishes ('khat cafés'), where men meet and chew khat.

Conclusion

Information about drugs and drug services for all age groups was identified as the major need by all the study reports. Of course, this need is not exclusive to members of Black and minority ethnic communities, but the project's results illustrate well how different responses may be required for different ethnic groups.

Although all the study reports stressed that the Black and minority ethnic communities they studied need information on drugs and drug services, there was less agreement between them on what this information should consist of, the media used to deliver it, who should deliver it, to whom it should be delivered and where it should be delivered. This is indicative of the diversity within and between the Black and minority ethnic communities the project targeted. In the South Asian communities, for instance, there are differences between genders, generations (especially between those who were born in the UK and those who were not), religions and languages (scores of official, regional and tribal languages and dialects are used across South Asia), as well as between those of Bangladeshi, Indian, Pakistani and Sri Lankan heritage. Therefore, initiatives need to be devised on a local basis, so that the heterogeneity of what have been described here as 'South Asian communities' is addressed: 'what works' for any one of these – or for any other Black and minority ethnic community – may be inappropriate for another.

Acknowledgements

Thanks are due to the Department of Health for funding the project from which the data presented in this article were obtained. Thanks are also due to all the community organisations who participated in the project and worked so hard to collect the data. The opinions expressed, however, are those of the author.

Further reading

This article can only summarise the findings from the community organisations' reports. Further details can be found in the following series of publications:

Fountain, J. (2009) *Issues surrounding drug use and drug services among the South Asian communities in England.* National Treatment Agency for Substance Misuse. Available at http://www.nta.nhs.uk/publications/documents/1_south_asian_final.pdf, accessed 18 September 2009.

Fountain, J. (2009) *Issues surrounding drug use and drug services among the Black African communities in England.* National Treatment Agency for Substance Misuse. Available at http://www.nta.nhs.uk/publications/documents/2_black_african_final.pdf, accessed 18 September 2009.

Fountain, J. (2009) *Issues surrounding drug use and drug services among the Black Caribbean communities in England.* National Treatment Agency for Substance Misuse. Available at http://www.nta.nhs.uk/publications/documents/3_black_caribbean_final.pdf, accessed 18 September 2009.

Fountain, J. (2009) *Issues surrounding drug use and drug services among the Kurdish, Turkish Cypriot and Turkish communities in England.* National Treatment Agency for Substance Misuse. Available at http://www.nta.nhs.uk/publications/documents/4_kurdish_turkish_cypriot_turkish_final.pdf, accessed 18 September 2009.

Fountain, J. (2009) *Issues surrounding drug use and drug services among the Chinese and Vietnamese communities in England.* National Treatment Agency for Substance Misuse. Available at http://www.nta.nhs.uk/publications/documents/5_chinese_vietnamese_final.pdf, accessed 18 September 2009.

Wider prevention: Poverty and social exclusion

James Egan

Introduction

Law enforcement or health approaches have historically, within many countries, dominated policy and practice responses towards harmful patterns of drug and alcohol use. Often this has led to a relative neglect of important socio-economic factors, such as poverty and inequality, and their negative impact on levels of harmful substance use. Overlooking these socio-economic factors has resulted in a tendency towards practice that locates the problem and potential solutions within the individual.

The relationship between the individual, wider social and health factors such as poverty, and harmful patterns of substance use is complex and cannot be reduced to a simple cause and effect – not everyone experiencing poverty will develop a substance-use problem, and equally not all problems with substances are shaped by poverty or indeed personal trauma. However, Buchanan (2004) has argued that a significant group of people with serious drug problems do face a disproportionate range of socio-economic disadvantages and inequalities: these are often associated with disrupted childhood, personal trauma, relationship breakdown, under-achievement and unemployment.

This article will attempt to look beyond enforcement or health approaches by examining the wider themes of poverty and inequality and their link to harmful patterns of substance use. There will be a focus on UK welfare policies that attempt to address poverty and unemployment among people with substance-use problems with reference to the current difficult economic climate. It will conclude by exploring how practitioners could strengthen their response by acknowledging and developing an active role in addressing the poverty, inequalities and discrimination that often prevents social integration for people with substance-use problems.

Poverty and substance use – The bigger picture

The UK has poverty levels almost double that of the Netherlands and one-and-half times that of both France and Germany (The Poverty Site 2009). Of the 27 European Union countries, only five have a higher proportion living in relative poverty. The latest UK poverty figures show that 13 million people, or one in five of the population, live in relative poverty, which is a significant increase from 7.8 million in 1982 (Palmer, MacInnes and Kenway 2008).[1] Within these new UK figures, unemployed adults without children are receiving welfare benefits that are 20 per cent below their value a decade ago. Consequently, a 25-year-old man on a weekly jobseeker payment of about £60 has to get by on just over half the threshold poverty figure of £112. This benefit payment is much less than the amount people think is required to offer a socially acceptable standard of living in Britain today, according to the first ever minimum income standards study (Bradshaw et al. 2008), which suggested that a single working-age adult needs a budget of £158 per week.

---

1   Relative poverty exists when household income is 60% or less of the average (median) income for that year. Using 2006/07 data, the weekly figure was £112 for an adult with no children; £193 for a couple with no children; £189 for a single adult with two children under 14; and £270 for a couple with two children under 14. The poverty threshold is measured after income tax, council tax and housing costs are deducted. It is the amount left to spend on everything else, such as food, heating and travel.

Despite the gap between the rich and poor in the UK reaching high levels last seen in the late 1960s (Dorling, Rigby *et al.* 2007), public attitudes towards poverty have hardened. A British attitudinal survey reveals that one in four attribute poverty to laziness or a lack of willpower, with over half of those surveyed thinking that benefit payments are too high and discourage people from finding work (Taylor-Gooby and Martin 2008). Yet those moving from benefits into work face the increasing likelihood of in-work poverty. The number of working adults experiencing poverty in the UK has increased since 2002 to such an extent that it 'exceeds, probably for the first time, "out-of-work" adult poverty' (Palmer *et al.* 2008, p.12).

With the latest poverty figures preceding the onset of the new recession, an economic update suggests that the UK will face the deepest recession of any large industrialised economy (International Monetary Fund 2009). This recession is being shaped by rising home repossessions, increasing unemployment levels and will create further hardship for many existing vulnerable groups, including people with substance-use problems.

The UK also has the highest prevalence of problem drug use within the European Union – three times that of Germany and the Netherlands (European Monitoring Centre for Drugs and Drug Addiction 2009). With a population of 16.6 million, the Netherlands has approximately 30,000 dependent heroin users (Reuter and Pollack 2006). In sharp contrast, Scotland, with less than a third of the Dutch population, has a significantly larger drug problem of about 52,000 users (Hay *et al.* 2005).

Caution is required when comparing the size of nations' drug or alcohol problems. EU countries use different methods to estimate the number of people with a drug problem. However, it is unlikely that differences in data collection methods can fully explain why UK drug prevalence is so severe compared to its European neighbours. It has been argued that although UK drug policy had a positive impact in reducing harm at an individual and community level (e.g. HIV infection among drug injectors), it has had very limited impact on the overall size of dependent drug use (Reuter and Stevens 2007). With nearly a sixty-fold increase in the number of dependent heroin users in England, from about 5000 in 1975 to a recent estimate of 281,000, Reuter and Stevens (2007) suggest that this has been influenced by factors such as socio-economic conditions. Their view echoes a previous UK study examining the influence of social class on alcohol-related deaths over a seven-year period. With young men involved in unskilled labour up to 20 times more likely to die than the professional classes, Harrison and Gardiner (1999) conclude that reducing poverty and inequality has the potential to reduce current levels of alcohol-related harm among the poorest members of society.

The association between deprivation and income inequality with drug-related deaths is also seen at an international level. Using mortality data from 1999 to 2002, Wilkinson and Pickett (2007) found significant correlation between drug-related deaths and state income inequality within the US. In England and Wales, between 1993 and 2006, drug-related deaths were five times higher in the most deprived areas compared with the least deprived (Brock *et al.* 2008). Other studies in Italy and Australia have also found an association between lower socio-economic status and higher drug death rates (Michelozzi *et al.* 1999; Najman 2008).

There is a growing body of international evidence demonstrating the negative health impact on populations with high levels of income inequality (Babones 2008; Dorling, Mitchell and Pearce 2007; Wilkinson 2005; Wilkinson and Pickett 2006; Wilkinson and Pickett 2007). With more equitable societies tending to be healthier, research suggests that inequitable societies often promote strategies that create more self-interest, poor family and community relations, high levels of antisocial behaviour, violence and poor health (Wilkinson 2005). Therefore, the extent to which increasing income inequalities and the developing economic recession will impact on the future size and shape of substance-related harms are important areas that require further policy maker attention. Shapiro (2009) has suggested that we may not see a repeat of the heroin epidemic that was shaped by the severe recession in the early 1980s. Instead, for those young people 'gearing up to be the next generation of "problem drug users", cheap alcohol and cheap cocaine, maybe along with cannabis, ecstasy like-drugs and tranquillisers are likely to provide the toxic mix that services will need to address' (Shapiro 2009, p.1).

Is welfare-to-work a route out of poverty and substance-use problems?

Within most highly industrialised regions, such as the US, Europe and Australia, moving people from welfare into work, using a mixture of support and sanctions, has become a key policy response to reducing poverty. With the UK experiencing a steady rise in overall levels of employment throughout the 1990s, a set of welfare-to-work reforms were developed towards 'making work pay'. These reforms involved significant investment in New Deal programmes, a shift from benefits towards in-work tax credits and an emphasis on work-focused personal responsibility.

Powell (2000) has pointed out that a declared aim of the UK government approach was to prevent poverty by ensuring that people have the appropriate education, training and employment support. Often called employability, this support was extended beyond New Deal programmes to reach out to disadvantaged groups furthest from the labour market, including people with substance-use problems. Programmes such as Progress 2 Work and the New Futures Fund (NFF) in Scotland were developed. Despite NFF achieving some degree of success, the funding from Scottish Enterprise, an economic investment agency, has been withdrawn.

Despite significant investment in mainstream New Deal programmes, high levels of unemployment among people with substance-use problems still persist. According to a recent Department of Work and Pensions (DWP) study, eight out of ten people with drug problems in England were unemployed and receiving some type of welfare benefit (Hay and Bauld 2008).[2] With comparable unemployment levels existing among people seeking drug treatment in Scotland (Information Services Division 2008), the DWP study found that just over a quarter of a million people with drug problems in England were on benefits with the majority receiving Income Support or Incapacity Benefit (Hay and Bauld 2008). With these two benefits paid to people unable to work because of carer duties, such as being a lone parent, or ill-health, the DWP study also revealed that only one in four drug users were receiving Jobseeker's Allowance (there are no comparable benefits data on people with alcohol problems).

More welfare-to-work reforms are currently being rolled out to address unemployment among drug users. These ambitious reforms, which include streamlining the benefits system and removing one million people from Incapacity Benefit by 2015, contain proposals to pilot drug and employment support programmes (Department for Work and Pensions 2008). Against the backdrop of a developing recession, rising unemployment and high levels of in-work poverty, there are plans to extend these pilots programmes to include people with alcohol problems. These approaches will involve Jobcentre Plus in creating working links with drug-treatment services and criminal justice agencies, including prisons; and offering drug users a treatment allowance. This new allowance will be given to those entering the pilot programmes and is an additional welfare payment with conditions attached – drug users would have to engage with a rehabilitation plan or face possible sanctions, including having their

2   Figures for 2006 show that an estimated 332,090 individuals were using opiates (such as heroin) and/or crack cocaine with 80 per cent (267,000) accessing the main Department of Work and Pension benefits.

benefit payments stopped. These penalties are part of a wide range of welfare sanctions being introduced.

The effectiveness of applying welfare sanctions among people with multiple disadvantages has been questioned. Evidence cited in a report from the Office of the Deputy Prime Minister found that sanctions could increase social exclusion and participation in the informal economy, push some into criminality and move already marginalised groups further from the reach of employment organisations (Social Exclusion Unit 2004). The report noted the potentially harmful impact on well-being:

> Emotionally, sanctioned jobseekers generally felt 'fed up' and 'stressed' about losing their benefits. Some jobseekers felt that the impact on their mental health had been quite serious; claiming Income Support because of depression, or relying on prescription drugs to cope. (Social Exclusion Unit 2004, p.76)

Despite people with drug problems being a relatively small part of the welfare bill – about 6 per cent of adult benefits – these new sanctions are part of a wider strategy that includes a media campaign targeting benefit cheats and the use of lie detectors to identify fraudulent welfare claims. These punitive approaches are occurring during a period when UK benefit fraud is at an all-time low, significantly dropping from £2 billion to £0.8 billion (National Audit Office 2008). In sharp contrast, an estimated £25 billion is lost through tax avoidance each year in the UK (Murphy 2008). Although not illegal, tax avoidance reduces the level of public funds available to address major social problems such as current high levels of poverty and harmful substance use, particularly during a period of economic recession.

Arguably, this picture of widespread poverty, severe drug problems and inadequate benefit payments, juxtaposed with an increasingly punitive welfare culture and soaring levels of tax avoidance, reinforces Wilkinson's (2005) view that countries with major inequalities often promote strategies that increase self-interest, high levels of antisocial behaviour, poor community relations and worse health.

Implications for practice

Addressing the wider socio-economic aspects of 'addictions' presents a range of challenges. With the bigger picture often considered too difficult to understand, implementing costly socio-economic changes can be of uncertain value and often fits poorly with political demands for immediate results (Spooner and Hetherington 2005). Notwithstanding these wider challenges, from the 1990s onwards three different approaches have influenced ways of working with substance users – harm reduction, Motivational Interviewing and the Cycle of Change.

Harm-reduction approaches were promoted as a means of reducing the threat posed by HIV in the 1980s (Advisory Council on the Misuse of Drugs 1988). Grounded within a public-health framework, this approach involves identifying harms and responding in a pragmatic way to reduce the risk of these harms occurring – for example, offering drug users sterile needle and syringes to reduce HIV infection risks or prescribing methadone to lessen the risk of involvement in acquisitive crime to buy drugs.

Motivational Interviewing (MI) is a psychological model which tries to avoid pressuring people to become drug or alcohol free. Instead MI encourages client empathy and works with the tensions between a person's current situation and how they would like their lives to be (Miller and Rollnick 2002). It also embraces client resistance as a natural part of the process and encourages personal autonomy, even when clients choose not to change.

Complementing these two approaches, the Cycle of Change model recognises that people struggling with dependent behaviours may be in one of six stages of change (Prochaska, DiClemente and Norcross 1992):

1. Not seeing a problem – *pre-contemplation*

2. Being in two minds about doing anything – *contemplation*

3. Taking steps to change – *preparation*

4. Making the change – *action*

5. Integrating it – *maintenance*

6. Return to old behaviours possibly occurring – *relapse.*

These three approaches have an important role to play in addressing psychological and physical aspects of substance-use problems, but may overlook socio-economic factors. With a recent policy shift towards the concept of recovery, social factors are increasingly being recognised as important aspects of treatment and rehabilitation (Scottish Government 2008). This is an important recognition as many people with substance-use problems have had such limited options in life and lack resources, that social *integration* not re-integration and *habilitation* not rehabilitation is often required: 'It seems that many have never really been able to get started in life in the first place. This makes living without drugs a very tough option indeed' (Buchanan 2004, p.393).

The struggle for social integration or reintegration is often a main cause of relapse, according to Buchanan (2004). Yet when vital support to establish alternative patterns of social and economic life, such as housing or managing daily activities, is needed, it is often inaccessible by virtue of exclusion that is shaped by stigma (Buchanan 2004). Endorsing this view, a World Health Organization study, which involved ranking 18 different conditions, found that 'alcoholism' and 'drug addiction' ranked near the top in terms of social disapproval or stigma in 12 out of 14 countries, above being dirty and unkempt (Room 2005).

Although most traditional drug services are operating within a context of severe social exclusion, there is a pressing need for more service focus on social integration or reintegration to prevent future relapse (Buchanan 2004). Vital social support, which may involve mentoring or buddying schemes, could create new habits and routines to help people find accommodation and undertake daily activities – like picking up children from school, shopping, cooking and managing personal finance. Additionally, although some may benefit from the welfare-to-work reforms, in an increasingly competitive labour market employment may not be a realistic immediate goal. A study involving a large sample of young, working-age drug users in treatment found that the overwhelming majority had such serious social and health problems, that most were a long way from being ready for education or training (Kemp and Neale 2005). The study suggested that preliminary activities – such as developing literacy and numeracy skills, voluntary work or sheltered employment – were a more realistic goal.

Conclusion

Substance-use policy and practice span a complex and often intractable set of problems, issues and solutions. Rather than being characterised as a narrow set of health or crime concerns, they must also be seen as social care, housing, education, employment, child and family welfare concerns. If we are to reduce the high levels of harmful drug and alcohol use, then we need to act upon co-existing high levels of poverty and widening inequalities that persist. Acknowledging the importance of these links will help define more realistic boundaries for health, criminal justice and social care responses. Moreover, it would enable practice to move beyond focusing on individual motivation and psychological strategies towards a more assertive role in addressing the economic disadvantage, social discrimination, isolation and powerlessness often faced by people with substance-use problems.

References

Advisory Council on the Misuse of Drugs (1988) *AIDS and Drug Misuse, Part 1*. London: HMSO.

Babones, S.J. (2008) 'Income inequality and population health: Correlation and causality.' *Social Science and Medicine 66*, 1614–1626.

Bradshaw, J., Middleton, S., Davis, A., Oldfield, N., Smith, N., Cusworth, L. and Williams, J. (2008) *A Minimum Income Standard for Britain – What People Think*. York: Joseph Rowntree Foundation.

Brock, A., Griffiths, C., Morgan, O. and Romeri, E. (2008) Geographical variations in deaths related to drug misuse in England and Wales 1993–2006. *Health Statistics Quarterly 39*, 14–21. Available at www.statistics.gov.uk/articles/hsq/HSQ39Geographicdrugmisuse.pdf, accessed on 26 June 2009.

Buchanan, J. (2004) 'Missing links: Problem drug use and social exclusion.' *Probation Journal* (Special Edition on Problem Drug Use) *51*, 4, 387–397.

Department for Work and Pensions (2008) *Raising Expectations and Increasing Support: Reforming Welfare for the Future*. London: The Stationery Office.

Dorling, D., Mitchell, R. and Pearce, J. (2007) 'The global impact of income inequality on health by age: An observational study.' *BMJ 335*, 873–875.

Dorling, D., Rigby, J., Wheeler, B., Ballas, D., Thomas, B., Fahmy, E., Gordon, D. and Lupton, R. (2007) *Poverty, Wealth and Place in Britain, 1968 to 2005*. York: Joseph Rowntree Foundation.

European Monitoring Centre for Drugs and Drug Addiction (2007) *Table PDU-1. Prevalence of Problem Drug Use at National Level: Summary Table, 2001–2005*. Available at www.emcdda.europa.eu/stats07/pdutab01a, accessed on 26 June 2009.

Fountain, J., Patel, K. and Buffin, J. (2007) 'Community Engagement: The Centre for Ethnicity and Health model.' In D. Domenig, J. Fountain, E. Schatz and G. Bröring (eds) *Overcoming Barriers: Migration, Marginalisation and Access to Health and Social Services* (pp.50–63). Amsterdam: Foundation Regenboog AMOC.

Harrison, L. and Gardiner, E. (1999). Do the rich really die young? Alcohol-related mortality and social class in Great Britain, 1988–94. *Addiction 94*, 1871–1880.

Hay, G. and Bauld, L. (2008) *Population Estimates of Problematic Drug Users in England Who Access DWP Benefits: A Feasibility Study*. Department for Work and Pensions Working Paper No. 46. Available at www.dwp.gov.uk/asd/asd5/WP46.pdf, accessed on 26 June 2009.

Hay, G., Gannon, M., McKeganey, N.P., Hutchinson, S. and Goldberg, D. (2005) *Estimating the National and Local Prevalence of Problem Drug Misuse in Scotland*. Edinburgh: Scottish Executive.

Information Services Division (2008) *Drug Misuse Statistics Scotland 2008*. Edinburgh: Common Services Agency.

International Monetary Fund (2009) *World Economic Outlook – Update*. January 28. Available at www.imf.org/external/pubs/ft/weo/2009/update/01/pdf/0109.pdf, accessed on 29 June 2009.

Kemp, P.A. and Neale, J. (2005) 'Employability and problem drug users.' *Critical Social Policy 25*, 1, 28–46.

Michelozzi, P., Perucci, C.A., Forastiere, F., Fusco, D., Ancona, C. and Dell'Orco, V. (1999) 'Inequality in health: Socioeconomic differentials in mortality in Rome, 1990–95.' *Journal of Epidemiology and Community Health 53*, 687–693.

Miller, W.R. and Rollnick, S. (2002) *Motivational Interviewing: Preparing People for Change* (2nd edition). New York: Guilford Press.

Murphy, R. (2008) *The Missing Billions – The UK Tax Gap*. TUC Publication. Available at www.tuc.org. uk/touchstone/Missingbillions/1missingbillions.pdf, accessed on 26 June 2009.

Najman, J.M. (2008) 'Increasing socio-economic inequalities in drug-induced deaths in Australia: 1981–2002.' *Drug and Alcohol Review 27*, 6, 613–618.

National Audit Office (2008) *Department for Work and Pensions: Progress in Tackling Benefit Fraud*. Available at www.nao.org.uk/publications/0708/progress_in_tackling_benefit_f.aspx, accessed on 26 June 2009.

Palmer, G., MacInnes, T. and Kenway, P. (2008) *Monitoring Poverty and Social Exclusion 2008*. York: Joseph Rowntree Foundation.

Powell, M. (2000) 'New Labour and the third way in the British welfare state: A new and distinctive approach?' *Critical Social Policy 20*, 1, 39–60.

Prochaska, J.O., DiClemente, C.C. and Norcross, J. (1992) 'In search of how people change.' *American Psychologist 47*, 1102–1114.

Reuter, P. and Pollack, H. (2006) 'How much can treatment reduce national drug problems?' *Addiction 101*, 3, 341–347.

Reuter, P. and Stevens, A. (2007) *An Analysis of UK Drug Policy*. A Monograph Prepared for the UK Drug Policy Commission. London: UKDPC. Available at www.ukdpc.org.uk/docs/UKDPC%20 drug%20policy%20review.pdf, accessed on 26 June 2009.

Room, R. (2005) 'Stigma, social inequality and alcohol and drug use.' *Drug and Alcohol Review 24*, 2, 143–155.

Scottish Government (2008) *The Road to Recovery: A New approach to Tackling Scotland's Drug Problem*. Edinburgh: Scottish Government.

Shapiro, H. (2009) 'Boom or bust on the drug market?' *Druglink 24*, 1, January/February, p.1.

Social Exclusion Unit (2004) *Jobs and Enterprise in Deprived Areas*. London: Office of the Deputy Prime Minister.

Spooner, C. and Hetherington, K. (2005) *Social Determinants of Drug Use*. National Drug and Alcohol Research Centre, Technical Report 228. Available at http://ndarc.med.unsw.edu.au/ndarcweb. nsf/website/Publications.reports.TR228, accessed on 26 June 2009.

Taylor-Gooby, P. and Martin, R. (2008) 'Trends in Sympathy for the Poor.' In A. Park, J. Curtice, K. Thomson, M. Phillips, M.C. Johnson and E. Clery (eds) *British Social Attitudes: The 24th Report*. London: SAGE.

The Poverty Site (2009) *European Union – Low Income by Age and Gender*. Available at www.poverty.org. uk/0a/index.shtml, accessed on 26 June 2009.

Wilkinson, R.G. (2005) *The Impact of Inequality: How to Make Sick Societies Healthier*. London: Routledge.

Wilkinson, R.G. and Pickett, K.E. (2006) 'Income inequality and population health: A review and explanation of the evidence.' *Social Science and Medicine 62*, 7, 1768–1784.

Wilkinson, R.G. and Pickett, K.E. (2007) 'The problems of relative deprivation: Why some societies do better than others.' *Social Science and Medicine 65*, 9, 1965–1978.

PART V

Integrated Services and Workforce Development

CHAPTER 12

Integrated Services
The Glasgow Experience

Neil Hunter

Introduction

Glasgow is Scotland's biggest city with a population of just over 650,000 people in the metropolitan city area. An article in *Community Care Works* profiling the work of drug and alcohol services in the city, said that 'if anywhere needs integrated alcohol and drug services it is Glasgow' (Stewart 2007). The reasoning behind this is clear. Glasgow is a city which has been built on steel, iron, ship building and heavy industry. The city faced significant economic decline in the 1970s and early 1980s and was affected more than most areas by the impact of the Thatcher era. Glasgow cleared its inner-city slums in the 1950s and 1960s and built housing estates the size of large towns on its periphery. The city has its disproportionate share of economic and social problems: unemployment, poor health and, in particular, addiction to alcohol and drugs, remain stubbornly higher than the Scottish and UK national average (Hanlon, Walsh and Whyte 2006). The particular problems faced by Glasgow in relation to drug misuse are well known and well covered, although not always accurately. The city has been undergoing a renaissance since the early 1990s when it reigned as the European City of Culture, rebuilding on its financial sector, tourism and world-renowned culture. Nonetheless, Glasgow faces significant problems, and drug misuse is one of the most serious. The most recent estimate of the number of serious problematic drug users, mainly heroin and benzodiazepine users, is at some 11,500 (Hay *et al.* 2004). This equates to 1 in 30 of the city's economically available adults, and in some of the most deprived parts of the city rises to 1 in 20. In some areas of Glasgow therefore, 1 in 20 adults you will meet walking down the street will have a serious addiction problem, usually to heroin. This is a huge economic and social burden for a city of Glasgow's size – and adding to that the estimated 35,000 people who have serious alcohol problems in Glasgow, it can be seen that the burden of addiction is one the most significant facing the health and social services in the city.

In response to the increased use of heroin in the 1980s, Glasgow began to develop small-scale community services for drug misusers. There were already some community-led alcohol services, which had been developed over many years. Throughout the late 1980s and early 1990s the health service also began to initiate its own responses in the form of two distinct clinically led directorates – one psychiatric directorate and another led by GP-trained medics. Throughout the 1990s, Glasgow did invest in services for alcohol and drug problems – some services developed for alcohol users, some for drug users and some for individuals with a range of addiction problems. The network of provision in the city was characterised by lack of any clear specifications for services, relatively poor communication and joint work, and by inter-professional rivalry, with significant parts of the city remaining uncovered by any appropriate services. Whilst immensely good work was going on in all of these services, it did not meet the needs and demands of the city as it faced up to economic and social crises of the late 1980s and early 90s. At the same time we saw a massive expansion in the use of heroin across Glasgow, as elsewhere in the UK.

It was clear that our health and social services, both of which had been trying on their own to tackle addiction problems in the city, required radical revision. In short, our health and welfare systems had been trying separately to tackle a growing problem for a decade and a half when in fact what was required was more joined-up responses, service planning and pooling of resources between the two statutory bodies. In 2001, the NHS and city council stopped trying to tackle alcohol and drug problems separately across their health and welfare systems and began to construct a single partnership for the delivery of health and care services that could meet the city's need and aspirations.

Why integrate services?

Integration of health and social care services, especially community care services, has been a priority for the government in Scotland since the advent of devolution (Stewart, Petch and Curtice 2003). Integrated team working has many features but principal amongst them are physical co-location of services, establishment of joint team leaders and single administrative processes, a single team culture and ethos (Glendinning 2002; Hudson 2006b). There is a slowly emerging body of evidence of what might be achieved by integrated team working, particularly with complex populations, of the improvement of service delivery and of service-user experience. Moves towards integrated working and the formation of partnerships to support these have also been subject of legislation in both Scotland and England, where NHS bodies have increasingly been asked to demonstrate partnership arrangements leading towards integrated front-line services (Evans and Forbes 2009).

In his evaluation of integrated nursing, social work and housing services in northern England, Hudson (2006a) suggests that there was real appetite amongst professionals to adopt more integrated forms of working and co-location within single teams. He remarks that such integration seemed to be both 'inevitable and desirable', with the 'holy grail' of integration being an 'acceptance of collective responsibility for a problem (between professionals in integrated teams) as opposed to the pursuit of narrow professional concerns'. Successful approaches to integration require knowledge sharing, respect for each other's autonomy, surrender of professional territory and a shared set of values. Petch (2006) also highlights the importance of respect for traditions, and acceptance of different levels of evidence from which professional foundations can be derived within integrated teams. The need to develop an understanding of the respective traditions in the physical or social sciences is a critical ingredient to supporting full integration of teams (Barnes, Green and Hopton 2007)

Integrated teams therefore go beyond multi-disciplinary working or simply co-location; but are aimed at providing structural change, support and drive towards better, more effective front-line clinical and practice delivery. They can take some time to show concrete results (Rosen and Ham 2008).

The challenge for Glasgow therefore was to work to develop a model and framework for combined professional effort to make our services more effective, accessible, flexible and accountable for delivery of care and treatment to a highly complex, vulnerable and stigmatised part of the city's population.

Constructing integrated services

We have described the challenge faced by a city like Glasgow where 1 in 30 of economically able adults has serious heroin problems. We estimate that there are somewhere around three million injecting episodes each year in Glasgow, and a prevalence rate of hepatitis C of 80 per cent amongst our injecting population, which numbers 4400. Psychiatric and physical co-morbidities stretch our services every day, both in terms of our capacity to respond and in relation to the degree of professional expertise we require to meet the needs of those individuals with the most complex problems.

In 2001, the city council and NHS Board agreed that Glasgow required to develop a single joint partnership to manage and deliver its alcohol and drug services across its respective organisations. This followed many years of frustration voiced by local politicians in relation to lack of focus of the alcohol and drug services on recovery and rehabilitation. The fact was that there was no common specification, and standards varied markedly – some services were long-term funded whilst others relied on short-term regeneration monies.

There had been a limited history of collaborative joint work and care planning amongst the city's addiction professionals. When we eventually put together some of our early joint teams we found that in many cases over 80 per cent of individuals who formed our newly combined caseload had previous involvement from at least two of three main statutory provider organisations: The Alcohol Directorate, Glasgow Drug Problem Services and Social Work Addiction Services. There had been virtually no instances of any identifiable joint work between those three providers. Joint care plans, integrated assessments or joint reviews were not routine features of the services in the late 1990s. There was inter-professional rivalry between the three statutory organisations, which led quite often to displacement of responsibility for poor performance, with no single identifiable individual responsible for leadership in the city's services, and a high level of buck-passing for critical operational or strategic decisions. There was a lack of coherence in the overall approach being taken to tackle the worst of the city's problems in relation to alcohol and drugs. Indeed, at times the approach being taken by the agencies concerned appeared to be oppositional – particularly in their adherence to either medical or social models. A Review Team was established and looked at the provision within the city. One of the findings of this Review Team was that sometimes the most expensive and resource-intensive services, and those with the most highly trained staff, were not seeing individuals with most complex needs in the city. This had happened partly as a result of real distortions in the ways that people found themselves coming into contact with these services, quite often determined by where you lived, who your GP was (or knew), what your local service did, or did not, provide and how long you were able to wait on a service.

The health board and city council ordered that these organisations become one single partnership responsible for the delivery of services to all of the city. This required an extensive period of unpicking professional and managerial structures across the three organisations, looking at new structural models, developing visions for a future service that would support a modernised service delivery and one which could help staff grow into new roles, taking on joint responsibility for delivery and performance.

The Addictions Partnership was created in 2001, and was aimed at forming alliances, building integrated management structures, creating joint teams, co-locating professionals and revising standards and performance for all of the services previously managed separately within the statutory sector.

There were some key steps along the way. The creation of a single Head of the Partnership with joint accountabilities to both the council and health services management structures, with authority to discharge legal duties and powers for both organisations, integration of human resources and finance functions, was a critical first step. In the next 12 months more joint posts were created at every level in the partnership organisation, including those to manage local services, to plan and to develop strategy and to ensure joined up personnel approaches. Such was the criticality of the agenda for the city, both the local authority and the health board were willing to re-draw their Scheme of Delegation in order to ensure that the single partnership could discharge its functions jointly on behalf of the board, based on a common vision, for the delivery of service.

The cornerstone of our approach has been the development of locality community addiction teams. These teams are now managed by joint heads of service, with responsibility for budget, caseload and performance across the health service and local authority. They are now delivered as part of local Community Health and Care Partnerships, which are an extension of the approach to be taken in relation to alcohol and drug services in other areas of health and social care provision – such as mental health, children services and older people services (see Freeman and Moore 2008 for a more detailed description). We piloted the introduction of integrated teams over the first 12 months of the partnership's life and created two pathfinder community addiction teams. A 12-month evaluation process (Keenan 2006) told us that our staff, who had been moved into single co-located bases over a three-month period, found working in an integrated service more difficult than working in uni-agency arrangements. They found it uncomfortable and also found that some of their core beliefs, professional identify and underpinning values were being challenged through co-location and integration. Our structures were important, but were overlaid by single processes such as joint assessment, care plans, single points of access for individuals from local communities and mixed professional teams. Many staff found the challenge of working in joint service too difficult and left the service. This was to be expected, and it was something that we were able to see as a positive rather than something that questioned the legitimacy of what we were trying to achieve. However, those staff that were surveyed across the 12-month period expressed clear support for joint-service arrangements and told us clearly that, despite the challenges and difficulties, they did not want to return to the previous uni-agency arrangements. The one unifying feature of this was that both staff and service users told us that they had experienced real benefits of services coming together in a single base, with different professionals able to provide a wider range of intervention based much more thoroughly on service-user need. Most staff and service users identified some tangible benefits, which turned out to be the biggest single driver in the further development of our services, post evaluation. These benefits were:

- increased access to a better range of coordinated services
- alcohol service users experiencing the largest single increase in access, particularly via referrals from GPs
- for the vast majority of service users, no difficulties with information sharing between professionals to improve the quality of their care, although all saw consent as being critical.

We found that the professional identify of staff (whether a social care worker or a nurse, medic, psychologist or occupational therapist, etc.) was important to service users in order that they could understand what interventions might be available from different professional staff members of the inter-disciplinary team.

We also came across something we have called the 'proximity premium' in relation to integrating services. What this meant was that transactions between professionals have become much more effective and efficient. Previously when people might have taken many hours or days to make contact with each other, make referrals, arrange different types of treatment (albeit this was very limited in the city prior to integration), staff found that being in the same physical location with different professional groups allowed much more streamlined and effective access to a wider range of skills and possible interventions to meet a wider range of needs at the point of access in local areas.

Our stakeholders also told us where previously their services had been provided by centralised directorates, using local resources on an out-patient basis, services following integration were run and managed more locally and could be much more easily influenced in order to meet local needs and demands. A wider range of needs could also be met from a single point, including wound management, hepatitis vaccination, prescribing service, homelessness and accommodation services, access to rehabilitation, employability and family support. In all of the statutory services, direct access to services had not been a common feature up to the point of development of an integrated partnership. There was now a clear commitment, however, that services should be very local, should cover all geographical areas in the city and should, as a principle, be available for people to walk in and have immediate access. This was a real challenge to many staff that had previously been used to quite rigid appointment systems to manage access. There was real anxiety amongst the staff group that services would be overwhelmed by demand.

Joint teams also started to bring together the basis of delivery of our joint organisational strategies and objectives – for example, those in relation to child protection, health improvement and inequalities. Previously, child protection had been seen as being mainly in the domain of, and of concern to, local authority social-care practitioners. Developing joint services with single management, working to a common specification, meant that child protection and support for vulnerable parents became a core objective of the whole service – of both local authority and NHS staff. Similarly, health and inequalities, public health protection and mental health improvement, previously seen as being mainly within the domain of health professionals, became a core service objective for all staff within a joint working environment. Whilst individual competencies are clearly different, the fact that joint services can bring people together and widen ownership of key strategic priorities of the parent organisation is one of the critical benefits of the approach.

Another key benefit found in the Glasgow experience was the ability of services to become more focused on agreed objectives and outcomes. The city of Glasgow, building on its physical and economic regeneration, had prioritised the issue of social renewal and employability, and had emphasised the need for public sectors to tackle worklessness. The integrated nature of our teams, the joint processes and increasing cohesion of professional practice meant that a strong focus on employability and social renewal was possible across the spread of our services. In previous years this would have been much more difficult to manage in anything other than a disparate way.

Managing interface arrangements with other client groups, such as children services, mental health services and criminal justice to name but three, is also an important priority for joint services. Joint managers developing and securing interfaces with other services on behalf of statutory partners make the use of strategic meetings, planning sessions and organisational development activity much more efficient and meaningful. Prior to integration of services, the management of these interfaces had been much more complex, unwieldy and inefficient.

Assessing integrated services: Four years on

Before the creation of a single partnership to manage and deliver alcohol and drug services in Glasgow, services had been patchy, inconsistent, suffered from lack of confidence and under-investment, lacked clarity of leadership, accountability for performance and did not have common purpose. In the period since the creation of a single partnership, development of joint teams, construction of single joint management posts and the focus on accountability and performance, a transformation has taken place in relation to Glasgow's addiction services.

First, services work to a clearly visible single specification of key service standards which are explicit and for which are services held accountable. This is in contrast with the previous arrangements whereby services often reflected the priorities of influential key senior people rather than being based on solid planning and assessment of local needs. Single managers have made a difference to our service because there is no doubt that the buck stops for them for the quality and performance of their services. They are charged with driving forward the agenda of the statutory partners in relation to alcohol and drug provision.

There is evidence from our experience (see p.202) and elsewhere (e.g. Cook, Gerrish and Clarke 2001) that professionals can work together co-operatively, enabling each other's skills to be maximised, and of the degree to which professional boundaries can be woven together at the same time as strengthening roles – this is the key success of services like ours. Our teams now comprise medical, nursing, social care, pharmacy, psychology and occupational therapy staff working together around common care plans, based on inter-disciplinary single assessment processes. The partnership has developed mechanisms to ensure overarching inter-disciplinary care governance, maintain focus on professional leadership within an inter-disciplinary management team and ensuring that service-user safety and service quality is at the forefront of our work.

The Addictions Partnership itself performs an important strategic function given the separation between it and its service delivery units in both community and secondary care settings. The partnership is responsible for performance management of services, supporting and holding managers to account, planning services, reviewing needs and distributing resources in a way that is both equitable and responsive to those areas of explicit priority.

In four years, our services have doubled the number of people who are in contact with treatment and care services in the city from 5500 in 2003 to just under 12,000 in 2007. The partnership has allowed integrated services to develop a clear focus on recovery, rehabilitation, education and employability as key policy priorities of the NHS Board and city council. Responses have improved in relation to protecting children, working with alcohol- and drug-related offenders, and in relation to redesigning our services around management of co-morbidity with mainstream mental health services. Waiting times have continued to drop over the four-year period, despite the fact that the number of people coming into the service increases quarter over quarter. Bringing professionals together makes perfect sense in the context of cities like Glasgow, where needs are so extreme and can be so overwhelming.

The true success of our partnership will be based on continued improvements and the quality and delivery of the Scottish drugs strategy (Scottish Government 2008). Having processes, structures and management arrangements in place is critically important to our ability to deliver on this new set of priorities, and will lead to our success. The needs and the demands of our city will continue to be the key drivers by which our managers and staff are motivated towards ever-improving outcomes for service users.

References

Barnes, H., Green, L. and Hopton, J. (2007) 'Social Work theory, research, policy and practice – Challenges and opportunities in health and social care integration in the UK.' *Health and Social Care in the Community 15*, 3, 191–194.

Cook, G., Gerrish, K. and Clarke, C (2001) 'Decision making in teams: Issues arising from two UK evaluations.' *Journal of Interprofessional Care 15*, 2, 141–151.

Evans, D. and Forbes, T. (2009) 'Partnerships in health and social care.' *Public Policy and Administration 24*, 1, 67–83.

Freeman, I. and Moore, K. (2008) 'Community health (and care) partnerships in Scotland.' *Journal of Integrated Care 16*, 3, 38–47.

Glendinning, C. (2002) 'Breaking down barriers: integrating health and social care services for older people in England.' *Health Policy 65*, 139–151.

Hanlon, P., Walsh, D. and Whyte, B. (2006) *Let Glasgow Flourish: A Comprehensive Report on Health and Its Determinants in Glasgow and West Central Scotland.* Glasgow Centre for Population Health.

Hay, G., Gannon, M., McKeganey, N., Hutchinson, S. and Goldberg, D. (2004) *Estimating the National and Local Prevalence of Problem Drug Misuse in Scotland.* University of Glasgow.

Hudson, B. (2006a) 'Integrated team working Part I: You can get it if you really want it.' *Journal of Integrated Care 14*, 1, 13–21.

Hudson, B. (2006b) 'Integrated team working Part II: Making the inter-agency connections.' *Journal of Integrated Care 14*, 2, 26–36.

Hudson, B. (2007) 'Pessimism and optimism in inter-professional working: The Sedgefield Integrated Team.' *Journal of Interprofessional Care 21*, 1, 3–15.

Keenan, P. (2006) *A Process Evaluation of Community Addiction Teams in North East and East Glasgow in the First Year of Operation.* Scottish Executive Substance Misuse Research Programme. HMSO.

Petch, A. (2006) 'Evidence-informed practice and integrated care: the launch of research in practice for adults.' *Journal of Integrated Care 14*, 1, 3–6.

Rosen, R. and Ham, C. (2008) *Integrated Care: Lessons from Evidence and Experience.* Report of the 2008 Sir Roger Bannister Annual Health Seminar. London: Nuffield Trust.

Scottish Government (2008) *The Road to Recovery: A New Approach to Tackling Scotland's Drug Problem.* Edinburgh: Scottish Government.

Stewart, A. (2007) 'Addiction services in Glasgow: A partnership.' *Community Care Works 64.* Database of practice in community care, Glasgow School of Social Work.

Stewart, A., Petch, A. and Curtice, L. (2003) 'Moving towards integrated working in health and social care in Scotland: From maze to matrix.' *Journal of Interprofessional Care 17*, 4, 335–350.

CHAPTER 13

Messages for the Workforce

Joy Barlow

Introduction

Significant changes are taking place in the substance misuse field. This chapter will consider the implications of those changes for the training and education of workers in that field. Major changes in policy, new knowledge and information all call for re-examination of the skills staff require to do their job. For instance, the policy emphasis on a multi-disciplinary, integrated approach to work in the care and related fields requires an integrated approach to workforce development; that is, how professionals in different disciplines learn to work together effectively and acquire the skills to do so. We are still some way from achieving that integration.

In this chapter questions about the workforce will be addressed – who they are, what sort of workforce is required, what do we mean by workforce development and what works in carrying it out. We will see that 'development' involves not just training but learning, acquiring new knowledge as well as skills, reflecting on one's own practice, examining values and attitudes, sharing insights and information, and being aware of what impact learning and development has on practice. The chapter will conclude with some suggestions for the future.

What is workforce development?

There are many definitions of workforce development in the literature. The key requisites for staff/workforce development are that it should be a planned process, aiming at both collective and individual effectiveness; it should be able to respond to new knowledge and changes, impact on the quality of service, and enable skills and knowledge to be brought together. Further, it should encourage staff to take personal responsibility for their learning.

The drug and alcohol fields may seem to have come somewhat late to understanding the importance of workforce development. This may be due to uncertainty in the past about what services are required, making it difficult to determine what skills and knowledge the workforce should have to deliver them. The current drive towards new types of services is now focusing minds on the new skills they demand.

Not an isolated activity

Specifically in Scotland, the learning and development needs of staff in drug and alcohol misuse services have to be seen in the context of continuous professional development in the wider workforce as a whole. For example, the *National Strategy for the Development of the Social Services Work Force in Scotland* (Scottish Executive 2005) sets the basis for other more specific workforce strategies.

Government policy stresses the importance, for public health and social care services in general, of involving users and carers in the design and development of services, of the location of services, and of personalisation and choice of services. These changes will impact on the substance misuse field in far-reaching ways. For example, choice and personalisation (promised as part of the 'recovery' focus) will affect the range of services offered and the way services will be commissioned. New services will be needed to demonstrate that people not only ought to have a choice of treatment options but know they will have a choice. Not every treatment intervention will be right for every service user. If more treatment options are made available, it is axiomatic that new skills will be needed to enable staff in all professions involved to deliver these interventions (McGrail 2006).

Other major policy frameworks on welfare development have made an impact on what and how learning and development is delivered to the substance misuse workforce. These include:

- The *NHS Knowledge and Skills Framework* – Delivered through 'Agenda for Change'. This will 'assist the goal of achieving a quality workforce with the right numbers of staff, with the right skills and diversity, organised in the right way' (Department of health 2004).

- *Joint Futures Agenda* – The establishment of the Joint Futures Agenda Group for Community Care by the Minister for Health in the Scottish Executive in 1999, set the agenda for joint work between the health and social care services. The development of Community Health and Care Partnerships follows on from this, with its focus on integration, on linking services and planning processes to address the wider health needs of communities.

Workforce trends in education, justice and the prison service also need to be taken account of in any learning and development strategy for the substance misuse workforce. Whatever professional background, or whichever occupational standards are required, the drug and alcohol workforce and its partner services need to be competent, confident, responsive and flexible in the joint delivery of a service to substance misusers.

Who are the workforce?

The substance misuse workforce is multi-professional and multi-faceted. The role of universal services (such as health, social care, or education) in identifying a problem or concern, their assessment of it, or making an appropriate referral, cannot be over-estimated. The necessary competencies, and in particular the attitudes required of the drug and alcohol misuse workforce, should encompass all who come into contact with substance misuse, whatever their profession, as well as the drug and alcohol specialist (Mills *et al.* 2005).

A number of typologies have been suggested to describe the substance misuse workforce, from that of 'Tiers' to that of 'Levels'. I prefer the description of levels. This categorises the workforce as working at different levels of engagement, ranging from Level 1 – those with a role in engagement with the public, through to Levels 2 and 3 where there is some level of direct service provision to those with drug and alcohol problems, to Level 4 where specialist support is provided.

What sort of workforce is required?

Substance misusers, their families and carers require well-trained, empathetic and confident workers. The workforce is multi-professional, therefore it should be trained on a multi-professional basis. The work they are required to do is complex, requiring a wide array of skills and core competencies reflected in levels of qualification and accreditation; it is challenging, and often it is difficult to achieve success. It is also often ethically fraught, involving hard decisions between the interests of service users and those of their families and communities. Work in this field requires sound professional judgement, often to be exercised autonomously. It has to recognise the theoretical basis for practice; and also the importance of attitudes and values in its work.

What do we know currently about workforce development?

In the drug and alcohol fields there is a paucity of research on how workforce development contributes to better outcomes for those with drug and alcohol problems. From a national – Scottish – perspective, we have gained the following insights from work undertaken for the as yet unpublished Alcohol and Drugs Workforce Development Plan for Action:

- At undergraduate and SVQ levels there is a lack of consistency of coverage, or absence of coverage, of alcohol and drugs within formal courses.

- There should be a greater link between academic learning and workplace practice.

- There is a need for a systematic approach to identifying training needs and appropriate learning and development provision, linked to agreed national and local priorities.

- There is a need for a clear set of competencies which state the knowledge, skills and attitudes that workers need in order to respond to Scotland's drug and alcohol problems.

- The importance of evaluating the impact of learning to ensure that it is transferred to workplace practice and is then assessed for effectiveness.

At an international level, the International Think Tank on Education and Training in Addiction (I-ThETA) has conducted a transnational survey of education and training across 11 countries, mostly within Europe but also including the US and Australia (for details of the structured questionnaire used by the survey see www.I-Theta.org). The survey's conclusions are summarised as follows:

> Since good practice is expected to be evidence-based... education and training have become more important. In most countries, therefore, continued education and training are fairly highly valued in principle, and the respective activities have increased. Training activities are mainly those chosen by providers in a 'top-down' fashion and are rarely based on... competence gaps and 'bottom-up' needs assessment. Incentives for services and professionals engaging in education and training are the exception rather than the rule. In a majority of countries there is little effort to systematise forms and content of continuing education in a conceptual framework, or to care about quality standards. Evaluation is mostly done by providers' self-evaluation, and only exceptionally are the effects of educational inputs researched. Professional associations and universities have a dominant role in developing educational programmes. Providers operate in a market competition rather than in a guided structure. A deficit is identified here and state-commissioned organisations are increasingly working on filling gaps in a number of countries. (Uchtenhagen 2006)

Current development of education and training
Introduction of 'competencies'
Everyone uses the word 'competency', but there is little difference between a 'skill' and a 'competency': a competency is a developed skill, and a skill is the ability to do something well.

In the UK, Drug and Alcohol National Occupational Standards have now been in place for some years for the drug and alcohol field. Known as DANOS, and produced by Skills for Health (2003), they represent a consensus of what competent people in the drug and alcohol sector are able to do, rather than simply what they know.

In other parts of the UK, DANOS has been used to define job remits, service specifications and training qualifications. It has also been the framework upon which to determine staff competence. In Scotland, the use of DANOS has been different, as it was agreed that a specific competence framework for those working in the drug and alcohol fields should not be necessary. In addition to the Scottish Vocational Qualification in Health and Social Care at Levels 3 and 4, DANOS skill sets were developed for the worker in the drug and alcohol sector. These skill sets guide employers, assessors, training providers and candidates in choosing units to work on which will extend the practice skills and/or knowledge in specific service areas. Staff will not undertake a separate SVQ; instead they will complete units for the relevant skill sets to add skills they do not already possess, and to equip them for new areas of work. STRADA courses (see below) are noted as providing the necessary knowledge to underpin the acquisition of DANOS skill sets.

National Vocational Qualifications and DANOS

There is a long history of 'vocation' in the alcohol and drug fields. Workers have often come into the field because of life or family experience, and a desire to do some good. Until quite recently such individuals dominated staff teams. Of course, social workers, nurses and those from the medical profession, had a role to play in the field; but those who did the perceived 'real work' were often unqualified.

There has now been a sea change brought about by the advent of National Vocational Qualifications and DANOS, bringing implications for the wider workforce such as registration of service staff, and inspection and regulation of services. These should be seen as positive developments, not negative. It is true that those with life experience can be the best of workers, but they should not be denied the right to become qualified and accredited. In England and Wales the NVQ in Health and Social Care will be redeveloped for the new qualifications and credit framework. The purpose is the same, to attest to occupational competence in the workplace as described in National Occupational Standards. There will be no change to SVQ in Scotland.

STRADA – Putting workforce development into effect

STRADA (Scottish Training in Drugs and Alcohol) has been in existence since 2001 when it was funded following its response to the Scottish Executive's tender specification. Its purpose is to provide training and educational activity in relation to drug and alcohol misuse across Scotland. It is a partnership between the University of Glasgow's Centre for Drug Misuse Research, the university's Department of Adult Education, and DrugScope – the UK-wide independent policy and practice body in the drugs field. Since 2001 it has been re-funded by the Scottish Government on the basis of competitive tender.

STRADA's aims are to ensure that the competence of professional staff addressing drug and alcohol misuse is raised throughout Scotland, and that practice skills of professional staff in addressing drug and alcohol misuse are further developed. Further, that interventions delivered to address drug and alcohol misuse are based on evidence of what works; and that its training programme is responsive and adapts as necessary to the Scottish Government policy agenda for drugs and alcohol.

Multi-disciplinary approach

STRADA's contribution to workforce development is made at different levels of staff engagement with substance misusers, and at different levels of learning – from academic courses to modules tailored to fit local needs (described below). What is common to them all is the multi-disciplinary basis of training and learning. Participants are invited from a wide range of professional backgrounds, and all courses and training events are attended to a greater or lesser degree by a mixture of disciplines. This feature is always particularly well evaluated by participants.

Theory and practice

The knowledge base of addictions and the theoretical basis of work are as important in this field as in those of law, medicine and education (McKeganey 2008). In STRADA's training-needs analyses conducted in various areas across Scotland since 2005, almost 40 per cent of respondents in some areas noted the need for training in the theoretical basis for the work undertaken. That finding should be acted upon by all concerned in education and training in addictions. In all of STRADA's courses, both at continuous professional development (CPD) and academic level, the link is made between theoretical knowledge and its use in practice. As one STRADA course participant said: 'A greater understanding of different theoretical models should assist the better delivery of services to the individual.'

Academic courses

In its academic programmes STRADA has sought to prepare a career pathway for those working in the fields of drugs and alcohol. STRADA's academic qualifications include:

- A *Certificate in Higher Education – Drug and Alcohol Practice* prepares students for work in these fields at a first-stage level.

- A *Postgraduate Certificate in Addictions* leads to further in-depth study, encouraging critique of policy and research. Here again, theoretical knowledge provides the basis for improved practice.

- A *Postgraduate Certificate in Management* – re-named Certificate in Leadership of Drug and Alcohol Services.

Whilst not all workers will be in a position to take up a university course, as many as are able must be encouraged to do so. Such a move towards an academic validation in the field of addictions should be matched by better links between vocational training and academic programmes. In this way we can begin to fashion an appropriate career structure for those who work in the most complex and highly charged situations. The staff and users of services deserve no less.

Continuous professional development

STRADA also provides a significant number of modules at CPD level, delivered across Scotland and, where appropriate, tailored for locality needs. STRADA sees CPD as a necessary driver for change in attitudes, values and principles of practice, as well as the acquisition of new learning. CPD is seen not only in terms of training and qualification, though these are important aspects of CPD. The definition from the Scottish Social Services Council is important here: 'On-going learning and development to improve and extend professional practice throughout an individual's career' (SSC 2004, p.30). As part of CPD, STRADA offers practice-based workshops which build on knowledge courses to develop and enhance skills.

In a changing world where new skills and knowledge are required to face new situations, it is vital that staff keep up to date with advances in policy and practice. Such workforce activity is needed to keep expertise longer at the front line, and to continue to develop staff in their existing roles.

Along with other academic providers of education in the drug and alcohol fields, STRADA's work is constrained by a lack of articulation between credit accumulation, transfer agreements between institutes of higher education, and a qualifications framework. Nevertheless, STRADA continues to work with professional and sectional bodies on general undergraduate courses to enhance drug and alcohol awareness. It also provides the underpinning knowledge and skill base for the acquisition of vocational awards.

The role of management in learning and development

Reid and Barrington (1994) describe the management of workforce development as 'an art and indeed a situation-specific art'. This means that the management of training should take account of situational learning needs, opportunities, problems, objectives, options, preferences and priorities.

All managers, without exception, should be at the forefront of identifying the training needs of their workforce, and should accept personal responsibility for their being met. This involves taking an active interest in staff members' careers, providing opportunities to improve and extend their abilities, especially by using day-to-day work tasks, and above all by encouraging them to continue learning. These assertions of good practice, however, are not universally accepted by managers. More urgent tasks and general pressure of work are cited as reasons why managers are not involved in the development of their employees.

Further, it is imperative to link learning and development of individual employees to service design and outcomes, leading to better outcomes for users of services.

It is for these reasons, and for the developing of managers themselves, that STRADA has provided both continuous professional development for managers, and an academic qualification at postgraduate level.

The CPD course 'Effective and Efficient Service Delivery for Managers', enables participants to implement key strategic documents required by effective services; and to consider performance management, evaluation processes, and staffing and supervision arrangements. Evaluation of these courses thus far have particularly valued the multi-disciplinary nature of the training; the emphasis on policy and its implementation; the analysis of service provision; and action planning for the implementation of learning in work-based practice.

> Possibly the best outcome for me and the organisation has been the positive effect on staff motivation and morale... On the Managers' course you were encouraged to bring along and share issues you were currently facing and wanted to see resolved... I think it helped refresh my thinking and gave me loads of tools to aid the new ideas... The results have been very positive and give us a new lease of life is how I'd probably describe it.
> (STRADA course participant)

The postgraduate certificate programme was formerly provided by Glasgow University's Department of Management, but has now been transferred to the Department of Educational Studies. The new course focuses on leadership for a changing world. It includes elements on leading people, leading organisations, and practitioner enquiry and decision making.

Evaluation of training – Do we know what works in workforce development?

STRADA has been concerned since its inception to try to capture the outcomes of its learning and development activity and its effect on work-based practice. This is a concept which is much discussed, defined and promulgated without a lot of systematic thinking about how it might be achieved. What is proposed by all writers on the subject is that learning and working are inextricably linked. People learn from what they do; and what they do is informed by their learning. Social learning theory shows that learning takes place more from seeing what others do, than what they tell us to do (Skinner 2005). This observation underscores the importance of modelling the kind of behaviours and practices which one hopes to develop in others. Such activity is included in STRADA's CPD and academic programmes.

As identified in the I-ThETA survey, evaluation of courses is largely conducted by those who provide the training. STRADA's experience is also of this type of evaluation, but it has on occasions also had external evaluation undertaken on its behalf. STRADA uses an adaptation of Donald Kirkpatrick's (1994) typology which includes:

- Immediate reaction to any course – asking by questionnaire specific questions about efficacy of training objectives, new learning and skill development, and future action planning

- Learning and behaviour – sampling of participants on a number of courses, using in-depth follow-up interviews to examine

  o participants' experiences of the training, as well as a perceived increase in knowledge, skills and confidence (i.e. 'internal learning')

  o participants' implementation of the increased knowledge and skills they report, and examples of where they have used these in practice to increase their effectiveness (i.e. 'external learning')

- Results – how participants' perceived increase in knowledge and skills have positive impact upon the organisation or service they work for.

Some examples of results from STRADA course participants:

> The training really benefited my knowledge and just gave me all sorts of things to actually use in practice and well...being able to do informed risk assessments helps us and our clients.

> ...because it's [identifying signs of overdose] something I'm not afraid to actually approach now with clients...service users. I have the confidence to talk about it and I have the knowledge to back it up in a lot of ways I just didn't have before. Like... actually being more confident now about the drugs involved, their effects, and just what to do. It's hard to explain but I just have the confidence now because I have the knowledge and it wasn't there before.

> Appreciating the effects of alcohol on my client and her ability to function daily, attending to practical tasks, financial situation and also the effect on her health. I feel this understanding has benefited my client as I can relate to her dependency and her ability to function and retain information. I have adapted and changed my approach and set firmer boundaries in relation to her care plan and level of support I give.

The results are also measured against managers' perception of the individual's increased knowledge and skills, and any impact on organisational practice.

From reviews of the literature on training and education, it is clear that there are only the beginnings of evidence as to whether or not training makes a difference to practice and therefore to better outcomes for users of services. However, some researchers note that inquiries of this nature are now being conducted (Ogilvie-Whyte 2006). The lack of robust evidence does not prevent the constant cry that this will improve practice. Whilst this may be the case, simple evaluation of courses (e.g. whether the participant enjoyed the experience) will not suffice. It is necessary to dig down into the workplace experience to discover the impact of training and development.

> I think it's changed my practice now because I'm more aware of the need to look at harm reduction from a different perspective

than maybe I did before. A lot of the clients I see, I know what to do now and so when they come back in and they are starting taking again, we are constantly reminding them that their resistance is very low, just be very, very careful. Stuff like that and actually being ready to put harm-reduction measures in place in a way I couldnae have before. I think that if I'm more aware I can pass that onto them and I know that my knowledge has helped some of them, 'cause I mean; they tell you. (STRADA course participant)

Education and training do not occur in isolation. They take place within different organisational environments, often with different perceived outcomes. The ability and willingness to put knowledge and skills into practice is not even across the drug and alcohol fields in Scotland. In an analysis of STRADA training needs, it was found that some organisations and individuals are thirsty for new knowledge and skills, whilst others see education and training, particularly if it is designed as mandatory, as somewhat of a chore.

A wide range of factors may influence course participants' capacity to benefit from education and training – motivation to learn, expectations, need, attitudes, existing knowledge and learning styles. In addition, factors in the work environment, such as the availability of support and encouragement from co-workers and supervisors, managerial culture, and organisational systems and cultures, may also impact on the learning and the transfer of learning into workplace practice.

Difficulties and barriers to evaluation

It is not always easy to engage people in evaluating the impact of their learning on their practice. These are some of the problems STRADA has experienced:

- lack of willingness to participate due to workload and pressure of time
- organisations not prioritising engagement with evaluation
- interviews, even by telephone, seen as time-consuming
- participants not feeling that there is a 'pay off' for their involvement
- participants not experiencing reflection on their practice and therefore finding it difficult to discuss or give examples of transfer of learning into practice

- the organisation providing the training finding the evaluation process time-consuming.

From an external perspective, Goldstein and Ford (2002) have identified four main barriers to the transfer of learning. First, failure to consider participants' personal characteristics when deciding on training. Then conducting training in isolation from the participant's work environment, managerial and learning culture. A further barrier is failure to consider strategies that may impede the participant in translating new skills into practice; and finally failure to consider role or aims of the organisation.

Nevertheless, we must not give up on the attempts to discover the impact of learning transfer. There are some potential facilitators for transferring learning into practice. These include good design of the training; readiness and motivation to learn by the participant; opportunities in the workplace for practice; and an organisational climate that values training and development. Supervisory support is essential to ensure that participants can access resources and strategies that will aid the transfer of learning into workplace practice.

Student beliefs and their impact on learning

An area of very little academic inquiry is that of the impact of beliefs about the aetiology of substance misuse on how people use their academic learning. I am indebted to Archie Fulton, STRADA's university teacher at the University of Glasgow, for allowing me to use the findings of his study for his MEd (Academic Practice) award. It is expected that papers from this research will follow in the near future, as it provides hitherto unknown insights into participant inquiry and learning transfer.

The study (Fulton 2007) considered whether student beliefs about substance misuse had an impact on their learning during a higher education course; and whether the experience of learning had an impact on their beliefs. The information collected by self-completion questionnaires and interviews took place at two time points: prior to teaching on models and theories of substance misuse, and during the weeks immediately after the teaching session.

The results of the study indicate that their learning experience had an impact on students' beliefs about substance misuse, either reinforcing their beliefs and promoting confidence in practice, or acting as a challenge to their beliefs. For example, one student with a belief in the disease model of addiction made a significant change in her belief during the course, due to conflict experienced. Three other students' beliefs were in a state of change; and the beliefs of five others were reinforced by their learning experience on the course.

These findings, as the author suggests, show the importance of relating learning in the university environment to the practical experience of students. The classroom environment, the value of peer discussion and challenging assumptions about substance misuse, contribute to the development or changing of student beliefs.

Conclusions and suggestions

It is hoped that this chapter has given the drug and alcohol workforce food for thought. It also contains messages for those of us who provide training and development to the workforce.

Reflection in practice

This has been stressed through this chapter, and is derived from various sources. The theoretical basis from which practice should follow is vital at all levels of training and development. 'Too often work is undertaken with no analysis of problems and no theoretical base for practice. The consequence is that staff may be ill-equipped to do the job, and have no framework for examining what goes on' (Beedell and Clough, cited in Clough 2000, p.1).

Allied to the theoretical base for practice must be the ability to reflect on practice. In Chapter 6, Joyce Nicholson illustrates the importance of reflection in her training programmes. Theory has to be combined with the workers' own reflection and how they interpret theory in the light of their own experience and practice. We learn best from our own experiences: 'Even when (the worker) makes conscious use of research-based theory and techniques, he is dependent on tacit recognition, judgements and skilful performances' (Schon 1983, p.50).

Attitudes and values

With the changing environment, particularly the recent focus on recovery from dependent drug and alcohol use, the attitudes and values of the entire workforce are a crucial ingredient in learning and development. Everyone has a view on what we should do about drug and alcohol misuse – ranging from 'banging them all up and throwing away the key', to 'do what thou wilt shall be the whole of the law' and people should be allowed to 'go to hell in a hand cart'.

That range of attitudes and values, from being harsh and condemnatory on the one hand, or permissive and 'laissez faire' on the other, is evident among staff who come for training from a wide range of professions. Staff have to be allowed to consider these attitudes and values, and be challenged. STRADA has found that work on attitudes is a vital part of drug and alcohol training and education. We know that better knowledge can lead to better practice. So can a change in attitudes bring about better practice?

> If somebody came in beforehand (i.e. before the training), if they came in with an addictive behaviour, I was probably very cold and closed about helping them. You know, it was their fault, their problem – they could deal with it without getting offered this, that and the next. I would say that I am a lot more sympathetic to their needs, and how they didn't necessarily want to be in the position they are in. (STRADA course participant)

Attitudes and values should be empathetic but also realistic and honest. Workers have to make judgements, but judgements made on the basis of evidence (e.g. of harm to self or others) not as judgements of character.

Attitudes, particularly in the process of recovery, include staff having hopes and aspirations for users and services. Staff have to believe that people can be helped to change. Without this, a culture of cynicism and even despair can prevail. Attitudes can go a long way towards helping service users feel valued. However, staff must also guard against over-optimism. Attitudes must reflect sound professional judgement, thorough assessment, and effective reflection on practice. The personal qualities of staff are important for the engagement of individuals with services, and it hardly needs saying that the relationship between worker and service user is likely to be a major factor in outcomes.

Career development

This chapter also touched on the importance of career development in the fields of drug and alcohol misuse, and the place of both vocational and academic qualifications. Workers need to know where their careers are going and have some belief that the job is valued and offers career prospects. Much more work needs to be undertaken on what is meant by a career pathway in the field of addictions.

One route to consider is that of a first degree in addiction studies, linked to work-based assessment, which would provide a first-stage qualification for those working in the field. This would also meet the necessary registration requirements for the wider workforce. In addition, in undergraduate programmes of the wider workforce, much greater stress should be laid on raising awareness on drug and alcohol issues, which could lead to more specialist qualification.

Hallmarks of good workforce development

To sum up, a good worker in this field should have

- skills
- knowledge, backed up by reflection and helped by sound supervision
- attitudes about substance misuse that are helpful towards both service users and other professionals
- a career pathway reinforced by management.

Those providing training and education should:

- pay attention to the design of training and development in the light of research, evidence of what works and policy
- recognise different learning styles and behaviour of participants
- relate theory to practice
- design training and education on the basis of identified training needs
- relate evaluation back to training participants
- use both participants and service users in training and programme design
- evaluate as far as possible how learning is put into practice.

None of the foregoing can be by-passed or treated as less important as any other. Competencies cannot exist on their own without knowledge and a theoretical base; reflection on practice cannot be done without a manager spending time on it with the member of staff; a career pathway cannot be pursued in isolation from the daily work covered; and the organisation has as much responsibility as the individual to seek out opportunities for learning and development for all its staff.

Users of services in the drug and alcohol fields are probably the most stigmatised, disenfranchised, socially excluded of all service-user groups. In the journey on the road to recovery they deserve staff who are competently trained, confidently skilled and valued.

> Your actions and perceptions need to aim at accomplishing practical ends; at the exercise of thought; at maintaining a confidence founded on understanding – an unobtrusive confidence, hidden in plain sight. (Marcus Aurelius, Emperor of Rome 161–180CE)

References

Clough, R. (2000) *The Practice of Residential Work.* London: Macmillan.

Department of Health (2004) *Agenda for Change.* Leeds: Department of Health.

Fulton, A. (2007) *Exploratory Study of Student Beliefs in Higher Education Studies in Substance Misuse.* MEd (Academic Practice) dissertation. University of Glasgow.

Goldstein, I.L. and Ford, K. (2002) *Training in Organisations: Needs Assessment, Development and Evaluation.* Florence, KY: Cengage Learning.

Kirkpatrick, D.L. (1994) *Evaluating Training Programmes: The Four Levels.* San Francisco, CA: Berrett-Koehler.

McGrail, S. (2006) 'Brave new world.' *DrugLink 21,* 1, 10–13.

McKeganey, N. (2008) '"Up to the Job?" Is the drug and alcohol workforce fit for purpose or fit for change?' *Drink and Drugs News,* 10 March, 13.

Mills, D., Jepson, A., Coxon, T., Easterby-Smith, M., Hawlins, P. and Spencer, J. (2005) *Demographic Review of UK Social Sciences.* Swindon: ESRC.

Reid, M. and Barrington, H. (1994) *Training Interventions – Managing Employee Development.* London: Institute of Personnel and Development/Prentice Hall.

Schon, D.A. (1983) *The Reflective Practitioner: How Professionals Think in Action.* London: Temple Smith.

Scottish Executive (2005) *National Strategy for the Development of the Social Services Workforce in Scotland, a Plan for Action 2005–2010.* Edinburgh: Scottish Executive.

Skills for Health (2003) *Drugs and Alcohol National Occupational Standards (DANOS) Guide, Skills for Health.* Bristol.

Scottish Social Services Council (2004) *Continuous Professional Development for the Social Services Workforce.* Dundee: Scottish Social Services Council.

Ogilvie-Whyte, C. (2006) *Baselines: A Review of Evidence about the Impact of Education and Training in Child Care and Protection on Practice and Client Outcomes.* Evaluation & Evidence, Discussion Paper 2. Dundee: Scottish Institute for Excellence in Social Work Education.

Skinner, K. (2005) *Continuous Professional Development for the Social Services Workforce in Scotland.* In Developing Learning Organisations, Discussion Paper Dundee: Scottish Institute for Excellence in Social Work Education/Scottish Social Services Council.

Uchtenhagen, A. (2006) *Continued Education: A Cross-national Comparison.* I-ThETA (International Think Tank on Education and Training in Addiction). Available at www.i-theta.org/fileadmin/pdf/reports/summary_countryreports_-_A.Uchtenhagen.pdf, accessed 24 June 2009.

The Editor

Joy Barlow MBE is Head of STRADA (Scottish Training on Drugs and Alcohol), a partnership between the University of Glasgow and Drugscope. Before setting up STRADA in 2001, Joy designed and developed unique residential and outreach services for women dependent on drugs and alcohol with their children, for the Aberlour Child Care Trust in Scotland. She has been a member of the Advisory Council on the Misuse of Drugs, being on the prevention working group that produced *Hidden Harm*. She has also been a member of the Scottish Advisory Committee on Drug Misuse, and is a long-standing adviser to government on substance misuse issues.

Joy has presented and written widely on the impact of parental substance misuse on children, and workforce development. With a background in teaching, training and lecturing, she has a Master's Research Degree in Advanced Professional Development, and is currently the chair of I-ThETA (International Thinktank on Education and Training in Addiction). She is a member of the Research Highlights in Social Work Advisory Group.

The Contributors

Margaret Black works for the NHS Greater Glasgow and Clyde Clinical Governance Support Unit as the Patient Involvement Facilitator, with a specific remit to help services include the experience and perspective of patients in their governance activities. She has worked in the health sector for many years and in a range of roles, including practice management, project-based improvement programmes, and freelance evaluation and research.

Anne Bryce works for the Corporate Inequalities Team of NHS Greater Glasgow and Clyde as the Development Lead for Inequalities Sensitive Practice. Prior to this she worked as the Tobacco Coordinator for NHS Argyll and Clyde. In both roles a key aspect of the work has been the development of equitable services within the NHS.

Maurizio Coletti is a clinical psychologist and family therapist, and is Professor of Family Therapy at Iefcos, Rome. He has been a researcher in the field of drugs since 1972 and is President of Itaca Europe – an association of professionals working in the drugs field. He is a former consultant to the Italian government on drugs, and has been a trainer and consultant for many treatment centres in Europe and South America.

James Egan is a Health Improvement and Inequalities Manager working in East Glasgow Community Health and Care Partnership. He was previously Head of Policy and Practice at the Scottish Drugs Forum. Earlier in his career, when working in NHS psychiatric nursing, he was involved in the first community-based methadone clinics in Edinburgh in the 1980s, set up in response to the then HIV epidemic among injecting drug users.

Vivienne Evans OBE is the Chief Executive of Adfam, the national organisation that works with, and for families affected by substance misuse. She is a former member of the Advisory Council on the Misuse of Drugs and chaired its working group on the implementation of *Hidden Harm*. She is currently chair of the advisory committee for the Family Drug and Alcohol Court Project, and a member of the NICE Alcohol Use Disorders (Prevention) Programme Development Group.

Donald Forrester is Director of the Tilda Goldberg Centre for Social Work and Social Care, University of Bedfordshire. In his earlier career as a practising social worker he worked continually with families in which there was parental substance misuse. This experience shaped and informed his research interests when he became an academic. He is also a lead consultant for the Welsh Assembly Government, who are reconfiguring services to address parental substance misuse.

Jane Fountain has been working in the drug research field since 1988 and became a Professor of Substance Use Research at the University of Central Lancashire in 2005. Her work uses mainly qualitative research methods, which have been most often used to research drug use, drug treatment, and other drug-related issues, particularly amongst so-called 'hidden' or 'hard-to-reach' populations and those vulnerable to problematic drug use.

Sally Haw has recently been seconded to the Scottish Collaboration for Public Health Research and Policy (SCPHRP) as Senior Scientific Advisor. Prior to this she was Principal Public Health Advisor with Health Scotland where she led a team of topic specialists who developed evidence-based advice and guidance to inform both policy and practice. Her specialist area is substance misuse and tobacco control and she has contributed to Scottish and UK policy development and evaluation in these areas.

Neil Hunter is Joint General Manager for Glasgow Addiction Services. He has worked in the field of addiction for 15 years, originally developing one of Scotland's first alcohol and drug services for young people in North Glasgow. He has also worked in the fields of youth homelessness and mental health.

Richard Ives is founder and Managing Director of the UK-based educational company *educari*. Since the early 1980s, his work has been concerned with prevention of and education about substance misuse, particularly in relation to children and young people. He is Vice-Chair of the charity DrugScope, and a member of the Responsible Gambling Strategy Board.

Lisa Jones is a senior researcher at the Centre for Public Health, Liverpool John Moores University. She has extensive experience of undertaking systematic reviews on a broad range of clinical and public health topics. Her current research interests include examining the evidence for the effectiveness of alcohol and drug prevention initiatives and interventions for young people, and methodological issues relevant to systematic reviews of public health interventions.

Peter Kemp is the Barnett Professor of Social Policy and a Fellow of St Cross College, Oxford. He has published extensively on housing, including housing allowances, private rental housing, and homelessness. His research interests now also include social security, particularly in relation to people on the margins of the labour market, such as carers, people with long-term ill-health, and problem drug users.

Brian Kidd is a consultant psychiatrist in NHS Tayside Substance Misuse Services and is Senior Lecturer in Addiction Psychiatry in the University of Dundee's Centre for Addiction Research & Education Scotland. He also chairs the Dundee City Drug & Alcohol Action Team. He has been a member of the Scottish Advisory Committee on Drug Misuse since 1998.

Megan Larken is Senior Policy Analyst at the Alcohol Advisory Council of New Zealand. Prior to this, she was employed for five years by the Ministry of Health in New Zealand, mainly in alcohol and drug policy and mental health.

Jack Law is Chief Executive of the voluntary organisation Alcohol Focus Scotland. He is a member of the Scottish Ministerial Advisory Committee on Alcohol Problems, and other advisory and working groups. He is a board member of the International Council on Alcohol and Addictions. He has worked in local authority social services, in Strathclyde Regional Council and Glasgow City Council, as a community worker and social work manager.

Charlie Lloyd is Programme Manager on Alcohol and Drugs with the Joseph Rowntree Foundation, and is Honorary Visiting Fellow, Health Sciences, University of York. Previously he was with the Home Office working on the Drug Prevention Initiative (later the Drug Prevention Advisory Service), where he managed their research programme and undertook some of his own research on drugs prevention and vulnerable groups.

Neil McKeganey is Professor of Drug Misuse Research and founding director of the Centre for Drug Misuse Research at the University of Glasgow. He has been undertaking research into drug misuse in Scotland and elsewhere over the last 20 years.

Linda McKie is Research Professor in Sociology at Glasgow Caledonian University. Her current research interests are organisations, work and care. She is a trustee for Evaluation Support Scotland and the Institute for Rural Health.

Bernadette Monaghan is a criminologist whose career culminated in appointments as Head of Operations with SACRO (Safeguarding Communities, Reducing Offending) and Chief Executive of Apex Scotland, delivering employability services to offenders and young people at risk. She has served on the Sentencing Commission for Scotland and the National Advisory Body for Offender Management.

Joanne Neale is Professor of Public Health at Oxford Brookes University, Senior Editor of *Addiction* and on the editorial board of the *International Journal of Drug Policy*. Her research into illicit drug use has explored topics such as non-fatal drug overdose, drug driving, drug users' views and experiences of treatment services, homelessness amongst drug users, and drug users' everyday lives and recovery processes.

Joyce Nicholson has been involved in the addictions field for almost 20 years, working as a counsellor and outreach worker. She has been working as a trainer with STRADA for three years and has a focus on delivering workshops on children affected by parental substance misuse.

Toby Seddon is Senior Research Fellow and Director of the Regulation, Security and Justice Research Centre, in the School of Law, University of Manchester. He has been researching in the area of drugs and crime for over 15 years and is author of *A History of Drugs: Drugs and Freedom in the Liberal Age* (Routledge-Cavendish).

Harry Sumnall is Reader in Substance Use at the Centre for Public Health, Liverpool John Moores University. He was research lead for the Department of Health and NICE funded National Collaborating Centre for Drug Prevention, and is currently pursuing prevention related projects across the EU.

Gerard Vaughan is Chief Executive of the Alcohol Advisory Council of New Zealand. Prior to this, he worked for the Ministry of Health as National Project Manager for a campaign to reduce stigma and discrimination associated with mental illness. As well as his involvement with social change campaigns, he has worked in both government and non-government organisations in New Zealand, Australia and the UK in areas of communications, employment, health promotion and community development.

Subject Index

Author Index

Printed in Great
Britain
by Amazon